FREE Test Taking Tips DVD Offer

To help us better serve you, we have developed a Test Taking Tips DVD that we would like to give you for FREE. **This DVD covers world-class test taking tips that you can use to be even more successful when you are taking your test.**

All that we ask is that you email us your feedback about your study guide. Please let us know what you thought about it – whether that is good, bad or indifferent.

To get your **FREE Test Taking Tips DVD**, email freedvd@studyguideteam.com with "FREE DVD" in the subject line and the following information in the body of the email:

   a. The title of your study guide.

   b. Your product rating on a scale of 1-5, with 5 being the highest rating.

   c. Your feedback about the study guide. What did you think of it?

   d. Your full name and shipping address to send your free DVD.

If you have any questions or concerns, please don't hesitate to contact us at freedvd@studyguideteam.com.

Thanks again!

ASWB Clinical Study Guide

Social Work ASWB Clinical Exam Prep and Practice Test Questions [3rd Edition Book]

TPB Publishing

Written and edited by TPB Publishing.

TPB Publishing is not associated with or endorsed by any official testing organization. TPB Publishing is a publisher of unofficial educational products. All test and organization names are trademarks of their respective owners. Content in this book is included for utilitarian purposes only and does not constitute an endorsement by TPB Publishing of any particular point of view.

Interested in buying more than 10 copies of our product? Contact us about bulk discounts:
bulkorders@studyguideteam.com

ISBN 13: 9781628459173
ISBN 10: 1628459174

Table of Contents

Quick Overview

As you draw closer to taking your exam, effective preparation becomes more and more important. Thankfully, you have this study guide to help you get ready. Use this guide to help keep your studying on track and refer to it often.

This study guide contains several key sections that will help you be successful on your exam. The guide contains tips for what you should do the night before and the day of the test. Also included are test-taking tips. Knowing the right information is not always enough. Many well-prepared test takers struggle with exams. These tips will help equip you to accurately read, assess, and answer test questions.

A large part of the guide is devoted to showing you what content to expect on the exam and to helping you better understand that content. In this guide are practice test questions so that you can see how well you have grasped the content. Then, answer explanations are provided so that you can understand why you missed certain questions.

Don't try to cram the night before you take your exam. This is not a wise strategy for a few reasons. First, your retention of the information will be low. Your time would be better used by reviewing information you already know rather than trying to learn a lot of new information. Second, you will likely become stressed as you try to gain a large amount of knowledge in a short amount of time. Third, you will be depriving yourself of sleep. So be sure to go to bed at a reasonable time the night before. Being well-rested helps you focus and remain calm.

Be sure to eat a substantial breakfast the morning of the exam. If you are taking the exam in the afternoon, be sure to have a good lunch as well. Being hungry is distracting and can make it difficult to focus. You have hopefully spent lots of time preparing for the exam. Don't let an empty stomach get in the way of success!

When travelling to the testing center, leave earlier than needed. That way, you have a buffer in case you experience any delays. This will help you remain calm and will keep you from missing your appointment time at the testing center.

Be sure to pace yourself during the exam. Don't try to rush through the exam. There is no need to risk performing poorly on the exam just so you can leave the testing center early. Allow yourself to use all of the allotted time if needed.

Remain positive while taking the exam even if you feel like you are performing poorly. Thinking about the content you should have mastered will not help you perform better on the exam.

Once the exam is complete, take some time to relax. Even if you feel that you need to take the exam again, you will be well served by some down time before you begin studying again. It's often easier to convince yourself to study if you know that it will come with a reward!

Test-Taking Strategies

1. Predicting the Answer

When you feel confident in your preparation for a multiple-choice test, try predicting the answer before reading the answer choices. This is especially useful on questions that test objective factual knowledge. By predicting the answer before reading the available choices, you eliminate the possibility that you will be distracted or led astray by an incorrect answer choice. You will feel more confident in your selection if you read the question, predict the answer, and then find your prediction among the answer choices. After using this strategy, be sure to still read all of the answer choices carefully and completely. If you feel unprepared, you should not attempt to predict the answers. This would be a waste of time and an opportunity for your mind to wander in the wrong direction.

2. Reading the Whole Question

Too often, test takers scan a multiple-choice question, recognize a few familiar words, and immediately jump to the answer choices. Test authors are aware of this common impatience, and they will sometimes prey upon it. For instance, a test author might subtly turn the question into a negative, or he or she might redirect the focus of the question right at the end. The only way to avoid falling into these traps is to read the entirety of the question carefully before reading the answer choices.

3. Looking for Wrong Answers

Long and complicated multiple-choice questions can be intimidating. One way to simplify a difficult multiple-choice question is to eliminate all of the answer choices that are clearly wrong. In most sets of answers, there will be at least one selection that can be dismissed right away. If the test is administered on paper, the test taker could draw a line through it to indicate that it may be ignored; otherwise, the test taker will have to perform this operation mentally or on scratch paper. In either case, once the obviously incorrect answers have been eliminated, the remaining choices may be considered. Sometimes identifying the clearly wrong answers will give the test taker some information about the correct answer. For instance, if one of the remaining answer choices is a direct opposite of one of the eliminated answer choices, it may well be the correct answer. The opposite of obviously wrong is obviously right! Of course, this is not always the case. Some answers are obviously incorrect simply because they are irrelevant to the question being asked. Still, identifying and eliminating some incorrect answer choices is a good way to simplify a multiple-choice question.

4. Don't Overanalyze

Anxious test takers often overanalyze questions. When you are nervous, your brain will often run wild, causing you to make associations and discover clues that don't actually exist. If you feel that this may be a problem for you, do whatever you can to slow down during the test. Try taking a deep breath or counting to ten. As you read and consider the question, restrict yourself to the particular words used by the author. Avoid thought tangents about what the author *really* meant, or what he or she was *trying* to say. The only things that matter on a multiple-choice test are the words that are actually in the question. You must avoid reading too much into a multiple-choice question, or supposing that the writer meant something other than what he or she wrote.

5. No Need for Panic

It is wise to learn as many strategies as possible before taking a multiple-choice test, but it is likely that you will come across a few questions for which you simply don't know the answer. In this situation, avoid panicking. Because most multiple-choice tests include dozens of questions, the relative value of a single wrong answer is small. As much as possible, you should compartmentalize each question on a multiple-choice test. In other words, you should not allow your feelings about one question to affect your success on the others. When you find a question that you either don't understand or don't know how to answer, just take a deep breath and do your best. Read the entire question slowly and carefully. Try rephrasing the question a couple of different ways. Then, read all of the answer choices carefully. After eliminating obviously wrong answers, make a selection and move on to the next question.

6. Confusing Answer Choices

When working on a difficult multiple-choice question, there may be a tendency to focus on the answer choices that are the easiest to understand. Many people, whether consciously or not, gravitate to the answer choices that require the least concentration, knowledge, and memory. This is a mistake. When you come across an answer choice that is confusing, you should give it extra attention. A question might be confusing because you do not know the subject matter to which it refers. If this is the case, don't eliminate the answer before you have affirmatively settled on another. When you come across an answer choice of this type, set it aside as you look at the remaining choices. If you can confidently assert that one of the other choices is correct, you can leave the confusing answer aside. Otherwise, you will need to take a moment to try to better understand the confusing answer choice. Rephrasing is one way to tease out the sense of a confusing answer choice.

7. Your First Instinct

Many people struggle with multiple-choice tests because they overthink the questions. If you have studied sufficiently for the test, you should be prepared to trust your first instinct once you have carefully and completely read the question and all of the answer choices. There is a great deal of research suggesting that the mind can come to the correct conclusion very quickly once it has obtained all of the relevant information. At times, it may seem to you as if your intuition is working faster even than your reasoning mind. This may in fact be true. The knowledge you obtain while studying may be retrieved from your subconscious before you have a chance to work out the associations that support it. Verify your instinct by working out the reasons that it should be trusted.

8. Key Words

Many test takers struggle with multiple-choice questions because they have poor reading comprehension skills. Quickly reading and understanding a multiple-choice question requires a mixture of skill and experience. To help with this, try jotting down a few key words and phrases on a piece of scrap paper. Doing this concentrates the process of reading and forces the mind to weigh the relative importance of the question's parts. In selecting words and phrases to write down, the test taker thinks about the question more deeply and carefully. This is especially true for multiple-choice questions that are preceded by a long prompt.

9. Subtle Negatives

One of the oldest tricks in the multiple-choice test writer's book is to subtly reverse the meaning of a question with a word like *not* or *except*. If you are not paying attention to each word in the question, you can easily be led astray by this trick. For instance, a common question format is, "Which of the following is…?" Obviously, if the question instead is, "Which of the following is not…?," then the answer will be quite different. Even worse, the test makers are aware of the potential for this mistake and will include one answer choice that would be correct if the question were not negated or reversed. A test taker who misses the reversal will find what he or she believes to be a correct answer and will be so confident that he or she will fail to reread the question and discover the original error. The only way to avoid this is to practice a wide variety of multiple-choice questions and to pay close attention to each and every word.

10. Reading Every Answer Choice

It may seem obvious, but you should always read every one of the answer choices! Too many test takers fall into the habit of scanning the question and assuming that they understand the question because they recognize a few key words. From there, they pick the first answer choice that answers the question they believe they have read. Test takers who read all of the answer choices might discover that one of the latter answer choices is actually *more* correct. Moreover, reading all of the answer choices can remind you of facts related to the question that can help you arrive at the correct answer. Sometimes, a misstatement or incorrect detail in one of the latter answer choices will trigger your memory of the subject and will enable you to find the right answer. Failing to read all of the answer choices is like not reading all of the items on a restaurant menu: you might miss out on the perfect choice.

11. Spot the Hedges

One of the keys to success on multiple-choice tests is paying close attention to every word. This is never truer than with words like almost, most, some, and sometimes. These words are called "hedges" because they indicate that a statement is not totally true or not true in every place and time. An absolute statement will contain no hedges, but in many subjects, the answers are not always straightforward or absolute. There are always exceptions to the rules in these subjects. For this reason, you should favor those multiple-choice questions that contain hedging language. The presence of qualifying words indicates that the author is taking special care with his or her words, which is certainly important when composing the right answer. After all, there are many ways to be wrong, but there is only one way to be right! For this reason, it is wise to avoid answers that are absolute when taking a multiple-choice test. An absolute answer is one that says things are either all one way or all another. They often include words like *every*, *always*, *best*, and *never*. If you are taking a multiple-choice test in a subject that doesn't lend itself to absolute answers, be on your guard if you see any of these words.

12. Long Answers

In many subject areas, the answers are not simple. As already mentioned, the right answer often requires hedges. Another common feature of the answers to a complex or subjective question are qualifying clauses, which are groups of words that subtly modify the meaning of the sentence. If the question or answer choice describes a rule to which there are exceptions or the subject matter is complicated, ambiguous, or confusing, the correct answer will require many words in order to be expressed clearly and accurately. In essence, you should not be deterred by answer choices that seem excessively long. Oftentimes, the author of the text will not be able to write the correct answer without offering some qualifications and modifications. Your job is to read the answer choices thoroughly and completely and to select the one that most accurately and precisely answers the question.

13. Restating to Understand

Sometimes, a question on a multiple-choice test is difficult not because of what it asks but because of how it is written. If this is the case, restate the question or answer choice in different words. This process serves a couple of important purposes. First, it forces you to concentrate on the core of the question. In order to rephrase the question accurately, you have to understand it well. Rephrasing the question will concentrate your mind on the key words and ideas. Second, it will present the information to your mind in a fresh way. This process may trigger your memory and render some useful scrap of information picked up while studying.

14. True Statements

Sometimes an answer choice will be true in itself, but it does not answer the question. This is one of the main reasons why it is essential to read the question carefully and completely before proceeding to the answer choices. Too often, test takers skip ahead to the answer choices and look for true statements. Having found one of these, they are content to select it without reference to the question above. Obviously, this provides an easy way for test makers to play tricks. The savvy test taker will always read the entire question before turning to the answer choices. Then, having settled on a correct answer choice, he or she will refer to the original question and ensure that the selected answer is relevant. The mistake of choosing a correct-but-irrelevant answer choice is especially common on questions related to specific pieces of objective knowledge. A prepared test taker will have a wealth of factual knowledge at his or her disposal, and should not be careless in its application.

15. No Patterns

One of the more dangerous ideas that circulates about multiple-choice tests is that the correct answers tend to fall into patterns. These erroneous ideas range from a belief that B and C are the most common right answers, to the idea that an unprepared test-taker should answer "A-B-A-C-A-D-A-B-A." It cannot be emphasized enough that pattern-seeking of this type is exactly the WRONG way to approach a multiple-choice test. To begin with, it is highly unlikely that the test maker will plot the correct answers according to some predetermined pattern. The questions are scrambled and delivered in a random order. Furthermore, even if the test maker was following a pattern in the assignation of correct answers, there is no reason why the test taker would know which pattern he or she was using. Any attempt to discern a pattern in the answer choices is a waste of time and a distraction from the real work of taking the test. A test taker would be much better served by extra preparation before the test than by reliance on a pattern in the answers.

FREE DVD OFFER

Don't forget that doing well on your exam includes both understanding the test content and understanding how to use what you know to do well on the test. We offer a completely FREE Test Taking Tips DVD that covers world class test taking tips that you can use to be even more successful when you are taking your test.

All that we ask is that you email us your feedback about your study guide. To get your **FREE Test Taking Tips DVD**, email freedvd@studyguideteam.com with "FREE DVD" in the subject line and the following information in the body of the email:

- The title of your study guide.
- Your product rating on a scale of 1-5, with 5 being the highest rating.
- Your feedback about the study guide. What did you think of it?
- Your full name and shipping address to send your free DVD.

Introduction to the ASWB Clinical Exam

Function of the Test

The ASWB Clinical Exam is one of five social work licensing exams given by the Association of Social Work Boards. The others are: Associate, Bachelors, Masters, and Advanced Generalist. Each is intended to determine entry-level proficiency for particular social work education and experience levels. These exams are utilized by the social work regulatory bodies throughout the United States and the Canadian provinces of Alberta and British Columbia, as one of the components to determine whether a social worker has the competency and knowledge to safely practice professionally. The total number of ASWB Clinical Exams attempted across all jurisdictions in 2016 was 13,958, with a pass rate of 78.2 percent.

There are several steps that need to be followed prior to registering for the ASWB Clinical Exam. It is first necessary to contact the social work regulatory board in the prospective test taker's region to request a license application. Once this is received, the application needs to be submitted to the appropriate social work board. The social work board will then alert the examinee with its approval to register for the ASWB Clinical examination.

Test Administration

The ASWB Clinical Exam is administered electronically by appointment at Pearson Professional Centers, with locations around the world. Registered candidates can arrange a day and time to take the test via Pearson VUE's website. There are no pre-scheduled dates for this exam. Examinees are given four hours to take the test, which is taken on a networked computer.

If an applicant receives a failing score, he or she must wait a period of ninety days prior to taking the exam again. Some regions place restrictions on the number of times a candidate may retake an ASWB examination. In order to take a retest, it is required to re-register and once again pay the examination fee in full.

Accommodations are available for candidates with disabilities. To make these arrangements, approval of the accommodation request must first be given by the appropriate social work board and ASWB. Most boards include the pertinent form in their application packet.

Some jurisdictions permit special arrangements for candidates for whom English is not a first language. It is necessary to contact the appropriate board to see whether such arrangements are permitted. ESL arrangements must be pre-approved by the board and ASWB prior to registering.

Test Format

Each ASWB Clinical test contains 170 selected response questions intended to gauge the candidate's proficiencies in the following clinical practice areas: Human Development, Diversity, and Behavior in the Environment; Assessment, Diagnosis, and Treatment Planning; Psychotherapy, Clinical Interventions, and Case Management; and Professional Values and Ethics

Questions are organized into content areas, competencies, and knowledge, skills, and abilities statements (KSAs). Content areas gauge broad areas of topic proficiency. Competencies measure the knowledge, skills, and abilities within each subject area that is crucial to a social worker's job. The KSAs provide additional specifics about the exam content included in the competencies. Each KSA features a distinct knowledge element that may be tested anywhere in the exam and forms the foundation for the individual test questions.

Content Area	Percent of Test	Subtopics
Human Development, Diversity and Behavior in the Environment	24%	• Human Growth and Development • Human Behavior in the Social Environment • Diversity and Discrimination
Assessment, Diagnosis, and Treatment Planning	30%	• Biopsychosocial History and Collateral Data • Assessment and Diagnosis • Treatment Planning
Psychotherapy, Clinical Interventions, and Case Management	27%	• Therapeutic Relationship • The Intervention Process • Service Delivery and Management of Cases • Consultation and Interdisciplinary Collaboration
Professional Values and Ethics	19%	• Professional Values and Ethical Issues • Confidentiality • Professional Development and Use of Self

Scoring

Of the 170 test questions on the ASWB Clinical exam, only 150 are included in the score; the remaining twenty are sample pretest questions to determine whether they should be included in future exams. They are randomly spread throughout the examination.

Like the other ASWB social work licensing exams, the Clinical test is scored on a pass/fail basis. All jurisdictions utilizing the ASWB exams recognize the same pass point (number of questions a candidate must answer correctly in order to pass the exam), but this number can vary, depending on the exam version and category. Typically, pass points range from 93 to 107 correct questions out of the 150 that are scored.

Each score report outlines the number of questions correctly answered and the number needed to pass the version of the exam that was taken. Each jurisdiction has different ways of listing a passing score: it can be depicted as a 70, a 75, or a pass. The 70 used in one region and the 75 used in another, are both used to depict the same pass point. The exams are NOT easier or more difficult to pass in one state or province versus another. The methods are just two different ways to report the same outcome.

Recent/Future Developments

Starting in January 2016, California's Board of Behavioral Sciences (BBS) replaced the Clinical Vignette Exam with the ASWB Clinical Exam to issue clinical social work licenses. However, according to state regulations, candidates for social work licenses are still required to take a law and ethics exam (formerly the Standard Written Exam). As a result, it is now necessary for applicants in California to take both the ASWB Clinical Exam and the California Law and Ethics Exam. The state of California also now accepts transfers from candidates who received a passing score on the ASWB exam in the past. Therefore, candidates who are from other U.S. states may request California clinical social work licenses without going through the retesting process. Additionally, licensed California social workers receiving passing grades on the ASWB Clinical Exam can transfer test scores to other states where the exam is accepted.

Human Development, Diversity, and Behavior in the Environment

Human Growth and Development

Human Development Throughout the Lifespan

There are a number of theories on human growth and development. The most important theories are addressed in this section.

Freud's Model of Development
Freud is known for his research on stages of human development and his assertion that there were five stages of psychosexual development:

Oral Stage (birth to 18 months)
- An infant's focus of gratification involves the mouth.
- The primary need is security.
- Security needs are met when caretakers provide the baby with essentials, such as food, shelter, warmth and cleanliness.

Anal Stage (18 months to age 3)
- A child's focus of gratification involves the anus and the bladder.
- These organs represent sensual satisfaction.
- Internal conflict arises when the child begins the process of toilet training.

Phallic Stage (age 3 to age 6)
- The child engages in exploration of his/her body with greater interest in genitals.
- Oedipus and Electra complexes may occur.
- There is a pseudo-sexual attraction to the parent of the opposite gender.
- Conflict arises when the child realizes he/she has failed to win control over the parents' bond with one another.

Latent Stage (age 6 to puberty)
- The child's sexual interests become subdued or dormant.
- Energy is focused on school, hobbies, athletics, and mastering social skills.

Genital stage (puberty until death)
- The teen becomes aware of physical changes and onset of sexual feelings.
- The individual is less egocentric and more compassionate.
- There's a motivation to seek relationships that are emotionally and sexually satisfying.
- Success in this stage lays groundwork for future relationships that are healthy and long lasting.

Erikson's Model of Development

Erikson devised eight stages of psychosocial development. He emphasized the importance of social context, asserting that family and environment are major contributors to child development.

Trust vs. Mistrust (birth to 18 months)
- The primary goal is to learn to trust others.
- Trust occurs when a caretaker appropriately responds to a need in a timely, caring manner.
- Mistrust occurs when caretakers fail to meet the infant's basic needs.

Autonomy vs. Shame and Doubt (18 months to age 3)
- The primary goal is the development of self-control without loss of self-esteem.
- The toddler develops cooperation and self-expression skills.
- Failure to reach this goal leads to defiance, anger, and social problems.

Initiative vs. Guilt (age 3 to age 6)
- Initiative means confidently devising a plan and following it through to completion.
- Guilt is generated by fear that actions taken will result in disapproval.
- Failure to achieve initiative can lead to anxiety and fearfulness in new situations.

Industry vs. Inferiority (age 6 to age 11)
- Industry refers to purposeful, meaningful behavior.
- Inferiority refers to having a sense of unworthiness or uselessness.
- The child focuses on learning skills, such as making friends and self-care activities—e.g., dressing or bathing.
- Failure in this stage could lead to negative social or academic performance and the lack of self-confidence.

Identity vs. Role Confusion (age 12 to age 18)
- This stage involves the desire to fit in and to figure out one's own unique identity.
- Self-assessment of sexual identity, talents, and vocational direction occurs.
- Role confusion is the result of juggling multiple physical changes, increased responsibility, academic demands, and a need to understand how one fits into the greater picture.

Intimacy vs. Isolation (age 18 to age 40)
- This stage pertains to an ability to take risks by entering the work force, finding a long term relationship, and possibly becoming a parent.
- Failure to navigate this stage leads to isolation, loneliness, and depression.

Generativity vs. Stagnation (age 40 to age 60)
- This stage involves developing stability in areas of finance, career, and relationships, as well as a sense that one is contributing something valuable to society.
- Failure to achieve these objectives leads to unhappiness with one's status and feeling unimportant.

Ego Identity vs. Despair (mid sixties to death)
- Important life tasks, such as child rearing and career, are being completed.
- Reviewing and evaluating how one's life was spent occurs.

- Success in this stage provides a sense of fulfillment.
- Failure emerges if one is dissatisfied with accomplishments, which leads to depression or despair.

Erikson's Psychosocial Stages of Devleopment

Stage	Age	Psychosocial Crisis	Basic Virtue
1	Infancy (0 to 1½)	Trust vs. mistrust	Hope
2	Early Childhood (1½ to 3)	Autonomy vs. shame	Will
3	Play Age (3 to 5)	Initiative vs. guilt	Purpose
4	School Age (5 to 12)	Industry vs. inferiority	Competency
5	Adolescence (12 to 18)	Ego identity vs. role confusion	Fidelity
6	Young Adult (18 to 40)	Intimacy vs. isolation	Love
7	Adult hood (40 to 65)	Generativity vs. stagnation	Care
8	Maturity (65+)	Ego integrity vs. despair	Wisdom

Piaget's Model of Development

Piaget is best known for his concept that children's minds are not just smaller versions of adult minds, but instead grow and develop in different ways. His work has been influential within academic settings and has helped educators better determine what and how children can learn at various stages of their educational process. The following are the key ideas related to his research into the way cognition develops in children:

- Assimilation: A process by which a person accepts and organizes information, then incorporates new material into existing knowledge
- Accommodation: A process by which old ideas must be changed or replaced due to obtaining new information from the environment
- Schemas: A set of thoughts, ideas, or perceptions that fit together and are constantly challenged by gaining new information and creating change through knowledge

Piaget also recognized and defined the following *four stages of cognitive development*:

Stage 1: Sensorimotor Stage (birth to age 2)
- The infant becomes aware of being an entity separate from the environment.
- Object permanence occurs as the baby realizes that people or objects still exist, even if they are out of sight.
- Object permanence builds a sense of security as the baby learns that though mommy has left the room, she will still return.
- This reduces fear of abandonment and increases his/her confidence about the environment.

Stage 2: Pre-operational Stage (age 2 to age 7)
- The child moves from being barely verbal to using language to describe people, places, and things.
- The child remains egocentric and unable to clearly understand the viewpoint of others.
- The process of quantifying and qualifying emerges, and the child can sort, categorize, and analyze in a rough, unpolished form.

SENSORIMOTOR STAGE
- constantly learning about their environment via their senses

0-2

PREOPERATIONAL STAGE
- can use symbols
- egocentric
- has trouble using logic & understanding differing viewpoints

2-6 or 7

CONCRETE OPERATIONAL STAGE
- can understand differing viewpoints & use logic
- has trouble dealing in the abstract

7-11 or 12

FORMAL OPERATIONAL STAGE
- can think in the abstract
- can solve problems systematically

12 - Adulthood

Stage 3: Concrete Operational Stage (age 7 to age 11)
- The ability to problem solve and reach logical conclusions evolves.
- By age 10 or 11, children begin to doubt magical stories, such as the Tooth Fairy or the Easter Bunny.
- Previously-held beliefs are questioned.

Stage 4: Formal Operational Stage (age 12 through remaining lifetime)
- More complex processes can now be assimilated.
- Egocentrism diminishes.
- One assimilates and accommodates beliefs that others have needs and feelings too.
- New schemas are created.
- The individual seeks his or her niche in life in terms of talents, goals, and preferences.

Ivan Pavlov (Classical Conditioning)

Another important concept of development has to do with learning and the way in which humans learn new behaviors. A famous psychologist, Ivan Pavlov, conducted research with dogs that proved to be ground-breaking in the field of classical conditioning. In his experiment, a ringing bell was paired with the presentation of food, which produced salivation in the dog. The ringing sound eventually produced salivation from the dog even in the absence of food. Salivation then became the conditioned response to hearing a bell, and thus, the theory of classical conditioning was developed. The important finding of this research is that we learn by association.

B.F. Skinner (Operant Conditioning)

Skinner also did important research in the field of learning, specifically operant conditioning. Operant conditioning theory focuses on behavioral changes that can be seen or measured. The basic concept is that behavior that is reinforced will increase, and behavior that is punished will decrease. There are several key concepts integral to an understanding of this form of learning:

- Positive Reinforcement: Anything that serves as a form of reward, including food, money, praise, or attention
- Negative reinforcement: An unpleasant stimulus that is removed when behavior is elicited, such as a man finally cutting the grass to stop his wife from nagging him about it
- Punishment: An unpleasant response from the environment—e.g., a slap, an unkind word, or a speeding ticket—that when encountered, increases the likelihood that a behavior will cease. Two problems arise with using punishment. Once the negative stimulus is removed, the behavior is likely to continue. Punishment can also cause humiliation, anger, resentment, and aggression.
- Superstition: An incorrect perception that one stimulus is connected to another. Skinner found that when teaching a rat to press a lever for food, if the rat chases its tail before pressing the lever, it will mistakenly believe that the tail chase is required and will do both behaviors each time it wants food.
- Shaping: The process of changing behavior gradually by rewarding approximations of the desired behavior, i.e., first rewarding a rat for moving closer to the lever

Skinner found that there are different schedules of reinforcement and that some work better than others. These include the following:

- Continuous rate: Person or animal is rewarded every time a behavior is demonstrated
- Fixed ratio: Reward is given after a fixed number of attempts
- Variable ratio: Reward is forthcoming at unpredictable rates, like a slot machine
- Fixed interval: Reward is given only after a specific amount of time has passed
- Variable interval: Reward is given after an unpredictable amount of time has passed
- Extinction: Occurs when a behavior disappears or is extinguished because it is no longer being reinforced. To stop tantrum behavior in toddlers, ignoring the behavior will decrease or stop the tantrum, if the desired reward is parental attention or parental aggravation.

Seasons of Life Theory (Levinson)

This theory of adult development is classified by development stages, with each stage defined by different, yet meaningful and developmentally necessary, tasks. There are transition periods where stages overlap.

The *pre-adulthood stage* ends at age twenty-two. Beginning at birth, this is the stage when a person develops and prepares for adulthood. It is a time of major growth and transition where the individual develops a state of independence.

The *early adulthood transition* is roughly age seventeen to twenty-two. Pre-adulthood is ending, and early adulthood is beginning, but the time of transition is actually part of both periods. Physical development is completed, but this time of transition can be compared to the infancy of a new period of development. During this stage, adolescence ends, and the individual begins to make decisions about adult life. He or she further develops independence and separates from the family of origin.

Early adulthood stage is roughly age seventeen to forty-five. This stage begins with the early adult transition. From a biological perspective, an individual's twenties and thirties are at the peak of the life cycle. This stage can be the time at which individuals have their greatest energy, but are also experiencing the greatest amount of stress as they try to establish families and careers simultaneously.

Midlife transition is roughly age forty to forty-five. This is a time of transition that bridges the end of early adulthood and the beginning of middle adulthood. At this time of life, people tend to become more reflective and compassionate and less concerned with external demands. Values may change, and it is possibly a time where crisis is experienced due to limited time to reach goals. Individuals become aware of death and leaving a legacy.

Middle adulthood stage is roughly age forty to sixty-five. There is a diminishment of biological capacities, but only minimally. Most individuals are able to continue to lead fulfilling and relatively energetic lives. Many take on a mentoring role and responsibility for the further development of young adults. Choices must be made about livelihood and retirement.

Late adulthood is at roughly age sixty. A transition period occurs from around sixty to sixty-five. Late adulthood is a time of reflection on other stages and on accomplishments. During this stage, retirement takes place, and the individual gives up his or her role in the workplace. Crisis occurs at this stage due to declining power and less accolades of work performed.

Social Clock Theory (Bernice Neugarten)

Neugarten proposed that every society has a *social clock*: an understood expectation for when certain life events should happen (e.g., getting married, buying a home, having children). When individuals do not adhere to this timeframe, they often experience stress, the sense of disappointing others, or the experience of an internal "clock ticking" and reminding them that time is running out.

Normal and Abnormal Physical, Cognitive Emotional, and Sexual Development Throughout the Lifespan

Typical and Atypical Physical Growth and Development

It is important to understand normal developmental milestones. While not all children progress at the same rate, one must have some guidelines in order to determine if the child has any developmental delays that prevent them from reaching goals by a certain age.

Infancy Through Age Five

During the first year of life, abundant changes occur. The child learns basic, but important, skills. The child is learning to manipulate objects, hold their head without support, crawl, and pull up into a standing position. The toddler should be able walk without assistance by eighteen months. By age two, the child should be running and able to climb steps one stair at a time. By age three, the child should be curious and full of questions about how the world works or why people behave in certain ways. The child should have the balance and coordination to climb stairs using only one foot per stair. By age four, the child is increasingly independent, demonstrating skills like attending to toilet needs and dressing with some adult assistance.

School Age to Adolescence

By age five, speech is becoming more fluent, and the ability to draw simple figures improves. Dressing without help is achieved. By age six, speech should be fluent, and motor skills are strengthened. The youth is now able to navigate playground equipment and kick or throw a ball. Social skills, such as teamwork or friendship development, are evolving. The child must learn to deal with failure or frustration and find ways to be accepted by peers. They become more proficient in reading, math, and writing skills. Towards the end of this phase, around age twelve, secondary sexual characteristics, such as darker body hair or breast development may occur.

Adolescence

This is a period of extraordinary change. The process of *individuation* is occurring. The teen views themself as someone who will someday live independently of parents. More time is spent with peers and less with family. Identity formation arises, and the teen experiments with different kinds of clothing, music, and hairstyles to see what feels comfortable and what supports their view of the world. Sexuality is explored, and determinations are being made about sexual preferences and orientation. Sexual experimentation is common, and some teens actually form long-term intimate relationships, although others are satisfied to make shorter-term intimate connections. There is often a period of experimentation with drugs or alcohol. As the thinking process matures, there may be a questioning of rules and expectations of those in authority. Moodiness is common, and troubled teens are likely to "act out" their emotions, sometimes in harmful ways.

Typical and Atypical Cognitive Growth and Development

Cognitive development refers to development of a child's capacity for perception, thought, learning, information processing, and other mental processes. The *nature vs. nurture* debate questions whether cognitive development is primarily influenced by genetics or upbringing. Evidence indicates that the interaction between nature and nurture determines the path of development.

Some commonly recognized milestones in early cognitive development:

- One to three months: focuses on faces and moving objects, differentiates between different types of tastes, sees all colors in the spectrum

- Three to six months: recognizes familiar faces and sounds, imitates expressions

- Six to twelve months: begins to determine how far away something is, understands that things still exist when they are not seen (object permanence)

- One to two years: recognizes similar objects, understands and responds to some words

- Two to three years: sorts objects into appropriate categories, responds to directions, names objects

- Three to four years: Demonstrates increased attention span of five to fifteen minutes, shows curiosity and seeks answers to questions, organizes objects by characteristics

- Four to five years: Draws human shapes, counts to five or higher, uses rhyming words

The *Zone of proximal development* is the range of tasks that a child can carry out with assistance, but not independently. Parents and educators can advance a child's learning by providing opportunities within the zone of proximal development, allowing the child to develop the ability to accomplish those actions gradually without assistance.

Typical and Atypical Social Growth, Development, and the Socialization Process
Social development refers to the development of the skills that allow individuals to have effective interpersonal relationships and to contribute in a positive manner to the world around them.

Social learning is taught directly by caregivers and educators, but it is also learned indirectly by the experience of various social relationships.

Social development is commonly influenced by extended family, communities, religious institutions, schools, and sports teams or social groups. Positive social development is supported when caregivers engage in these behaviors:

- Attune to a child's needs and feelings
- Demonstrate respect for others
- Teach children how to handle conflict and solve problems encountered during social experiences
- Help children learn to take the perspective of another person and develop empathy
- Encourage discussion of morals and values and listen to the child's opinions on those topics
- Explain rules and encourage fair treatment of others
- Encourage cooperation, rather than competition

Social development begins from birth as a child learns to attach to their mother and other caregivers. During adolescence, social development focuses on peer relationships and self-identity. In adulthood, social relationships are also important, but the goal is to establish secure and long-term relationships with family and friends.

Another important contributor to social development are social institutions, such as family, church, and school, which assist people in realizing their full potential. Lev Vygotsky was a pioneer in this field with his concept of cultural mediation. This theory emphasizes that one's feelings, thoughts, and behaviors are significantly influenced by others in their environment.

Typical and Atypical Emotional Growth and Development
Emotional development encompasses the development of the following abilities:

- Identifying and understanding the feelings that one experiences
- Identifying and understanding the feelings of others
- Emotional and behavioral regulation

- Empathy
- Establishing relationships with others

Caregivers who are nurturing and responsive enable children to learn to regulate emotions and feel safe in the environment around them.

- By age two to three months, infants express delight and distress, begin smiling, and may be able to be soothed by rocking.

- By three to four months, infants communicate via crying and begin to express interest and surprise.

- Between four to nine months, infants respond differently to strangers in comparison to known individuals, solicit attention, show a particular attachment for a primary caregiver, and have an expanded range of expressed emotions that include anger, fear, and shyness.

- At ten to twelve months, babies show an increase in exploration and curiosity, demonstrate affection, and display a sense of humor.

- Children at age twelve to twenty-four months often demonstrate anger via aggression, laugh in social situations, recognize themselves in a mirror, engage in symbolic play, and have a complete range of emotional expression.

- Around age two, children begin using different facial expressions to show their emotions, begin to play cooperatively, and may transition from being calm and affectionate to temperamental and easily frustrated.

- At age three, children engage in more social and imaginative play, show interest in the feelings of others, begin to learn to manage frustration, and are often inconsistent and stubborn.

- Children at age four show improved cooperation, express sympathy, and may exhibit lying and/or guilty behavior.

- At age five, children can play rule-based games, often want to do what is expected of them, express emotion easily, and choose friends for themselves.

- Children at age six typically describe themselves in terms of their external attributes, have a difficult time coping with challenges and criticism, prefer routines, and show inconsistent self-control.

- Around age seven, children can typically describe causes and outcomes of emotions and show better regulation of emotions in most situations.

- From ages eight to ten, children have an increased need for independence, want to be viewed as intelligent, experience and better understand emotional subtleties, and may be defiant.

- During adolescence, children begin to master emotional skills to manage stress, increase self-awareness, develop identity, show increased ability for empathy, and learn to manage conflict.

Normal versus abnormal behavior is difficult to distinguish because each person is unique, so creating a standard of normal can be challenging. Though labeling behaviors as normal or abnormal can be problematic, it is important to have some standard by which it is possible to identify those behaviors that are indicative of an underlying psychological condition. Notwithstanding the challenges, it is possible and helpful to have general definitions of normal and abnormal behavior.

Normal behaviors are those that are common to the majority of the population, as related to emotional functioning, social interactions, and mental capacity. *Abnormal behavior* is generally considered that which is maladaptive, dysfunctional, and disruptive to life. These behaviors may be an exaggeration of a normal behavior or even an absence of a typical response. They do not conform to the accepted patterns or common behaviors of society. Sadness over the death of a loved one is considered normal, but disabling depression that interferes with school and work responsibilities is not. The *DSM-5* is the current standard for determining the diagnostic criteria that distinguishes abnormal behavior from normal.

Typical and Atypical Sexual Growth and Development

While not everyone develops sexually on exactly the same timeline, there are certain expectations that define healthy and unhealthy sexual development. These expectations differ based on age. During the early stage of life, from birth until age two, the child is focused on developing a relationship of trust with caregivers. Eventually, children become aware of their genitals and explore these through self-touch. By ages two to five, they begin to develop the ability to name and describe genitalia. They understand that male and female bodies are different. They have little inhibition about nudity.

As children enter middle childhood (ages six to eight or nine), they begin to understand the concept of puberty and what to expect about future body changes. They have a more sophisticated knowledge of reproduction, and may become more inhibited about nudity.

By the age of nine or ten, some children show signs of puberty, although the typical age of onset is eleven for girls and thirteen for boys. During puberty, there is a dramatic development in both primary and secondary sex characteristics. Children at this age show an increased interest in sex and may have questions about sexual orientation, sexual practices, or how the opposite sex behaves. By age twelve or thirteen, they begin to understand the consequences of sexual behavior, such as pregnancy or STDs. As they enter later adolescence, they may form longer relationships with their love interests, but many prefer casual dating. They are beginning to form an identity in terms of sexual orientation, preferences, and values.

It is important to understand red flags that may be signs of unhealthy sexual development. These may be brought on by abuse or by exposure to sexually explicit scenes. Children who are pre-occupied with sexuality at an early age and whose behaviors differ from peers their own age may be at risk. Other indicators include attempting adult-like sexual interactions. These behaviors may include oral to genital contact or some form of penetration of another person's body.

These issues should raise concerns:

- A child overly pre-occupied with sexual thoughts, language, or behaviors, rather than in more age-appropriate play
- Child engaging in sex play with children who are much older or much younger
- Child using sexual behavior to harm others
- Child involved in sexual play with animals
- Child uses explicit sexual language that is not age appropriate

A sexually-reactive child refers to one who is exposed to sexual stimuli prior to being sexually mature enough to understand the implications. The child becomes overly pre-occupied with sexual matters and often acts out what they witnessed or experienced.

Sexual Development Throughout the Lifespan

Sigmund Freud's Psychosexual Stages of Development

Sigmund Freud was an Austrian neurologist who is considered the father of psychoanalysis. Freud developed important concepts in Western psychology such as the id, ego, and super ego, and wrote literature focusing on what he called the *unconscious* and the repression and expression that stems from it.

Freud also focused on human development, especially relating to sexuality. Freud theorized that each stage of human development is characterized by a sexual focus on a different bodily area (*erogenous zone*), which can serve as a source of either pleasure or frustration. He believed that *libido* (psychosexual energy) is the determinant of behavior during each of five fixed stages, and that if a developing child experiences frustration during one of these stages, a resulting fixation (or lingering focus) on that stage will occur.

To understand Freud's developmental stages fully, one must also understand his conceptualization of the human personality.

Freud describes three levels of the mind as follows:

- Consciousness: the part of the mind that holds accessible and current thoughts
- Pre-consciousness: the area that holds thoughts that can be accessed by memory
- Unconscious: where the mind motivates behavior and contains thoughts, feelings, and impulses not easily accessible

Freud believed that the personality, or psyche, consists of three parts called the Psychic Apparatus, each of which develops at a different time.

Id

The id is the most basic and primitive part of the human psyche, based on instincts and all of the biological aspects of a person's being. An infant's personality consists only of the id, as the other aspects have not yet developed. The id is entirely unconscious and operates on the pleasure principle, seeking immediate gratification of every urge. It has two instincts: a death instinct called *thanatos* and a survival instinct called *eros*. The energy from eros is called the libido.

Ego

The ego is the second personality component that begins to develop over the first few years of life. The ego is responsible for meeting the needs of id in a socially acceptable, realistic manner. Unlike the id, the ego operates on the reality principle, which allows it to consider pros and cons, to have awareness that other people have feelings, and to delay gratification when necessary.

Super Ego

The super ego is the final personality component, developed by about age five. The super ego is essentially a person's internal moral system or sense of right and wrong. The super ego suppresses the instincts and urges of the id, but also attempts to convince the ego to act idealistically, rather than realistically.

In a healthy personality, there is balance between the three personality components. The individual has *ego strength*—the ability to function well in the world despite the conflicting pressures that the id and super ego place upon the ego.

Five Stages of Psychosexual Development

Oral Stage (Birth to Eighteen Months)
The infant satisfies its libido by feeding and by exploring the environment, primarily by putting objects in its mouth. The id dominates the oral stage of development, and every action an infant undertakes is guided by the pleasure principle. The key task of this phase is weaning from the breast, which also results in the infant's first experience of loss. Too much or too little focus on oral gratification at this stage was theorized to lead to an oral fixation and an immature personality. Examples of an oral fixation were believed to be excessive eating, drinking, or smoking.

Anal Stage (Eighteen Months to Three Years)
The key task of this stage is toilet training, which causes a conflict between the id (which wants immediate gratification of the urge to eliminate waste) and the ego (which requires delay of gratification necessary to use the toilet). A positive experience with toilet training was believed to lead to a sense of competence that continues into adulthood. Anal-retentive personality results from overly-strict toilet training, characterized by rigid and obsessive thinking. Likewise, anal-expulsive personality results from a lax approach to toilet training, characterized by disorganization and messiness.

Phallic Stage (Three to Six Years)
The libidinal focus during this stage is on the genital area, and it is during this stage that children learn to differentiate between males and females. The Oedipus Complex develops during this stage; Freud believed that a young boy views his father as a rival for his mother's attention and wants to eliminate his father in order to take his place. Similar to the Oedipus Complex, the Electra Complex says that a young may view her mother as her rival. Freud also believed that girls experience penis envy. The key task of this stage is identification with the same-sex parent.

Latency (Six years to Puberty)
During this period, libidinal energy is still present, but the child is able to direct that energy toward school, friendships, and activities.

Genital Stage (Puberty to Adulthood)
The libidinal focus is once again on the genital area (as it is during the phallic stage), but at this point, the psyche is more developed. During the genital stage, an individual achieves sexual maturation, becomes independent of his or her parents, resolves any remaining conflict from the earlier stages, and is able to function as a responsible adult in terms of both work and relationships.

Spiritual Development Throughout the Lifespan

Spiritual development refers to the way a person grows and changes spiritually over the course of their life, and particularly toward a sense of the purpose of their existence. This process may have conscious or unconscious origins, and it may be affected by other factors of their growth and development. Spiritual development is often linked to the stages of cognitive development, but evidence-based research pertaining strictly to spiritual development is limited. Theories often focus on the influence of psychosocial constructs (such as morality), cognitive beliefs, and religious or faith-based influences.

Jean Piaget (1896–1980) is renowned for his work in the field of cognitive development. He examined social, biological, and psychological constructs that influence cognitive development and intellect. He theorized four stages of cognitive development, from birth through adulthood. He believed that a multitude of constructs influences a person's moral beliefs and values, and this leads to their ultimate perspective on themselves and the environment.

Lawrence Kohlberg (1927–1987) studied moral psychology and development, and he developed a theory of the stages of moral reasoning. He theorized that individuals model behavior around them and behavior patterns to develop concepts of right and wrong as they progress through life. The more aware a person becomes of the effects of their thoughts, actions, and decisions, the more capacity they have for moral decision making. This may be connected to what shapes an individual's spiritual beliefs.

James Fowler (1940–2015), a theologian and university professor, contributed his "stages of faith" development, which breaks spiritual evolution down into six stages. He believed in the importance of safety and nurturing in the early years, which lead individuals to feel they are in touch with a greater good. Comparatively, individuals who feel unsafe or do not feel nurtured in their younger years are less likely to focus on spiritual aspects of life. Fowler made connections between his stages of faith and the developmental stages of Piaget and Kohlberg.

Racial, Ethnic, and Cultural Development Throughout the Lifespan

Racial, ethnic, and cultural identities are developed over the course of a lifespan and influenced by a number of factors. Atkinson, Morten, and Sue's racial and culture identity development model is accepted as one of the fundamental theories of racial and cultural development. This theory states that most individuals try to conform to the primary culture with which they're surrounded or which they believe is considered superior by peers. However, as the individual develops, they begin to seek out and reflect upon any underlying differences. Ideally, the developed individual ultimately becomes comfortable identifying in the way that feels best to him or her while respecting others' differences. Theorists have also focused on how specific minority groups develop racial, ethnic, and cultural identities. For example, Jean Kim's theory of Asian racial identity development focuses on Eastern populations. Minorities from Asian countries such as India, China, or Japan who grow up in the United States may act in traditional ways at home with their family unit, but they may struggle immensely to identify and assimilate with peers at school. This may be due to the fact that Asian culture is largely rooted in a collective, community identity (as opposed to the more individualistic Western culture). Additionally, Eastern and Western languages, traditions, and foods are different. While younger individuals may try to assimilate, older Asian individuals may tend to group together as they age. Bernardo Ferdman and Placida Gallegos's model of Latino identity development states that for Latino groups, ethnicity plays a larger role than race in self-identification. Finally, a number of researchers have theorized constructs and influences of white and black racial identity and culture. Often, these two racial identities are interrelated. Researchers have focused on the two races co-exist, based on historical interactions and contemporary narratives.

Physical, Mental, and Cognitive Disabilities Throughout the Lifespan

Approximately 7 percent of U.S. children have some type of disability. The most common physical disabilities that impact development are cerebral palsy, hearing issues, and visual issues. Learning

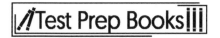

disabilities are also common—these could be Down's syndrome or other developmental delays. Common psychiatric disabilities are ADHD and autism spectrum disorders. Others include mood disorders, oppositional disorders, anxiety disorders, and, in rare cases, schizophrenia. The impact upon the child and family corresponds to the family's ability to adapt to the condition, and their ability to connect to community resources.

How the individual develops and copes with the disability depends greatly upon the social context and the child's own personal attributes. Raising a disabled child puts tremendous stress on parents and siblings. There are issues of stigma, financial burden, missed days of work for parents, and the time and energy needed to seek useful resources. Siblings may be called upon to take roles of parenting to help out. These siblings may be bullied by peers who make fun of their disabled family member. They may feel neglected by parents. Additionally, there may be a need for special housing and special schools. Low-income families may face barriers to accessing services such as transportation, medical specialists, or assistance with childcare.

The impact of disabilities on development depends largely on (1) the extent of the disability and (2) whether that disability is experienced across the lifespan or for a limited amount of time. Positive coping skills and sufficient social support may lessen the impact of a disability. Although the tendency is to focus on negative impact, disabilities may also leave a positive impact in terms of the strengthening of relationships or the development of skills that an individual may not have otherwise acquired.

Interplay of Biological, Psychological, Social, and Spiritual Factors

The interplay of an individual's biological, psychological, social, and spiritual factors is an indicator of overall health and happiness. If one or more of these factors are imbalanced, the individual is unlikely to feel as though they are at their highest level of well-being or personal fulfillment (even if a clinically diagnosed disease is not present). This framework is often utilized in social work settings where mental or emotional health appears to be compromised. Practitioners address the issue in the client's life by examining their physical and physiological health, medical history, personal history, moods, reactions to events, environment, family life, home life, cultural beliefs, personal relationships, faith or belief system, spirituality, personal desires, and other factors to provide holistic drivers for any necessary interventions. A number of these factors strongly influence each other. For example, a client who feels tremendous stress daily at work may find themselves constantly falling sick with colds, as stress negatively affects the immune system's ability to perform. Clients with clinically diagnosed mood disorders may have a more difficult time coping with major stressors, such as a divorce. Clients who report having some level of faith or spiritual belief system often appear to have higher levels of positivity and healthier coping mechanisms in the face of adverse personal events. As practitioners intervene in such scenarios, they must address not only the individual client, but all the systems in which the client exists and interacts. Practitioners may also need to work with the client's families, in communities, or in other group settings in order to effectively create balance between biological, psychological, social, and spiritual factors.

Basic Human Needs

Abraham Maslow is the most notable researcher in the area of basic human needs. Maslow theorized that human needs could be described in the form of a pyramid, with the base of the pyramid representing the most basic needs and the higher layers representing loftier goals and needs. Unless the basic needs are met, a person cannot move on to higher needs. For example, a homeless woman living under a bridge will need food, shelter and safety before she can consider dealing with her alcoholism.

23

The foundational layer in Maslow's hierarchy is physiological needs, and the final layer at the pinnacle of the pyramid is self-transcendence.

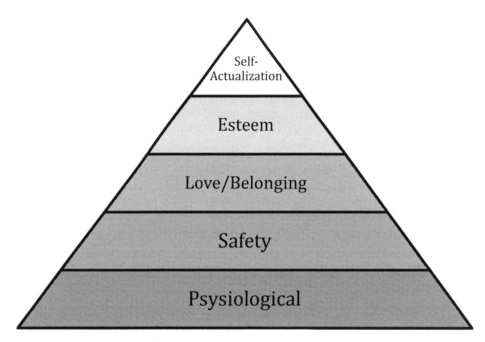

Maslow's Hierarchy of Needs

Physiological Needs: These needs must be met first and pertain to what humans need to survive. This includes basics, such as food, water, clothing, and housing.

Safety Needs: Once primary needs are met, the person may now focus on safety issues. This would include safety from abuse and neglect, natural disaster, or war.

Love and Belonging: Once the first levels of need have been satisfied, people are next driven to find a sense of acceptance and belonging within social groups, such as family, community, or religious organizations. Maslow suggests that humans have a basic need for love, affection, and sexual intimacy. Failure to achieve this level can lead to difficulty in forming and maintaining close relationships with others.

Esteem: The need for esteem is driven by a desire for recognition, respect, and acceptance within a social context.

Self-Actualization: The U.S. Army slogan, "Be All You Can Be," expresses this layer of need. Reaching one's highest potential is the focus. According to Maslow, this cannot be achieved until all the others are mastered.

Self-Transcendence: Devised by Maslow in his later years, he felt self-actualization did not completely satisfy his image of a person reaching their highest potential. To achieve self-transcendence, one must commit to a goal that is outside of one's self, such as practicing altruism or finding deeper level of spirituality.

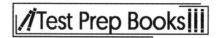

Attachment and Bonding

Understanding attachment and bonding has become more important than ever, especially in relation to changes within the U.S. culture's attitudes about child welfare over the last fifty years. Child Protective Service Teams have become more active in every city. The medical profession, the educational system, and the mental health profession are more informed about children at risk. As a result, more children are being taken from parents, sometimes as early as the day of birth. An older child victim may travel from relative to relative, back to the mother, then into foster or group homes. These children do not have an opportunity to form attachments with their caregivers, nor do caregivers have the opportunity to bond with the children.

Bonding refers to a mother's initial connection to her baby. This generally occurs within the first hours or days of the birth. Mothers who are able and willing to hold their child close to them shortly after birth generally have more positive relationships with the child. When a mother fails to bond, the child is at greater risk for having behavioral problems.

Attachment, on the other hand, refers to a more gradual development of the baby's relationship with his or her caretaker. A secure attachment naturally grows out of a positive, loving relationship in which there is soothing physical contact, emotional and physical safety, and responsiveness to the child's needs. The baby who has a secure attachment will venture out from his or her safe base, but immediately seek his or her mother when fearful or anxious, having learned that mommy will be there to protect him or her. This type of secure relationship becomes impossible if the child is moved from home to home or has experienced abuse or neglect.

A child whose needs have not been met or who has learned through mistreatment that the world is unfriendly and hostile may develop an avoidant attachment or ambivalent attachment. An *avoidant attachment* is characterized by a detached relationship in which the child does not seek out the caregiver when distressed, but acts independently. A child with *ambivalent attachment* shows inconsistency toward the caregiver; sometimes the child clings to him or her, and at other times, resists his or her comfort. Establishing a secure, positive attachment with a caregiver is crucial to a child's life-long emotional and social success. The development of attachment disorder is often present in foster children or those adopted later in life and can create much frustration and heartache as the more stable parents step in and attempt to bond with them.

Effect of Aging on Biopsychosocial Functioning

Biological Aging
Biological aging is based on physical changes that have an impact on the performance of the body's organs and systems.

Psychological Aging
Psychological aging is based on changes in personality, cognitive ability, adaptive ability, and perception. Basic personality traits appear to be relatively stable through the lifespan, as does an individual's self-image. One aspect that does tend to change, however, is the tendency to become more inwardly focused, which may also result in reduced impulsivity and increased caution.

Studies have shown that a pattern of age-related changes in intelligence can typically be observed after age sixty, although changes vary widely across individuals. Furthermore, the somewhat poorer testing results are reflected in fluid intelligence (i.e., reasoning, problem-solving, and abstract thinking unrelated to experience or learned information), but not in crystallized intelligence (i.e., knowledge based on skills, learning, and experience). Normal age-related changes in memory typically involve acquisition of new information and retrieval of information from memory storage. *Sensory decline* is also a common experience for aging individuals.

Social Aging

Social aging is based on changes in one's relationships with family, friends, acquaintances, systems, and organizations. Most older persons experience a narrowing of their social networks. However, they are more likely to have more positive interactions within those networks, and they are more likely to experience more positive feelings about family members than younger persons do.

Disengagement theory states that it is natural and inevitable for older adults to withdraw from their social systems and to reduce interactions with others. This theory has been highly criticized and is incompatible with other well-known psychosocial aging theories. *Activity theory* proposes that social activity serves as a buffer to aging; successful aging occurs among those who maintain their social connections and activity levels. *Continuity theory* proposes that with age, individuals attempt to maintain activities and relationships that were typical for them as younger adults.

Gerontology

Gerontology is the study of biological, cognitive, and psychological features of the aging process. It includes the study of the impact of an aging population on social and economic trends. Gerontologists practice in the fields of medicine, psychology, physical and occupational therapy, as well as social work. Geriatric social work practice refers to a range of services provided to the population of those over age 60. Geriatric social workers are found in nursing homes, counseling programs, advocacy centers, and other programs serving seniors. Aging adults must deal with the very real issues of palliative care, hospice, and other end of life issues. The job of social workers is to support them through difficult decision-making processes and to counsel them as they deal with the complicated emotional and spiritual concerns of aging.

Personality Theories

There are several noted theories as to how personality is formed. In 400 B.C.E., Hippocrates attempted to identify personalities based on four temperaments. He called these *humors*, and these were associated with body fluid presence, such as phlegm or bile.

In the 1940s, William Sheldon came up with his body type theories that included the *endomorph*—an overweight individual, with an easy-going personality, the *mesomorph*—a muscular person, with an aggressive personality—and the *ectomorph*—a thin individual, with an artistic or intellectual personality.

Gordon Allport developed the trait theory of personality development. He believed that certain personalities were comprised of clusters of traits and that these traits could be categorized into cardinal, central, and secondary traits.

Freud believed the personality was composed of the id, the ego and superego. The *id* refers to a person's unconscious, with its suppressed desires and unresolved conflicts, whereas the *ego* and *superego* are more influenced by the conscious mind. He believed that these three components were often in conflict with one another and that how one resolved these conflicts determined personality. He also stressed the importance of childhood experience in personality development.

Carl Rogers was a proponent of the humanistic theory of personality development. This approach emphasized self-perception and a desire for striving to become the best person one can become. His theory was based on the basic goodness and potential of each person.

The behavioral theories of B.F. Skinner and others related to personality development implies that one's persona is developed as a result of classical or operant conditioning. Reinforcement and punishment guide behavioral choices.

Factors Influencing Self-Image

Self-image has to do with how people view themselves. This concept includes *self-esteem*, whether a person has feelings of high or low worth. The concept of self evolves throughout the life span, but it always plays a significant role in a how a person functions in life.

Impact of Cultural Heritage on Self-Image

Although personal factors play a large role, self-esteem is also based on how closely a person matches the dominant values of his or her culture. For example, Western society tends to value assertiveness, independence, and individuality. Living up to these values is seen as an important accomplishment, and thus, children receive messages about their personal competence and success based on whether or not they are living up to these ideals.

Children who are able to exhibit behaviors that are valued within their home and family, as well as those valued by their culture, are more likely to develop a positive self-concept.

One study suggests that across culture, self-esteem is based on one's control of life and choices, living up to one's "duties," benefiting others or society, and one's achievement. However, the degree to which one's culture values each of those factors has an impact on how the individual derives his or her self-esteem.

A widely cited example of the way that a culture can affect a person's self-image is in the portrayal of women's bodies in the media. In the United States, young women are exposed to underweight models and unrealistically drawn cartoon "heroines," which can lead to the development of unachievable expectations and significant negative perceptions about their bodies.

Impact of Race and Ethnicity on Self-Image

Culture, race, and ethnicity can greatly impact one's self-image, whether one is part of a privileged population or a minority population. One's ethnic and racial background provides a sense of belonging and identity. Depending on a country's treatment of a particular group, self-image can be negatively impacted through racism and discrimination. As mentioned, non-whites are more likely to be arrested than whites and often receive harsher sentences for similar offenses. Racial jokes and racial slurs are common. Stereotypes abound, and some people judge entire racial groups based on the behavior of a few. Such treatment consistently impacts the self-esteem of minority groups. As children become aware of the environment and the culture in which they live, they inevitably notice a lack of prominent nonwhite politicians, entertainers, CEOs, or multi-millionaires. Non-white Americans—who grew up in the fifties or earlier—were denied access to restaurants, theaters, high schools, professions, universities, and recreational activities. Even within the last fifty to sixty years, African Americans who had achieved great status in the fields of music, sports and entertainment were still denied access to certain clubs, hotels, or restaurants.

Every person must explore and come to terms with his or her own culture, ethnicity, and race. Sometimes, this even means rejecting cultural aspects with which he or she disagrees and embracing new and evolving cultural norms. This is a significant part of self-identity development among teenagers and young adults as they are part of a new generation that may be culturally different from their parents. Those that have more exposure to other cultures and backgrounds will have a more open perspective and are better able to evaluate their own culture and ethnicity objectively.

Effects of Spirituality

Spirituality is sometimes mistaken for religion, but in fact, they are quite different terms. Religion is an organized system of beliefs that generally contain a code of conduct and often involve specific devotional or ritual observations. Spirituality is more abstract and includes participation in spiritual activities such as meditation, chanting, prayer, or unselfishly serving others. A spiritual person may or may not belong to a religious organization. Spirituality places emphasis on the growth and well-being of the mind, body and spirit.

Studies have shown that persons who embrace spirituality tend to live both longer and happier lives. Several benefits of being a spiritual person include the following:

- Encourages individual to strive towards being a better person
- Increases likelihood of connections with others
- Offers hope to the hopeless through strong faith
- Provides a path to heal from emotional pain
- Helps reduce anxiety through meditation and other spiritual activities
- Leads to greater life commitment via the optimism spiritual persons tend to have

Impact of Age on Self-Image

Aging is an inevitable phase of human development, and the impact is physical, psychological, social, and economic. Self-image is the perception of how one views oneself, but the perception is influenced by societal values. Some cultures revere the elderly and look to them for wisdom and strength. These cultures include the Native Americans, Chinese, Koreans, and Indians. In the United States, there is a different perception of aging. Many elderly Americans feel less valuable or important once they enter retirement. At the same time, they are coping with undesirable body changes and learning to accept that, physically, they can no longer do what they once did. In the U.S., youth and physical attractiveness are highly valued. The elderly are seldom seen as important social figures. They are also less connected with families today with only 3.7% of homes reporting multigenerational households, per Census Bureau reports. Family support and family contact is less available, currently. For some segments of the population, though, technology has allowed relatives to visit regularly with grandchildren and even participate in family meals or get-togethers.

Infancy: The ego is in charge. The baby thinks primarily of basic needs, such as food or warmth.

Childhood: In early to middle childhood, children tend to rate themselves higher than peers in terms of talents and intellect. As middle school approaches, there is a decline in self-evaluations. This could be related to feeling unattractive due to physical changes or being teased or bullied by peers in that age group.

Adolescence: In the early stage of adolescence (ages 9 to 13), another drop in self-esteem occurs. This is thought to be related to the need to let go of childish pleasures, such as a beloved toy or previous interests and step up to the plate of becoming a more responsible person. This can be a painful sacrifice

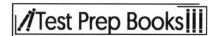

for some youth. The next drop in self-worth occurs at the end of adolescence and beginning of young adulthood (ages 18 to 23). It is during this period that the young adults realize that they truly are responsible for their own lives, yet they have not yet achieved a sense of mastery in the academic or vocational world. They are fearful and full of doubt about the ability to be successful as an independent adult.

Adulthood: Studies indicate a small but steady increase in self-image by mid-twenties. In general, during this period, men tend to have higher self-esteem than women. Persons who live in poor socioeconomic conditions tend to have lower self-esteem than their more financially stable peers. As later adulthood nears (the 70s), women tend to catch up with men in terms of how they evaluate themselves. Women in their eighties tend to have a more positive self-image than male counterparts. As a general rule, for both genders, there is a gradual increase in one's sense of self-worth throughout the life span until late middle age. Research shows that most adults' self-image peaks at around age 60.

Impacts of Disability on Self-Image
Disabilities impact self-image regardless of age; however, an individual who is born with a disability tends to fare better than one who acquires one later in life. Responses vary based upon severity of impairments. Some later life medical conditions cause the individual to give up independence as the person is forced to retire the car keys or move to an institutional setting. Less severe acquired disabilities, which still allow the person to maintain much of his or her previous lifestyle, are painful, but easier to accept. An individual's personality make-up and resilience to coping with change are also important factors. It is not uncommon for older adults to lapse into depression. This is often generated by a combination of losses. As one enters the later stages of life, loss of friends and family members is common. There may be declines in status, earning capacity, or physical abilities, all of which contribute to depression and negatively impact self-image.

Effects of Trauma on Self-image
Trauma can have a significant impact on self-image as a person's entire identity becomes intertwined with the traumatic event and the subsequent emotions. Some victims of trauma report a sense of isolation from others, feeling that they are not good enough or that they are less competent or less attractive than their peers. This generates feelings of shame and unworthiness, which, in turn, can lead to depression or anxiety. Some trauma survivors—especially victims of child or domestic abuse—feel a deep sense of betrayal and label the world and people as unsafe. They have trouble trusting others, and they may perform poorly in major areas of functioning, such as work or relationships. Some abuse survivors describe themselves as "damaged goods." Some individuals may engage in self-harm behaviors or may feel so depressed that suicide is seen as the only solution. These persons are prone to substance abuse as a means to numb the emotional pain. Addictive behavior can also negatively impact one's self-esteem. The more resilient will use their painful experiences as a tool for self-growth and may eventually learn to help others who have been through similar experiences.

Body Image

Body image refers to the thoughts and feelings about the appearance of one's body, as well as thoughts and feelings about how one's body is perceived by others. Body image is shaped by the messages that we receive from the people around us, the culture we live in, and the media.

Persistent negative body image can be associated with these factors:

- Low self-esteem
- Depression and/or anxiety
- Sexual risk-taking
- Impaired relationship satisfaction
- Withdrawal from activities where one's body may be visible to others (e.g., exercise, sexual activity, swimming, seeking medical care)
- Development of eating disorders

Parenting Skills and Capacities

Good parenting practices are essential for raising emotionally healthy children. Child psychologists vary on what types of parenting styles are most effective, but there are four generally recognized styles of parenting.

Authoritarian parenting style: This style of parenting reinforces the role of parent as controller and decision maker. Children are rarely given input into decisions impacting their lives, and the parent takes on a dictatorial role. Children raised by this kind of parent are often obedient and tend to be proficient. The drawback is that they do not rank high on the happiness scale.

Authoritative parenting style: This style of parenting allows for a greater sense of democracy in which children are given some degree of input into issues that impact their lives. There is a healthy balance between firmness and affection. Children raised in this environment tend to be capable, successful, and happy individuals.

Permissive parenting style: This type of parenting allows children to be more expressive and freer with both feelings and actions; they are allowed to behave in whatever manner they please. There are very few rules, and no consequences will be given, even if a rule is violated. These children are more likely to experience problems in school and relationships with others. In the long run, they are often unhappy with their lives.

Uninvolved parenting style: This form of parenting often occurs in dysfunctional families in which parents are emotionally or physically unavailable. They may be remiss in setting clear expectations, yet they may overreact when the child misbehaves or fails to understand what is expected. This is often seen in families where poverty is extreme or addictions or mental illnesses are present.

The authoritative style of parenting is considered to be the most effective form of parenting, yet much depends on the individual child or parent and the economic situation or cultural setting. One rule of thumb is that whatever style one chooses, it is helpful to remain consistent. A parent who is permissive one day and authoritarian the next sends mixed and confusing messages to the child. It is also important that the child is completely aware of rules, expectations, and what consequences may follow if the rules are broken. Communicating a sense that children are loved, wanted, and accepted is one of the most important parts of parenting.

Basic Principles of Human Genetics

Social workers will begin to see more work done in the area of human genetics in the coming years. Since social workers are often the first individuals to diagnose mental disorders, it's imperative for workers to understand the ethical and legal implications behind a genetic diagnosis. The following is a list of social work *practice skills* related to genetics:

- Biopsychosocial assessment of clients who may have genetic disorders
- Providing assistance to clients with genetic disorders by identifying and/or developing programs for them
- Providing risks-benefits counseling before a client undergoes genetic testing
- Providing post-test counseling following diagnosis of a disorder
- Providing counseling related to family planning
- Providing adoption-related counseling pertaining to implications of an adoptee's genetic information

The following is a list of social work values related to genetics:

- Accessibility: availability of genetic screening to those who need it
- Self-determination: protection of rights when individuals are asked to take part in population screening
- Autonomy: the right and ability for an individual to choose whether or not to undergo genetic testing
- Confidentiality: assurance and maintenance of the privacy of genetic testing results
- Research: data from screening used for the purpose of developing services that may benefit others

Ethical dilemmas may arise as the result of genetic testing. Social workers should refer to the NASW Code of Ethics (1996) for guidance, paying particular attention to the ethical standards of self-determination, informed consent, and social and political action.

Family Life Cycle

Family life cycle theories assume that, as members of a family unit, individuals pass through different stages of life. Although various theories will break down the stages somewhat differently, the following is a common conceptualization of the stages:

Unattached Young Adult
The primary tasks for this stage are selecting a life style and a life partner. Focus is on establishing independence as an adult and independence from one's family of origin.

Newly-Married Couple
The focus in this stage is on establishing the marital system. Two families are joined together, and relationships must be realigned.

Family with Young Children
The focus in this stage is on accepting new family members and transitioning from a marital system to a family system. The couple takes on a parenting role. Relationships must again be realigned with the extended family (e.g., grandparents).

Family with Adolescents

The focus here is on accommodating the emerging independence of the adolescents in the family. The parent-child relationship experiences changes, and the parents may also begin to take on caregiving roles with regard to their own parents.

Launching Family

The focus in this stage is on accepting the new independent role of an adult child and transitioning through the separation. Parents also must face their own transition into middle or older age.

Family in Later Years

In this stage, spousal roles must be re-examined and re-defined. One focus may be the development of interests and activities outside of work and family. Another focus is on navigation of the aging process and losses that may occur.

The basic family life cycle can vary significantly as a result of cultural influences, expectations, and particular family circumstances (e.g., single-parent family, blended family, multi-generational family).

Family Life Education in Social Work Practice

Family life education is an important aspect of social work practice in the psychoeducational realm of treatment. Families sometimes need to be educated concerning their biopsychosocial structure and other kinds of family structures. Family life models have changed in recent years and continue to change at a rapid pace with the advent of the legalization of gay marriage and the increase in extended and blended families. Family life has become very diverse, and social workers need to be educated on these models so they can further educate clients.

Aging Parents on Adult Children

There are about 10 million Americans over the age of fifty who are caring for aging parents. In the last fifteen years, thanks to modern medicine, the adult population has begun living longer. As a result, the number of adult children between the ages of fifty and seventy who provide care to aging parents has tripled. This amounts to about 25 percent of adult children who provide either personal or economic assistance.

Research indicates that becoming a personal caregiver to a parent increases the rates of depression, substance abuse, and heart disease. These adult children sometimes take significant financial blows in the form of lost income, earlier than planned retirement, and reduced pension plans, due to leaving the workforce earlier. At the same time, these adult children are assisting their own children as they move towards independence. Those in the youngest generation may still be in college or in the early stages of starting a career and still look to parents for some financial assistance. From a different perspective, the positives of this situation are that children are able to form deeper bonds with grandparents, and the longevity of life in loved ones can have very positive impact on all involved.

Systems and Ecological Perspectives and Theories

Systems Theory in social work refers to the view that human behavior is explained by the influences of the various systems to which individuals belong. When evaluating and conceptualizing an individual's behavior, that behavior must be considered in the context of the individual's family, society, and other systems.

All systems are seen as possessing interrelated parts and exerting influence on each other. There are many iterations of the premise of the basic systems theory. In practice, systems theory allows a social worker to understand the dynamics of a client's systems better, while also creating an appropriate intervention approach. The originator of systems theory in social work was Ludwig von Bertalanffy, a biologist, who was influenced by sociologists Max Weber and Emile Durkheim.

Talcott Parsons expanded on earlier work with his framework of structural functionalism, which proposes that a system is defined by its function in its social environment.

The four states of social systems are adaptation to the social environment, goal attainment, integration with other systems, and latency or homeostasis (social patterns and norms are maintained). It's also important to note the designations of social systems in social work. Microsystems are small systems, like an individual or a couple. Mezzosystems are medium-sized systems made up of extended families or groups to which the individual belongs. Macrosystems are large systems made up of organizations or communities.

The *ecological systems perspective* is concerned with the transactions between systems. It says that people and families must be considered within cultural and societal contexts, which also necessitates examining the events that have occurred in an individual's life. Changes made by the individual that cause the entire system to shift must also be considered.

The following lists common interventions based on systems theory:

- Strengthening a part of the system in order to improve the whole system

- Creating a genogram: a family tree constructed with a client in order to improve understanding of the familial relationships and to identify recurring patterns

- Connecting clients to organizations or individuals who can help them to function better within and between their systems

- Developing an ecomap: an Illustration of client's systems, such as family and community and how it changes over time

Strengths-Based and Resilience Theories

Rather than focusing on problems and pathology, the strengths perspective (or *strengths-based approach*) in social work encourages social workers to focus on a client's strengths or assets and to build upon the client's inherent resiliency and positive characteristics. Outcome studies regarding use of the strengths perspective are limited; however, it is posited that a strengths-based approach could help to remove some of the stigma attached to groups or conditions (e.g., mental illness, poverty).

Resilience theories account for risk factors that may threaten an individual's ability to cope with adverse events. Risk factors include lack of support, diagnosis of mental health disorders, and resource constraints. Protective factors that support high levels of resiliency include the ability to think positively about situations, the ability to feel hope, strong confidence in one's self-reliance, problem-solving abilities, and competence. Developing resilience should be treated as a preventative approach, rather than a reactive approach.

Strengths- and resilience-based approaches allow individuals to feel empowered and maintain a sense of self-efficacy, both of which are crucial components for lasting behavior change and resolution. Additionally, they minimize client's self-identification with a problem or issue, which can cause the client to fall into a self-fulfilling prophecy. It is important to note that clients can build the capacity to be resilient as a healthy method of coping. This type of skill building can often serve as a crucial component of an intervention. Exercises may include reframing perspectives, journaling, learning new abilities (such as problem-solving skills), practicing flexibility when unexpected changes arise, and examining public stories of strength and resiliency with the client. Finally, practitioners can support clients by providing positive reinforcement and feedback when the client displays strong and resilient behaviors.

Loss, Separation, and Grief

The concept of loss is at the root of many depressive episodes. Losses can include anything one holds dearly. Losing a loved one, a pet, a job, housing, or financial or social status can all bring emotional pain. Other losses include the loss of physical or mental health. Separation is a form of loss that can occur in many forms, including divorce, military deployment, a job that requires one to move far away, or the loss of custody of a child. Grief is the emotional response to loss. Grief includes the main emotion of sadness, but other strong emotions may be present as well. Other feelings include confusion, anger, frustration, anxiety, or guilt.

The five stages of grief is a concept developed by Elisabeth Kubler-Ross in her book *On Death and Dying* in 1969. The five stages model originally pertained to those experiencing the dying process as the result of a terminal illness, but the model has been widely used to understand the grief reactions that people have in response to a number of situations, including loss of a loved one. The stages were first posited to be linear, but Kubler-Ross later stated that they are five common experiences that may or may not be experienced during grieving.

Denial
This is the first stage. It occurs at the point that the person on some level becomes aware that they have lost someone or something dear, but on another level, they refuse to accept the truth. This stage is generally brief as the person begins to process irrefutable evidence.

Anger
This is a period of venting anger at anyone who the person feels contributed to the loss occurring. It may be towards God, the drunk driver who caused an accident, or the CPS worker who takes a child from the home. In the case of a suicide, there could be anger at the deceased for choosing to leave.

Bargaining
This stage is almost a form of magical thinking. A person may think that if they promise to do better, work harder, or pray harder, the loss process can be reversed. This again is generally a short-lived phase as one realizes that promises made will still not bring back that which has been lost.

Depression
During the fourth stage, a person allows themself to feel the sadness, and they may experience an even deeper emotional pain while learning to accept the loss and move forward. It may be a time of crying, despondency, and anguish. It must be experienced in order to move to the next stage.

Acceptance

The last stage is the point at which the grieving person recognizes that, while the pain is tremendous, they will be able to handle it. Those at this stage understand that time will ease some of the suffering. They are learning to make peace with the experience and move forward with their lives.

Human Behavior in the Social Environment

Person-In-Environment (PIE) Theory

Carel Germain described person-in environment interaction, based upon earlier work in systems theory. This perspective takes into consideration an individual's environmental and systemic influences. It is specific to social work, which differentiates it from other like professions.

- Life stress: the normal tension that occurs as the result of both external demands and internal experiences

    o What is experienced as stressful varies across people and their perceptions. For example, two people placed in the same environment may have completely different experiences due to the ways in which they experience and perceive the situation.

- Adaptation: when the environment and the individual change in response to the interaction with each other

- Coping: individual use of one's own strengths and problem-solving abilities to navigate life stress and develop self-esteem and hope

- Power: a source of stress to the individual and the larger system misused by groups

- Human Relatedness: the ability of individuals to cultivate relationships

- Three related concepts are *self-direction*, *competence*, and *self-esteem*. These attributes are interdependent and occur cross-culturally.

Family Dynamics and Functioning

Family dynamics are the interactions between family members in a family system. As discussed previously, under "Family Theories," each family is a unique system; however, there are some common patterns of family dynamics.

Common influences on family dynamics:

- The type and quality of relationship that the parents have
- An absent parent
- A parent who is either extremely strict or extremely lenient
- The mix of personalities in the family
- A sick or disabled family member
- External events, particularly traumatic ones that have affected family members
- Family dynamics in previous generations or the current extended family

Common roles in the family that may result from particular family dynamics:

- The problem child: child with problematic behavior, which may serve as a distraction from other problems that the family, particularly the parents, do not want to face

- Scapegoat: the family member to whom others unjustly attribute problems, often viewed as "bad," while other family members are viewed as "good"

- Peacekeeper: a family member who serves to mediate relationships and reduce family stress

The Effects of Family Dynamics on Individuals

There are many ways in which the family influences the individual socially, emotionally, and psychologically. All family systems have their own unique characteristics, with both good and bad functional tendencies. The family interactions are among the earliest and most formative relationships that a person has, so they define the relational patterns that the individual develops and utilizes with all subsequent relationships. Parenting styles, conflict resolution methods, beliefs and values, and coping mechanisms are just a few things that a person learns from their family of origin. It is also within the family that a person first develops an image of self and identity, often having to do with the role that they are given within the family system and the messages communicated by parents. If a child has a secure and healthy relationship with the family members, this will likely lead to overall well-being and emotional stability as an adult.

When it comes to physical or mental illness, the role that the family plays is critical in lowering risk factors and minimizing symptoms. A strongly supportive family will help a person function at the highest level possible. Oftentimes, family members can serve as caregivers or play less formal—but still critical—roles in supporting a person's health.

Dynamics of Interpersonal Relationships

Interpersonal relationships refer to interactions (often of a close, friendly, romantic, or intimate nature) between people. They can form due to shared personal, professional, social, charitable, or political interests. Strong interpersonal relationships are built over time as participants are willing to honestly communicate on a regular basis, support one another's well-being, and develop a shared history. Psychological, evolutionary, and anthropological contexts suggest that humans are an inherently altruistic, community-oriented species that relies on interpersonal relationships to survive and thrive. These types of relationships (when healthy) provide security, a sense of belonging, an exchange of benefits and rewards, and a sense of self-esteem. Healthy interpersonal relationships are characterized by mutual respect, care, and consideration between members. Almost all groups assemble into a power structure of some kind, with natural leaders taking over decision making, resource sharing, and other tasks that affect the group as a whole. Dysfunctional interpersonal relationships may be characterized by an extreme power imbalance and dominance by one or more involved members, often leading to submissiveness, learned helplessness, and feelings of low self-esteem in the relationship's less powerful members. Submissive members of a group may find themselves without material resources or respect from the rest of the group.

Abuse and Neglect Throughout the Lifespan

Indicators and Dynamics of Sexual Abuse

Sexual abuse is forced or coerced sexual contact or exposure, usually by someone older or in a position of authority over the victim. Sexual abuse can also include forcing someone to watch sexual acts or receive messages involving unwanted sexual content. The impact of sexual abuse is complex, and the emotional and psychological response to the trauma may evolve as the victim gets older and understands more fully what happened to them. Children who suffer sexual abuse may struggle from confusion about the abuse, especially if they are told by the perpetrator that it is right and good and if that person is someone with whom they have a relationship of trust. They may be blamed by the perpetrator for the abuse, which leads to further feelings of confusion and guilt. If they report the abuse to someone who does not believe it, the long term effects of the abuse may be even greater, as well as the guilt, self-doubt, and shame. A history of sexual abuse will normally impact a person's relationships with others throughout life, and there may be issues of trust as well as confused feelings toward sex.

Indicators of Sexual Abuse (Child)
- The statement that one has been sexually assaulted
- Mistrust or fear of those who bear resemblance to the abuser, potentially due to gender or size (children may be mistrustful of all adults)
- Changes in behavior
- Depression
- Anxiety with presenting symptoms (hair loss, fluctuations in weight)
- Increased fearfulness (possible night terrors and enuresis/bed wetting from children)
- Withdrawal from preferred activities/social isolation
- Compulsive masturbation
- Substance abuse
- Overly-sexualized behavior
- Parent, spouse, or caregiver demonstrating inappropriate behaviors
- Role confusion, distortion of child's role in the family
- Jealousness or over-protection of the victim
- Excessive, abnormal alone time with the child
- Lack of appropriate social and emotional contacts outside the home
- Substance and/or alcohol abuse
- Parent or caregiver reports being sexually abused previously (possible normalization or continuation of the cyclic behavior)

Indicators and Dynamics of Psychological Abuse and Neglect

Psychological abuse—or emotional abuse—is more difficult to define than sexual or physical abuse, but it can be just as damaging to the victim. Psychological neglect, especially as a child, involves withholding the love, affection, and emotional security that a child needs in order to grow and thrive. Psychological abuse involves emotional manipulation that uses strategies of shame, fear, and guilt to control someone's behaviors. Another aspect of psychological abuse can be verbal abuse which takes the form of yelling, constant criticisms or belittling, threats, or name-calling. Alternatively, the child may be ignored, be made the witness of violence, or isolated as a punishment. These are all forms of psychological abuse and neglect. Because of the often vague or indefinable aspects of psychological abuse, it may be difficult for victims to understand or believe that they are being mistreated. Even if they do, they may be convinced that no one will believe them because of the manipulation of the

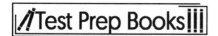

perpetrator, who may either threaten or undermine the victim to such an extent that they are unwilling to take any action. Long-term, a victim of psychological abuse is more likely to be fearful and withdrawn as a result of the many insecurities that have developed because of the abuse.

Indicators and Dynamics of Physical Abuse and Neglect

Physical abuse can be defined as bodily mistreatment, including hitting, slapping, kicking, burning, unnecessary constraints, strangling, or other acts of physical violence. Physical abuse is often perpetrated out of anger or frustration, as is the case with parents who use physical abuse to inappropriately discipline their children. In cases where there is a higher level of family stress or conflict or when parents have not received adequate training in parenting strategies, the levels of physical abuse may be higher. Physical abuse can also take place in adult relationships, most usually in an intimate relationship where one person struggles with anger management. Victims of physical abuse may show obvious signs of the abuse, such as injuries or multiple trips to the emergency room. However, there are other less obvious signs of physical abuse, such as fearful withdrawal, aggression, or other acting-out.

Physical neglect is withholding anything that is necessary for physical health and safety, as well as educational and medical needs. If a parent, for example, does not provide a child with enough food or with warm clothes in the winter, this would be considered neglect. This type of neglect can sometimes be deliberate, but may also be the result of ignorance or a lack of resources.

Effects of Physical, Sexual, and Psychological Abuse

People may experience abuse at the hands of strangers, caretakers, or close friends and family. The effects of abuse are traumatic, pervasive, and long lasting. Beyond affecting the abused parties, abuse often impacts those who are close to the victims. Physical, sexual, and psychological child abuse can lead to impaired intellect, learning abilities, deficits in trust and language skills, and long-term inappropriate behaviors or lack of coping mechanisms. As abused children grow, they may be unable to make healthy friendships or desire or maintain intimate relationships. They may have failed marriages, or they may perpetuate the cycle of abuse when they become parents. They may often feel unworthy or that they did something to cause the abuse. This often has an impact on their attachment styles and how they relate to others.

In adults, abuse may cause permanent or temporary physical damage, low self-esteem, shame, despair, or feelings of helplessness. Victims of abuse as an adult may experience mental health disorders such anxiety and depression. If children witness their loved ones experiencing abuse, it may be traumatic for them, or they may normalize the behavior and perpetuate abuse themselves. Elder abuse, especially in nursing homes, often goes undetected as victims may be weak or losing mental faculties. Elders are especially vulnerable to physical and financial abuse. Effects may include rapid physical or mental deterioration, submissiveness, bedsores, increased rate of illness, or premature death.

In traumatic cases, both children and adults may become severely depressed or anxious. They may abuse substances or commit suicide.

Perpetrators of Abuse, Neglect, and Exploitation

Abuse perpetrators are individuals who cause or allow mistreatment of a child or other dependent. Common characteristics of abuse perpetrators are having experienced or witnessed abuse during childhood; lack of coping skills to manage anger and frustration; isolation or lack of a substantial support system; immaturity with poor regulation of emotions; abuse of alcohol or other substances; inappropriate expectations for the behavior of others; and poor social skills.

Effects of Life Events, Stressors, and Crises

Life events are experienced by all families and can be both positive and negative—everything from marriage or childbirth to death or divorce. If the life event is more negative and sudden, it may be considered a crisis, such as the unexpected loss of a family member, diagnosis of a major illness, a car crash, financial trouble, or something even more intense like a natural disaster or terrorist attack. Even positive life events can become crises for families if they have difficulty adjusting to the changes. Crises often involve both hard decisions and emotional turmoil.

The *ABCX Model*, introduced by Reuben Hill, seeks to explain how families deal with stressful situations that arise. A is the event that occurs, B is the family resources, C is the family perception, and X stands for a crisis. It claims that the event, plus the family resources and plus the family's perception, all combine to determine whether the event is viewed as a crisis and whether the family is able to cope with it. Depending on the family's ability to adapt their normal functioning patterns, a life event or crisis can either strengthen their relationships and the family unit or tear them apart. A family can effectively deal with the crisis if they utilize *positive coping mechanisms*, such as pursuing practical solutions to deal with the issues that arise, seeking counseling from a therapist or clergy, engaging social supports, and communicating openly with each other. *Negative coping strategies* could involve drug or alcohol use, isolation, or displacement of anger and frustration onto family members. Though all families will face a period of disordered chaos in trying to deal with a crisis, the families that are successful are those that can engage in new and positive coping methods.

Impact of Stress, Trauma, and Violence

Trauma affects everyone differently. The reaction depends on the person's emotional resiliency, history of past trauma, and other factors. Some trauma survivors exhibit symptoms that clearly meet the criteria for PTSD, while others exhibit smaller clusters of symptoms, such as anxiety or depression. Others show little or no symptoms. Below is an overview of common responses:

- Foreshortened future: This refers to the sense that one's life is shortened or forever altered and that a normal life may never be experienced again.

- Emotional responses: These may be fear, sadness, shame, anger, guilt, and/or anxiety.

- Physical reactions: Survivors of trauma often have multiple somatic issues, including gastrointestinal complaints, neurological problems, poor sleep, and muscle pain.

- Hyperarousal: Trauma survivors often become hypervigilant. They are frightened by neutral stimuli, such as a dog barking or a child screaming. They may experience a continual feeling that something terrible is going to happen.

- Intrusive thoughts: Survivors can become flooded with unwanted thoughts and memories about the trauma.

- Trigger/flashbacks: Triggers are stimuli that set off memories and provide a sensory reminder of the traumatic event.

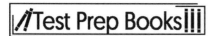

- Dissociation: This coping mechanism allows the person to "check out" temporarily. This process severs connections to the painful memories.

- Self-harm: Some survivors use self harm as a means of distraction from emotional pain. This could transition into more serious self harm and can result in suicidal behaviors if not treated.

- Substance abuse: Many survivors use substances to medicate unpleasant emotions, such as fear or shame.

Common Effects of Stress, Trauma, and Violence

Many people equate stress with an emotional experience, but stress can actually have a profound effect on the body, cognition, and behavior as well.

Common Effects of Stress		
Body	**Mood**	**Behavior**
Headache	Anxiety	Overeating or under eating
Muscle tension or pain	Restlessness	Angry outbursts
Chest pain	Lack of motivation or focus	Drug or alcohol abuse
Fatigue	Irritability or anger	Tobacco use
Change in sex drive	Sadness or depression	Social withdrawal
Stomach upset		
Sleep problems		

Although everyone experiences some degree of stress, stress becomes trauma when the intensity of the stress causes a person to feel helpless and seriously threatened, either physically or psychologically. Unfortunately, trauma and violence are common experiences for both adults and children, and the risk for traumatic and/or violent events is particularly high for individuals suffering from mental illness. Some people will experience a trauma with little to no lasting impact, while others may struggle with the aftermath of the trauma for the rest of their lives.

Many variables can either exacerbate or ameliorate the impact of trauma:

- Whether the event occurred once or was ongoing
- Whether the event occurred during childhood or adulthood
- Intensity of the traumatic event
- Personal experience vs. observation
- Ability to access supportive resources
- The way in which people and systems respond to the individual who has been traumatized

Potential effects of trauma and violence:

- Substance use and abuse
- Mental health problems
- Risk-taking behavior
- Self-injurious behavior
- Increased likelihood or exacerbation of chronic illnesses, including cardiovascular disease
- Difficulties with daily functioning, including navigating careers and relationships

Post-Traumatic Stress Disorder (PTSD)

Some people who have experienced trauma or violence will experience an impact significant enough to be diagnosed with PTSD. Symptoms must last for more than one month before the diagnosis of PTSD is considered and must include the following:

- One or more *re-experiencing symptoms* (flashbacks, disturbing dreams, frightening thoughts)

- One or more *avoidance symptoms* (avoiding reminders of the trauma, experiencing emotional "numbing," losing interest in activities that one previously enjoyed)

- Two or more *arousal and reactivity symptoms* (startling easily, experiencing tension, hypervigilance, difficulty falling or staying asleep, eruptions of anger)

- Two or more *cognition and mood symptoms* (difficulty remembering the traumatic event, persistent negative thoughts, excessive feelings of blame or guilt)

Crisis Intervention Theories

Crisis intervention is typically a short-term treatment usually lasting four to six weeks and is implemented when a client enters treatment following some type of traumatic event that causes significant distress. This event causes a state of disequilibrium when a client is out of balance and can no longer function effectively.

Gerald Caplan's Stages of Crises

Caplan theorized that individuals need to maintain homeostasis or remain in balance with their environment. A crisis is caused by an individual's reaction to a situation, not by an actual incident. Following a crisis event, an individual experiences the following stages:

Stage 1

Increase in feelings of stress immediately following the event. Client may experience denial and typically tries to resolve the stressful reactions using past problem-solving and coping skills.

Stage 2

Client experiences higher levels of stress as the usual coping mechanisms fail. Client may employ higher-level coping skills to alleviate the increasing stress levels.

Stage 3

As stressful feelings continue to escalate, client experiences major emotional turmoil, possible feelings of hopelessness, depression, and anxiety.

Stage 4

The final stage is marked by complete psychological and emotional collapse, or the individual finds a method to resolve the situation; however, there may be remaining emotional and psychological dysfunction or impairment if the coping mechanisms used were maladaptive.

Social workers can either use generic crisis intervention models for varied types of crises or can create an individualized plan for assisting the client. The main goal of crisis intervention should be to help clients develop and use adaptive coping skills to return to the level of functioning prior to the crisis.

The Crisis Intervention Process

Engage and Assess

Social workers participate in client engagement by helping to de-escalate volatile emotional states through establishing rapport, using empathy, employing emotional management techniques, and accessing outside systems (family, friends, and support groups). Additionally, the social worker assesses the crisis situation to determine the level of care required (general triage may include intensities ranging from one to three) and how the client has been impacted.

Set Goals and Implement Treatment

Goal setting should occur in collaboration with a client's treatment plan. Intervention strategies, tasks, and timeframes should correspond with the desired goal and objectives. The primary goal should be to assist clients in returning to pre-crisis functioning. However, there will likely be additional and related goals and tasks as the plan of action is implemented.

Evaluate and Terminate

Worker concludes treatment and evaluates completion of goals. It is important to discuss with the client what coping skills have been developed and how they might be able to use those skills for future crises and challenges.

Effect of Poverty

Poverty is often the foundation of a number of other socioeconomic and health problems faced by individuals, families, and communities. Without resources such as money, transportation, or housing, it becomes difficult to buy healthy food, access medical care, drive to work, have quality childcare, or live in a safe area. For adults in poverty, the extreme level of stress that arises from trying to pay bills, provide basic necessities for themselves and their families, and manage multiple jobs often leads to a number of mental, physical, and emotional problems. These can include substance abuse, domestic violence, inability to maintain family units and romantic relationships, hopelessness, depression, and desperation. Children who live and grow up in poverty are prone to traumatic and catastrophic health risk factors, such as experiencing or witnessing violence, chronic malnutrition, higher rates of illness, and mood disorders. Experiencing such adverse events in childhood is associated with high levels of stress, impaired functioning, and impaired cognitive ability that can be irreparable. Individuals experiencing poverty are more likely to visit the emergency room for health problems (and often be unable to pay), require government assistance, and commit crimes (often in order to obtain necessary resources). These outcomes create a financial burden on the community and local economy.

Impact of the Environment

The Impact of the Physical Environment on Client Systems

The ecological perspective focuses on the *person in environment,* or the interaction between the individual and the environment around them (including physical environment and family). Privilege, or lack thereof, may also have a large impact on the development of individuals.

As mentioned, the *person-in-environment (PIE) theory* emphasizes the importance of viewing and treating a person within the context of their environment, rather than as a completely independent entity. In order to understand and effectively treat a person, it is critical to evaluate the environment they are in and the physical, emotional, and psychological impact that it has had as related to individual strengths and needs. The environment includes the dynamics of family, school, work place, culture, and social relationships. Rather than being exclusively person-focused or environment-focused, the PIE theory looks at the interplay between the two. If a person is displaying anxiety or depression, for example, the goal would be to determine what cultural, social, or familial factors may be playing a role. PIE seeks to have a holistic view, which then leads to broader and more comprehensive treatment options.

The importance of the PIE theory can be seen when working with children. Often children are identified as the primary problem, with behavioral or emotional issues. However, when the situation is explored more closely, there are almost always other factors that are contributing to the child's behaviors, including parental conflict, abuse and neglect, or some traumatic experience. Without evaluating the context the child is in, but instead focusing exclusively on that child's behaviors, it is impossible to determine the root cause of the presenting problem or the most appropriate steps to take. Similarly, it would be futile to merely change or address the child's environment without also dealing directly with the child's emotional and behavioral needs. The person, their emotions and behaviors, as well as their environment and the context in which they live, are all significant when it comes to planning a treatment.

The Impact of the Political Environment on Policy-Making and Client Systems

Social welfare legislation can have a dramatic effect on social work practice. Some legislation may help solve social problems that social workers encounter and other legislation may create more problems, challenges, and barriers through which social workers must help clients navigate. To be effective, social workers must be knowledgeable about legislative measures that affect clients. Another possible role of a social worker is that of legislative advocate, which is working to change, modify, or create legislation for the benefit of a group of people.

Significant Social Welfare Legislation:

- Civil Rights Act of 1964
- Older Americans Act of 1965
- The Child Abuse and Prevention Act of 1974
- Adoption Assistance and Child Welfare Act of 1980
- Americans with Disabilities Act of 1990
- The Family Medical Leave Act of 1993
- The Health Insurance Portability and Accountability Act of 1996 (HIPAA)
- The Patient Protection and Affordable Care Act of 2010

Impact of Social Environment on Client Systems

Social institutions exist to meet the needs of individuals, promote pro-social behavior, define social norms, and create order.

There are five major social institutions:

Family
- Regulates sexual behavior (monogamy)
- Creates and provides for new society members
- Socializes new society members

Religion
- Provides explanations for the unexplainable

- Supports societal norms and values
- Provides a means of coping with life situations

Government
- Institutionalizes norms (by creating laws)
- Enforces laws
- Protects members of society
- Provides a means of resolving conflict

Education
- Prepares society members to contribute to the society in specified roles
- Teaches skills necessary to function within the society

Economics
- Produces and distributes goods needed by society members
- Provides services necessary to the society

Impact of Economic Changes on Client Systems
Economic changes, particularly negative ones, can have a substantial impact on client systems.

- In times of economic turmoil, people tend to cut back on spending and stop seeking services in order to conserve money. Over time, this can lead to a backlog of individuals with major problems that need to be addressed, burdening many components of society.

- A poor economic climate can also exacerbate pre-existing problems, such as depression or substance abuse, and can create significantly more stress on the family unit, which may spill over into work or school.

- Unemployment has been linked to a withdrawal from social activity, low self-esteem, an increased sense of hopelessness, poorer mental health, and an increase in substance use.

- Such change has an impact within a family, and when enough families are affected, entire communities can experience shifts in attitude and behaviors.

- The experience of living in poverty for many years or at crucial points in time is linked to certain individual outcomes. Children living at the poverty level during preschool and elementary school years are less likely to finish their schooling than are those who experience poverty during later childhood or adolescence only.

- When economic factors are at play with regard to a client's well-being, social workers must be prepared to assist with the development of appropriate coping skills and identification of resources for the client and family system.

The Impact of the Cultural Environment on Client Systems
As mentioned, it is important not to use information about culture, race, and ethnicity in a stereotypical or overgeneralized manner. There are vast differences within groups. For example, group members holding a traditional viewpoint are likely to identify very strongly with their group and to reject the practices of other groups. In contrast, other individuals may be acculturated into a dominant group culture and may not identify with their culture of origin.

Race refers to biologically distinct populations within the human species. *Ethnicity* is a cultural term referring to the common customs, language, and heritage of a category of people. *Ethnic identity* is the identification with a particular group of people who share one's culture and heritage.

William Cross's Stages of Identity Development

William Cross is a theorist and researcher in the field of ethnicity identity development. He is known for his Nigrescence model and for his novel *Shades of Black.* The following depicts William Cross's Stages of Identity Development for people of color:

- Pre-encounter: Unless prompted to do so, children do not critically evaluate the race-related messages that they receive from the world around them.

- Encounter: Often experienced in early adolescence, the individual has one or more experiences that are related to race. Though it is possible for the experiences to be positive, this is often when an individual first experiences racism or discrimination and begins to understand the personal impact of their race.

- Immersion-Emersion: After experiencing a race-related incident, the individual strongly identifies with their racial group and may seek out information about history and culture.

- Internalization: Racial identity is solidified, and the individual experiences a sense of security in identifying with their race.

- Internalization-Commitment: Racial identity is taken one step further into activism pertaining to issues related to the experiences of the individual's racial group.

Sue & Sue's Stages of Racial/Cultural Identity Development

Derald Sue and David Sue developed *Stages of Racial/Cultural Identity Development*. Derald Sue is a professor of counseling psychology at Colombia University. David Sue is a professor emeritus of psychology at Western Washington University. Their works revolve around multicultural issues in counseling and multicultural therapy. The following are the stages of racial-cultural identity development:

- Conformity: The individual displays a distinct preference for the dominant culture and holds negative views of their own racial and/or cultural groups. They may also experience shame or embarrassment.

- Dissonance: The individual undergoes a period of re-thinking or challenging their beliefs. For the first time, the individual examines and appreciates positive aspects of their own racial/cultural group.

- Resistance and Immersion: The individual shows preference for minority views and actively rejects the views of the dominant culture, experiencing pride about and connection to their racial or cultural group.

- Introspection: The individual becomes aware of the negative impact of the resistance and immersion stage and may realize that they do not actually disagree with all majority views or endorse all minority views.

- Integrative Awareness: The individual is able to appreciate both their own culture and differing cultures.

Social and Economic Justice

Professional Commitment to Promoting Social Justice

Social justice is defined as equal rights, opportunities, and privileges for all members of society. The Code of Ethics of the National Association of Social Workers (revised 2008) specifically lists social justice as a core value. The NASW Code of Ethics states, "Social workers pursue social change, particularly with and on behalf of vulnerable and oppressed individuals and groups of people. Social workers' social change efforts are focused primarily on issues of poverty, unemployment, discrimination, and other forms of social injustice. These activities seek to promote sensitivity to and knowledge about oppression and cultural and ethnic diversity. Social workers strive to ensure access to needed information, services, and resources; equality of opportunity; and meaningful participation in decision making for all people."

Social Change and Community Development

Community development theory focuses on oppressed people who are in the process of overcoming social problems that were imposed upon them by external forces. In the process of community development, members of a community learn how to improve that community and gain control of their local environment. *Community-level change* brings people together and demonstrates the power of solidarity. This theory also acknowledges the reality that many problems are at the social, rather than individual, level. An implication of the theory is that therapy addresses only the symptoms of a problem and not the underlying causes.

Impact of Social Institutions on Society

Social institutions exist to meet the needs of individuals, promote pro-social behavior, define social norms, and create order.

There are five major social institutions:

Family
- Regulates sexual behavior (monogamy)
- Creates and provides for new society members
- Socializes new society members

Religion
- Provides explanations for the unexplainable
- Supports societal norms and values
- Provides a means of coping with life situations

Government
- Institutionalizes norms (by creating laws)
- Enforces laws

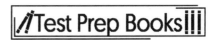

- Protects members of society
- Provides a means of resolving conflict

Education
- Prepares society members to contribute to the society in specified roles
- Teaches skills necessary to function within the society

Economics
- Produces and distributes goods needed by society members
- Provides services necessary to the society

Impact of Globalization on Clients

Globalization, or the process of working and operating in a hyper-connected, international capacity, has affected nearly every industry, including social work. Social workers are no longer limited to working with clients who are in close geographical proximity. They now have the ability to connect with audiences and clients all over the world through social media, email, virtual consultation, and web platforms. This expanded level of outreach can be positive, in that mental health and behavioral interventions, support, and awareness are more easily accessible. However, connecting online with clients can sometimes hinder the quality of personal interaction that practitioners cultivate with their clients. Additionally, it can be tricky to navigate the financial, legal, and security aspects of working with clients online, as these standards vary by geographical location.

Globalization has also opened new topics of interest for social workers. Globalization has led to increased working time, increased use of technology, and increased interactions across cultural, socioeconomic, and gender lines. In many ways, these changes have been associated with higher levels of work-related stress, health problems such poor sleep, increased rates of mood disorders such as depression and anxiety, and higher awareness of harassment against women and subordinate employees. These are all issues that social workers may not have typically handled with clients in previous decades. They must now become skilled in addressing these issues. Finally, the use of technology, screens, and social media in children has been potentially linked with addictive behaviors, cyberbullying, and increased depression and anxiety rates. This is yet another avenue in which social workers must develop interventions that work in a relatively new context with variables about which research is still emerging.

Criminal Justice Systems

Social workers can have an important role in the criminal justice system. Prison and jail systems are full, and less than a third of incarcerated individuals who are released remain free. Most end up back in the criminal justice system. Additionally, a number of incarcerated individuals have mental and emotional disorders that often contribute to unlawful behavior. These can include substance abuse problems or high levels of personal stress. Social workers are trained to understand these contexts, and therefore they can provide valuable insight and counsel before, during, and after legal cases. Therefore, social workers can intervene and offer support during all phases of the justice system. Social workers can work with individuals who were the victims of criminal activities. They are also able to work with perpetrators who have been released, thereby helping to prevent re-incarceration. Social workers can also provide support to the families of both victims and perpetrators, assist with the transition of having family member in jail, assist with the transition of having a family member released, and support in educational and professional activities after release. Finally, social workers can have a meaningful impact in the lives of children who may be at risk of ending up in the criminal justice system. By focusing interventions on vulnerable youth, such as education, positive recreational activities, mentoring programs, support for parents, and so on, social workers potentially have the ability to prevent youth and families from ever entering the criminal justice system. This is much more powerful approach for positive behavior and social change, rather than addressing individual, family, and community issues after crimes have already been committed. Social workers will need to remember to show compassion and withhold judgment when working with criminal offenders; however, they must also be mindful to protect their personal safety in these situations.

Impact of Out-of-Home Placement

Children and elderly or disabled persons are sometimes legally removed from homes when it is determined there is a safety concern such as abuse or neglect. In these situations, the goal of removal is to secure the health, safety, and well-being of the displaced individual. It is likely that many other interventions have been attempted and have not worked, with removal being a last resort. These individuals, particularly children, who have lived in chaotic, dysfunctional environments will already have psychological and behavioral problems, including anxiety, depression, acting out, and displays of aggression. Following removal, these behaviors will likely escalate. Additionally, the parents or other caregivers who have had dependents taken away will also experience anger, confusion, guilt, and an assortment of challenges. Social workers can assume many roles in out-of-home placement, including working with the family of origin, the individual who has been displaced, or the respite caregivers.

Couples Development

Many couples enter treatment after experiencing long-standing problems and may seek help because all other options have failed. One of the goals of couples' therapy is to help clients develop effective communication and problem-solving skills so they can solve problems throughout and after treatment. Other goals include helping the couple form a more objective view of their relationship, modifying dysfunctional behavior/patterns, increasing emotional expression, and recognizing strengths. Workers should create an environment to help the couple understand treatment goals, feel safe in expressing their feelings, and reconnect by developing trust in each other. Interventions for couples are often centered on goals geared toward preventing conflicting verbal communication and improving empathy, respect, and intimacy in a relationship. Therapeutic interventions, along with exercises, are designed to help couples learn to treat each other as partners and not rivals. Cognitive Behavioral Therapy is also used in working with couples. It uses cognitive restructuring techniques to help change distorted thinking and modify behavior.

Impact of Physical and Mental Illness on Family Dynamics

In some ways, physical illness is easier for a family to understand and deal with than mental illness because the symptoms and diagnosis are usually more obvious. When a person is diagnosed with a mental illness, the family may have a hard time accepting its reality. They may deny the diagnosis or try to find alternative explanations. There may be feelings of confusion or embarrassment, especially when those outside the family become aware of the illness. Because of the stigma that comes with mental illness, family members may become judgmental toward the individual who has been diagnosed. Since symptoms of mental illness often manifest themselves as emotional or behavioral responses, the family members can be tempted to blame the person with the mental illness and become frustrated with the perceived lack of responsibility and willingness to change.

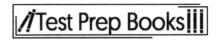

As with physical illness, mental illness may impact the responsibility structure of the family as well as the financial situation, since all family members must adjust to caring for the mentally ill person. Beyond this, there may be irritation or bitterness toward the person suffering, which may be exacerbated by every episode of anxiety, anger, depression, or psychosis on the part of the mentally ill individual. It may be helpful for the social worker to provide the family with education about the illness, as well as involve them in treatment, when possible. It also helps to engage the family in counseling. Support groups or services for the family are also critical in helping them deal with the stressors they face. While families need to acknowledge the reality and seriousness of the mental illness, they also must recognize that, with their help and support, the ill person can thrive and successfully cope with the illness.

Co-Occurring Disorders and Conditions

Co-occurring disorders may also be known as *dual disorders* or *dual diagnoses*. Co-occurring disorders are more prevalent in clients who have substance use history (or presently use substances). Substance use is diagnosed when the use of the substance interferes with normal functioning at work, school, home, in relationships, or exacerbates a medical condition. A substance use diagnosis is often made in conjunction with a mood or anxiety related disorder, resulting in a dual diagnosis.

Co-occurring disorders or dual diagnoses may be difficult to diagnose due to the nature of symptom presentation. Some symptoms of addiction or substance abuse may appear to be related to another mental health disorder; conversely, some symptoms of mental health disorder may appear to be related to substance use. On the contrary, there are some signs that a co-occurring disorder is present:

Mental health symptoms worsening while undergoing treatment: For example, a client suffering from depression may be prescribed anti-depressants to address depressive symptoms. However, if the client is using substances, he or she may mix other medications with anti-depressants. This can be dangerous in itself, but may also create a prolonged false sense of well-being while under the influence. Once this feeling fades, it can be confusing for the client to realize whether the prescribed medications are working. Even worse, the client may increase recreational substance use, leading to worse overall mental health symptoms over time.

Persistent substance use problems with treatment: There are some substance use treatment centers that transition clients off of one medication and place them on another, for example, methadone. This may result in a transfer of dependence and ongoing substance use while the client is receiving treatment for mental health disorders.

Another scenario is that a client may seek treatment from a substance use treatment center with clinicians that are not equipped to provide adequate mental health treatment for the client. As the mental health problems persist or worsen while undergoing withdrawal, the client may continue to engage in substance use as a coping skill, therefore making the substance use problem appear resistant to treatment.

It is important for co-occurring disorders or dual diagnoses to be treated together because they occur simultaneously. This may be done utilizing a multidisciplinary team approach in an outpatient or inpatient setting. Treatment of dual diagnoses or co-occurring disorders at the same time in the same setting by the same treatment team is also known as an *integrated treatment* approach.

Impact of Caregiving on Families

There are about 10 million Americans over the age of fifty who are caring for aging parents. In the last fifteen years, thanks to modern medicine, the adult population has begun living longer. As a result, the number of adult children between the ages of fifty and seventy who provide care to aging parents has tripled. This amounts to about 25 percent of adult children who provide either personal or economic assistance.

Research indicates that becoming a personal caregiver to a parent increases the rates of depression, substance abuse, and heart disease. These adult children sometimes take significant financial blows in the form of lost income, earlier than planned retirement, and reduced pension plans, due to leaving the workforce earlier. At the same time, these adult children are assisting their own children as they move towards independence. Those in the youngest generation may still be in college or in the early stages of starting a career and still look to parents for some financial assistance. From a different perspective, the positives of this situation are that children are able to form deeper bonds with grandparents, and the longevity of life in loved ones can have very positive impact on all involved.

Psychological Defense Mechanisms

Sigmund Freud's *psychoanalytic theory* focused on the conflicts, drives, and unacceptable desires in the unconscious mind and how they affect a person. One method of dealing with unconscious conflicts is through *defense mechanisms*, which are the mind's way of protecting a person from unacceptable thoughts. Here are some of the most common defense mechanisms:

- *Repression* is when a person suppresses thoughts or memories that are too difficult to handle. They are pushed out of the conscious mind, and a person may experience memory loss or have psychogenic amnesia related to those memories.

- *Displacement* takes place when someone displaces the feelings they have toward one person, such as anger, and puts it on another person who may be less threatening. For example, someone may express anger toward a spouse, even if they are really angry with a boss.

- *Sublimation* is when the socially unacceptable thought is transformed into healthy, acceptable creativity in another direction. Pain may become poetry, for example.

- *Rationalization* is when unacceptable feelings or thoughts are rationally and logically explained and defended.

- *Reaction formation* occurs when the negative feeling is covered up by a false or exaggerated version of its opposite. In such a case, a person may display strong feelings of affection toward someone, though internally and unconsciously hate that person.

- *Denial* is refusing to accept painful facts or situations and instead acting as if they are not true or have not happened.

- *Projection* is putting one's own feelings onto someone else and acting as if they are the one who feels that way instead of oneself.

Addiction Theories

Addiction is a complex process involving biological, social, cultural and genetic factors. There is some disagreement in the addiction treatment community about the causes and best treatments for substance abuse disorders. There are several models of addiction.

The earliest theory of addiction is called the *Moral Model*. This model implies that the person abuses substances because they are morally weak. The addict is viewed as a sinner or criminal and one who does not have the intestinal fortitude to change negative behaviors, therefore choosing to wallow in the misery of their sins.

The *disease model* or *medical model* of addiction, upon which the twelve-step program of Alcoholics Anonymous (AA) is based, specifies that the addict suffers from an illness that will never be cured and is progressive in its development. Even if the individual ceases alcohol intake, the disease remains. AA literature indicates that when one relapses, even after years of sobriety, the addict picks up, not where he left off, but where the disease would have taken him if the drinking had continued. It is seen as a medical disorder and, at times, referred to in the Big Book of AA as having an allergy, with alcohol as the identified allergen. This theory is accepted and understood by many successful AA participants who have maintained sobriety throughout this program for years and who have shared their experience of strength and hope to help others struggling with addiction.

The *bio-psychosocial model* of addiction focuses on the role of the environment. Cultural and social factors influence one's beliefs and attitudes about substance use. In certain religions, it is unacceptable to use alcohol. In others, it may be encouraged—such as the huge sale and consumption of beer at Catholic picnics and fish fries. An addict's observation of others and their patterns of alcohol ingestion influences their attraction to drug or alcohol use as a means for tension relief or a form of celebration. Exposure to family or community members who use large quantities of intoxicants may serve to normalize dysfunctional patterns of use. Some youth observing parents consuming a quart of vodka each night may believe their family members are just normal drinkers, whereas other youth are raised in environments where alcohol is unacceptable or served only on rare occasions.

The *learning theory* of addiction is based on concepts related to positive reinforcement. The assumption underpinning this model is that addiction is a learned behavior through operant conditioning, classical conditioning, and social learning. Social learning takes place through observation. Learning theory posits that the interplay between these three factors contribute to the initiation, maintenance, and relapse of addictive behaviors. The intoxicant serves as an immediate reinforcement in the form of increased euphoria or relaxation. In some cases, it also deters withdrawal symptoms. Both of these forms of reinforcement increase the likelihood that the behavior will be repeated in an effort to recreate the sensation of feeling better.

Genetic theory is based on research indicating that biological children of parents who struggle with addiction or alcoholics are more prone to addiction than children of non-alcoholics. According to genetic therapy, this genetic predisposition towards addiction accounts for about half of one's susceptibility to becoming an addict. Theorists of this model agree that other factors, such as social experiences, have an impact upon the formation of an addiction.

Effects of Addiction and Substance Abuse

The repercussions of the addict's behavior can affect many significant aspects of life. The impact of addictions is felt not only by the addict, but everyone in that person's family and circle of social support. Those most powerfully affected are the immediate family members—particularly those who live under the same roof as the addict. Friends, extended family, co-workers, and employers also experience fallout from the addict's behaviors.

The spouses or partners of parents who struggle with addiction often feel depressed, anxious, and angry. Persons in the throes of addiction often lie and steal to to maintain their habit. It is not uncommon for parents who struggle with addiction to steal from friends, family, or employers. Families must deal with the anxiety of not knowing when their loved one will come home or what mood or condition the person may demonstrate upon arriving home. Some families must deal with the shame of seeing their loved one arrested or knowing that this person harmed others while under the influence. Others simply become embarrassed by behaviors loved ones exhibit in public or their failure to show up for an important event, such as a graduation.

Children of parents who struggle with addiction experience embarrassment, fear, anxiety, and sadness. They are more likely to be abused or neglected, especially in single parent homes. Children may suffer when money intended for basic needs is spent on drugs or alcohol instead. When abuse and/or neglect are reported to CPS, these children may be taken from parents and placed in a series of group or foster homes. In some cases, custody is completely severed. Such experiences may lead to deep psychological scars for those closest to the addict.

Indicators of Addiction and Substance Abuse

Substance abuse and addiction problems come in many forms. These problems are often undetected or incorrectly attributed to other causes. Indicators include:

- Problems at work or school
- Friction with romantic partners, friends, or colleagues
- Neglect of household responsibilities, self-care, or hygiene
- Reckless behavior leading to legal trouble or financial problems
- Violence
- Tolerance of the substance/behavior over time
- Inability to stop using the substance/engaging in the behavior
- No longer engaging in normal activities in order to spend time/resources on the substance or behavior

Role Theories

Different role theories have culminated in the social role theory, which emphasizes that people's behaviors are motivated by the roles they are given within society. These roles can include aspects of race, gender, employment, position in the family, etc. When a person assumes a particular role, they tend to adopt the expectations of that role as governed by social norms and conventions. Some roles, such as gender, may affect many domains of life, while others—like being a student—may be confined to a particular situation or environment. The roles that a person adopts can strongly impact self-image and behaviors. Philip Zimbardo illustrated this role dynamic when he conducted the Stanford Prison Experiment, in which individuals given the roles of prisoners and guards assumed their positions so

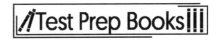

completely that the experiment became dangerous. The guards became violent and aggressive, and the prisoners became overly submissive and afraid.

Social roles can both negatively and positively impact the individual. While the smooth functioning of society is dependent on different people fulfilling different roles and responsibilities, certain role expectations can limit a person's individuality and self-determination. For example, typical gender roles may cause a woman to feel that her role in society is restricted by the expectations placed upon her.

Feminist Theory

Feminist theory is the study of relations between the sexes, especially in the context of inequality. Discussions often include the topics of gender roles, gender in work-life contexts, societal norms for the genders, and cultural perceptions of gender. Feminist theory also focuses gender relations and certain power relationships. Feminist pioneers have fought for equal political and social rights for men and women (such as the right to vote or the ability to work outside the home), for making previously male-oriented terms gender neutral (such as using "firefighter" instead of "fireman), for female body positivity and acceptance, for sexual and reproductive rights and protection, and for encouraging supportive relationships between the genders. Feminist theories also support equality for men in such areas as paternity leave, stay at home parenting for fathers, and a redefined masculinity that includes heightened emotional intelligence, awareness, and expression. Feminist theory researchers have been striving to reinvigorate feminist studies, believing that prior theories formed by primarily male researchers should be reexamined.

Influential Feminist Theorists

A number of American female psychologists, psychiatrists, and psychoanalysts have been influential in shaping psychological research that pertains to development in women and in serving as leaders in feminist theory.

Anna Freud (1895–1982) made significant contributions to the field of psychoanalysis, especially regarding the ego and child development. She was the youngest daughter of Sigmund Freud. Some of her works include *Introduction to Psychoanalysis: Lectures for Child Analysts and Teachers* and *Ego and the Mechanisms of Defense*.

Jean Baker Miller (1927–2006) is best known for authoring the revered text *Toward a New Psychology of Women* (1976). She is also known for her work with relational-cultural theory, which focuses on how culture affects relationships and how healthy connections with others are an integral part of psychological health and personal growth. These ideas often played a role in diagnosing and treating depression in women.

Carol Tavris (1944–) promotes critical thinking and evidence-based research in psychology, focusing on cognitive dissonance. She believes many of women's so-called psychological issues are actually social beliefs about women's limitations, and that these social beliefs are not backed by science.

Nancy Chodorow (1944–) authored the renowned text *Psychoanalysis and the Sociology of Gender* (1978). Her research focuses on mothering, gender systems, how the family influences female roles in society, and gender identity formation.

Harriet Lerner (1944–) is best known for her work regarding gender roles in marriage, cultural gender norms, and how women can balance self-care with other competing priorities in their lives.

Carol Gilligan (1936–) was a research assistant to Lawrence Kohlberg. She argues that his theories of moral development are male-focused and do not apply to women. Her research focuses on the development of morals and ethics in women. She initially published her findings as *In a Different Voice* in 1982.

Gail Sheehy (1937–), an author and journalist, wrote *Passages* (1976), which supports many of the beliefs and ideas of feminist psychologists. This book covers the different periods of life that women progress through and the emotions they experience in each one. The Library of Congress honored *Passages* as one of the top ten most influential books of its time.

Group Development and Functioning

Some aspects of planning interventions for a group will be similar to planning for an individual. Other aspects are unique to groups. Methods for planning interventions with a group may include:

- Conducting a needs assessment for the group to determine issues
- Ensuring that key stakeholders are involved in data collection and planning
- Continuously involving and updating all stakeholders
- Delegating components of the intervention appropriately by individuals' strengths and resources
- Establishing SMART objectives for changes (specific, measurable, achievable, relevant, time-based)
- Setting goals
- Developing an evaluation plan to assess progress

Techniques for Managing Group Process and Maintaining Group Functioning

Group therapy process involves members becoming familiar with each other before getting to work on issues. There should be group rules that the entire group agrees upon before entering therapy. The social worker acts as a guide and mediator for the group, and may also act as an instructor for the group. There are phases of group therapy process and functioning that include forming, norming, and storming elements. Groups may be open and allow members in at any time, or closed, which means that a group is specifically formed and only select participants are allowed entrance. Both the social worker and the group members are responsible for managing group dynamics.

The group and the social worker are involved in managing group process and maintaining group functioning. Group participants may be invested in maintaining group coherence and functioning, and someone may take the role of gatekeeper in maintaining the group. The social worker may assume the role of leader concerning group process and functioning and may be responsible for group growth and termination. Sometimes group members take specific roles within the group, such as helper, peacemaker, or gatekeeper. At times, group members may also take negative roles within the group setting. These should be ameliorated by the social worker.

Communication Theories and Styles

One of the main names associated with communication theory is Niklas Luhmann, a sociologist and systems theorist. In Luhmann's theory, it is the communication *between* people and not the people themselves that makes up a social system.

Luhmann uses the term *autopoiesis* to define social systems as self-creating. By this he means the social system has the ability to produce itself and maintain itself. Luhmann believed that communications make up the system, and communications create other communications. The meaning of a communication is the response it generates.

The Shannon and Weaver model of communication, though its origins are mathematical and technical, is cited as one of the primary communication models. This model was the first to conceptualize the activity of the sender and the receiver. For communication to occur in this model, the sending entity has to prepare and actively deliver information, and the receiver has to wait and actively accept information. The Berlo model of communication added that all communication also needed a channel over which to travel.

There are four primary communication styles. Passive communication refers to senders who avoid full, direct, and clear verbal or written expression to send a message. Rather, their body language and behaviors may provide a large chunk of the intended message. Passive communicators tend to avoid direct communication; they are unassertive, quiet, and anxious. Aggressive communicators are overly direct senders, so much so that their communications may harm those who are listening to them. Aggressive communicators are characterized as dominating, impulsive, and critical. Passive-aggressive communication refers to senders who outwardly show mildly expressive communication but inwardly feel aggression that is manifested in body language or behavior. Passive-aggressive communicators often have a difficult time with confrontation, expressing powerful feelings, and understanding anger. Assertive communication refers to senders who are clear and firm yet considerate when stating their message. Assertive communicators tend to speak clearly, feel in control, and respect themselves and others.

Theories of Conflict

Conflict theories center on the premise that all human interactions involve some degree of power struggle, and this struggle may be exacerbated by differences in ideologies, acquisition of resources, culture and class differences, or other variables. Eventually, some groups end up controlling resources and decision making, therefore limiting opportunities for more submissive or resource-constrained groups. These dynamics eventually shape the culture and interpersonal relationships of a group, whether it is a small team or a country's entire society.

Karl Marx (1818–1883) contributed one of the most widely recognized social conflict theories, Marxism, which sees conflict between socio-economic classes as the driver of history. Marx saw capitalist societies as necessarily entangled in conflicts between the working class and the ruling class over resources and opportunities. As privileged groups leave wealth and other resources to their descendants, those descendants have more opportunities, compared to groups who possess lesser quantities and quality of resources. Marx also believed these class conflicts would eventually unseat the ruling class.

Ludwig Gumplowicz (1838–1909) focused on conflicts that arise between different cultures. They arise as one group's desired way of living is threatened by a group with vastly different ideals, especially if one group tries to force its cultural and ethnic norms, beliefs, and systems on another group. These norms may encompass religious views, social views, financial views, family views, and racial views.

C. Wright Mills (1916–1952) developed conflict theories that focus on class structures and political parties. Inspired by Karl Marx, Mills focused his theories on ruling classes in societies and how their behaviors influence the larger group. He states that those in authority shape a society's culture and beliefs; however, the majority of the society does not have the same resources to uphold these behaviors. This is likely to eventually lead to conflict.

Diversity and Discrimination

Biopsychosocial Functioning Throughout the Lifespan

Disability can be a difficult adjustment, especially when it comes on acutely. People may experience disability from a traumatic incident, or it may come on gradually from a chronic disease. Some individuals are born with disabilities; they and their families and caregivers must adjust traditional ways of living. The biopsychosocial model is a view that accounts for biological factors, psychological factors, social factors, and their interplay within certain contexts. With regard to disability, an individual who experiences a disability is likely to feel biological changes, psychological adjustments, and social issues. From a biological perspective, an individual with a disability may have a body part that does not function typically. This in turn may affect adjacent body parts or other biological functions. For example, a patient with a heart disability is also likely to have certain vascular dysfunctions. From a psychological standpoint, an individual with a disability may have trouble adjusting if the disability is sudden (i.e., an unanticipated amputation). This individual may struggle with feelings of depression or low self-worth, or they may simply feel a general sense of limitation. Socially, people with disabilities may feel it is more difficult for them to do things that other people can do easily. They may worry about making friends or finding romantic relationships, or they may worry that they will be unfairly discriminated against in public or in the workplace. Children, especially, may experience teasing or exclusion from peers who are not developmentally mature enough to regularly exhibit sensitivity and compassion. Adults and elders with disabilities may mourn losses of freedom or changes in their lifestyles more than children who were born with disabilities and therefore have not experienced any other way of living. Practitioners who work with individuals experiencing disability should use strengths-based approaches to empower the client to live as well as they can with a disability. Acceptance, positive reinforcement, positive perspective and mindsets, and fostering a sense of community among individuals who are facing similar struggles are ways to support individuals with disabilities.

Effect of Culture, Race, and Ethnicity on Behaviors, Attitudes, and Identity

It is important not to use information about culture, race, and ethnicity in a stereotypical or overgeneralized manner. There are vast differences within groups. For example, group members holding a traditional viewpoint are likely to identify very strongly with their group and to reject the practices of other groups. In contrast, other individuals may be acculturated into a dominant group culture and may not identify with their culture of origin. With that caution in mind, some broad statements may be made to help social workers gain a better understanding of the ways in which race, culture, and/or ethnicity can influence behavior and attitude:

Native Americans
Core values include sharing, honor, respect, interdependence, obligation to family, group cohesion, and co-existence with nature.

Latinos
There is enormous variability among the various Latino groups, due to the differences in their histories and cultural experiences. Values include family, avoidance of conflict, respect for others, religiosity, and patriarchy.

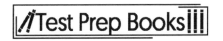

Asian Americans
Great diversity among groups should be noted, as this is a very broad category. Typically shared values across Asian cultures include family honor, deference to authority and to elders, humility, and avoidance of confrontation.

White Americans
Personal preferences or desires frequently supersede those of the family unit. Values may include capitalism, individuality, and freedom.

African-Americans
Extended family is held as very important; women are viewed as the center and strength of the family unit. Church and the extended church community may play a large role in an individual or family's life. There is a distrust of government and authority figures.

Pacific Islanders and Native Hawaiians
Values include the interconnectedness between all people, not just family, that is related by blood, community, and sharing. They are often polytheistic, with a belief that spirits exist in animals and in objects.

Effects of Discrimination and Stereotypes on Behaviors, Attitudes, and Identity

Discrimination is the unfair or unequal treatment of a person or group, based upon a characteristic, such as race, ethnicity, religion, age, sex, or sexual orientation. There are several forms of discrimination that minorities experience.

Direct discrimination refers to unfair treatment based on someone's characteristics. An example would be refusing to hire someone because of their ethnicity.

Indirect discrimination refers to situations in which a policy applies the same to everyone, but a person or group of people are negatively impacted due to certain characteristics. For example, a company might require that everyone help unload shipments that come to the office. The policy is the same for everyone, but it's discriminatory towards any disabled employees. In a workplace environment, indirect discrimination can sometimes be allowed if there's a compelling reason for the requirement. For example, firefighters have to meet certain physical criteria due to the nature of their work.

Another form of discrimination is *harassment*. This involves unwanted bullying or humiliation intentionally directed to a person of minority status. *Victimization* refers to the unfair treatment received when a person reports discrimination and is not supported by authorities.

Effects of discrimination on the individual may include depression, anxiety, and other mental health issues; and medical/health-related problems caused by lack of access to health resources. Effects of discrimination on society include diminished resources (e.g. employment, educational opportunities, healthcare) and a culture characterized by fear, anger, or apathy.

Influence of Sexual Orientation on Behaviors, Attitudes, and Identity

Even with today's advances in technology, medicine, and genetics, scientists have not clearly established how sexual orientation develops. It is believed that sexual orientation is a complex interplay of environmental, hormonal, and genetic influences. According to the American Psychological Association,

57

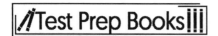

sexual orientation refers to an innate attraction. As such, the Association opposes psychiatric treatments such as *conversion therapy*—a form of treatment designed to help homosexuals become heterosexuals through therapy and, sometimes, medical interventions.

Research indicates that family composition may play a role in sexual orientation. For example, homosexual males are more likely to have older male siblings than homosexual women. For men, other factors include being the youngest child, having older mothers, absent fathers, or divorced parents. In women, examples include being an only child, youngest child, being the only girl in the sibling group, or the death of a mother during adolescence. Setting and culture also influence homosexual behavior, i.e., urban areas vs. rural areas.

Impact of Transgender and Transitioning Process on Behaviors, Attitudes, Identity, and Relationships

Being transgender can be defined as identifying as a gender other than they the gender one was assigned at birth. Publicly sharing that one is transgender can be difficult for some individuals. Transgender individuals may live in a community where their identity is not positively accepted or is misunderstood, and they may feel shamed or ridiculed. It may be a difficult experience for close family members to understand the perspective of a transgender individual, which can affect the cohesiveness of family relationships and the family unit. Transgender individuals may also feel a lack of acknowledgement when others fail to use the correct pronouns or respect other identity wishes.

Some transgender individuals choose to medically transition to the gender they identify as. This is a procedure that requires physical, emotional, and psychological support. Individuals not receiving support during their transition can experience extreme feelings of sadness, isolation, and lack of belonging. Medically transitioning individuals also undergo hormonal changes in addition to surgical procedures, and these can cause unexpected feelings and reactions in the individual. There are also medical risks that go along with both the surgical and hormonal procedures of transitioning that the individual has to be aware of and manage. Finally, after the transition is complete, individuals may struggle with living as someone who is relatively unfamiliar to their friends, family members, and colleagues. The transgender person may or may not experience support and acceptance in these groups and relationships, and some group members may even act aggressively toward the transgender person. If this is the case, it may be helpful to find support groups where transgender individuals can find not only friendship and community, but also guidance on how to navigate their new life, society, friends and relationships, and medical recovery.

Systemic Discrimination

Systemic (institutionalized) discrimination refers to discrimination taking place within a society or other institution (e.g., a religion or educational system). Such discrimination can be either intentional or unintentional and results from the majority of people within the institution holding stereotypical beliefs and engaging in discriminatory practices.

Systemic discrimination is often reflected in the laws, policies, or practices of the institution. Systemic discrimination creates or maintains a disadvantage to a group of people by way of patterns of behavior; it can have wide-reaching effects within a region, profession, or specific institution.

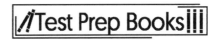

The following are example of systemic discrimination:

- Hiring practices that create barriers or result in lower wages for certain groups
- U.S. Supreme Court case, *Plessy vs. Ferguson* (1896) – "separate but equal" public facilities for African-Americans
- Oppression of women in certain countries (e.g., being unable to vote, obtain education, or hold jobs)

Culturally Competent Social Work Practice

Social workers must be culturally competent to meet the needs of all clients. One way to do this is to have the staff demographics reflective of the community served. Workers must also recognize the differences in individuals of the same culture and not use a cookie-cutter approach to deal with people of the same demographic group. Social workers must also work to create agency policies that encourage culturally sensitive treatment and do not allow discriminatory practices. When choosing interventions, treatment methods, and evaluation techniques, workers must also consider the appropriateness of the selection for the client's cultural background.

According to the NASW Code of Ethics, social workers must:

- Understand and be knowledgeable of their clients' culture and demonstrate sensitivity in providing services.

- Become educated as it relates to oppression and diversity regarding race, ethnicity, nationality, gender, disability, sexual orientation, age, and religion.

- Be aware of their own biases and prejudices and use culturally sensitive language in communications with clients.

Gender, Gender Identity, and Sexual Orientation Concepts

The term *gender* refers to a range of physical, behavioral, psychological, or cultural characteristics that create the difference between masculinity and femininity. *Gender identity* is a person's understanding of his or her own gender, especially as it relates to being male or female. *Sexual orientation* is a more complex concept as it refers to the type of sexual attraction one feels for others. This is not to be confused with *sexual preference*, which refers to the specific types of sexual stimulation one most enjoys.

Types of Sexual Orientation
- Heterosexual: An individual who is sexually and emotionally attracted to members of the opposite gender, also known as "straight"

- Homosexual: An individual who is sexually and emotionally attracted to members of the same gender, sometimes referred to as "gay" or "lesbian"

- Bisexual: A male or female who is sexually attracted to both same and opposite gender sex partners

- Asexual: An individual who has a low level of interest in sexual interactions with others

Types of Gender Identity

- Bi-gender: An individual who fluctuates between the self-image of traditionally male and female stereotypes and identifies with both genders

- Transgender: A generalized term referring to a variety of sexual identities that do not fit under more traditional categories, a person who feels to be of a different gender than the one he or she is born with

- Transsexual: A person who identifies emotionally and psychologically with the gender other than that assigned at birth, lives as a person of the opposite gender

Those who are transgender or transsexual may be homosexual, heterosexual, or asexual.

Practice Questions

1. What is the last stage of Freud's model of the five stages of human development?
   a. Latent stage
   b. Adult stage
   c. Genital stage
   d. Self-Actualization stage

2. In Erikson's eight stages of development, Identity Versus Role confusion begins at age twelve and contains all but which of the following challenges?
   a. Working through and understanding multiple changes and demands placed upon the child as he or she moves towards adulthood.
   b. Increasing understanding of sexual, hormonal, and other physical changes that are occurring.
   c. Finding a long-term partner and starting a family.
   d. Assessment of one's talents, sexual preferences, and vocational interests.

3. According to Piaget, what is the process by which old ideas or beliefs must be replaced with new ones due to obtaining new and more factual information?
   a. Schemas
   b. Assimilation
   c. Object permanence
   d. Accommodation

4. Ivan Pavlov is best known in the field of psychology for his concepts regarding which of the following?
   a. Classical conditioning
   b. Training dogs to behave obediently
   c. Development of sexual identity and orientation
   d. How positive reinforcement helps developmentally developed children.

5. According to B.F. Skinner, providing positive reinforcement increases the likelihood that a desired behavior will be repeated. Which of the following is NOT a form of positive reinforcement when working with children?
   a. A trip to the park with Mom following a week of good behavior
   b. Praise in response to a task well done
   c. Taking TV and computer privileges for a week
   d. Putting a colorful sticker on a poster each time the child goes to bed on time

6. As an elementary school social worker, you are interacting with an eight-year-old child who is unable to speak clearly or coherently, who sometimes has issues with bladder control, and who cannot yet tie his own shoes. The child should receive further assessment for which of the following?
   a. Developmental Delays
   b. Conduct Disorder
   c. Genetic Deficiencies
   d. Oppositional Defiant Disorder

7. Most researchers divide adult development into three sections of life following the end of adolescence. What are these three sections called?

    a. Early adulthood (ages eighteen to forty), middle adulthood (ages forty to sixty-five), and late adulthood (age sixty-five until death)

    b. Post adolescence (ages eighteen to twenty-four), middle adulthood (ages twenty-five to forty), and mature adulthood (age forty until death)

    c. Initial adulthood (ages eighteen to thirty-five), middle adulthood (ages thirty-six to sixty) and later life stage (age sixty until death)

    d. Stage one adulthood (ages eighteen to twenty-eight), stage two adulthood (ages twenty-nine to fifty-eight), and stage three adulthood (age fifty-nine until death)

8. Biological, psychological, and social factors all interact together as an individual transitions through various life stages. As a clinician evaluating biological factors that may contribute to the person's current psychological issues, the areas to review should include which of the following?

    a. A parental history of psychiatric illness and/or addiction

    b. Family income and social status

    c. Years of education completed

    d. Employment history

9. For therapists working primarily with adolescents, it is helpful to share which of the following with clients?

    a. Sexual Identity and preferences will probably never change throughout one's lifetime.

    b. It is important to offer a diagnosis to the adolescent of their sexual orientation so that they can be reassured of where they stand.

    c. Disclosure of oneself or others' sexual orientation to help the client feel empowered to share their own experience.

    d. Sexual development is a unique and individual process, and not everyone reaches sexual milestones at the same time.

10. Gerontology is the study of what?

    a. The biological aspects of aging, economic trends of the aging, population, and the impact of aging on social trends.

    b. Economic trends of youth, consumer spending as it pertains to children, and the focus on youth in the media.

    c. The impact of social trends on schools, how schools function in the technology age, and the evolution of administration within schools.

    d. The biological aspects of mental illness, and how substance abuse is viewed within social trends.

11. For many years, Abraham Maslow, who developed the hierarchy of human needs, described self-actualization as the highest level of achievement. In later years, he adjusted the model in order to add another level, which is referred to as what?

    a. Peace and Serenity

    b. Spiritual Attainment

    c. Self Determination

    d. Self-Transcendence

12. Those who research self-image throughout the life cycle report which of the following?
  a. Most people's self-image tends to peak around the age of sixty.
  b. Adolescents have the highest likelihood of a positive self-image than other age groups.
  c. There is very little change in self-image once middle school is completed.
  d. Young adults who are completing high school and entering the work force or college show an increase in self-image.

13. According to Elizabeth Kubler-Ross, there are five stages of grief. They occur in what order?
  a. Denial, anger, bargaining, acceptance, depression
  b. Anger, depression, denial, isolation, and bargaining
  c. Refusal, denial, isolation, anger, acceptance
  d. Denial, anger, bargaining, depression, acceptance

14. Receiving a diagnosis of a serious pulmonary illness can have many biopsychosocial impacts. Some things a therapist will want to address with a client who has just received a diagnosis of this nature may include which of the following?
  a. Asking why he or she continued to smoke, even after being told by a doctor it was affecting the respiratory system.
  b. Insisting that the client discuss the diagnosis with all immediate family members within twenty-four hours.
  c. Providing support and encouraging ventilation of emotions, especially grief and anger.
  d. Accompanying the client to his next medical appointment to make sure the information is accurate.

15. Changes that occur in a normal family life cycle tend to cause a re-alignment of relationships and roles within the family unit. This is because of what?
  a. At some point, the adult child is expected to provide more care and support to the parent than the parent can provide to the adult child.
  b. Families often split apart due to disagreements over money and relationships.
  c. Most parents view their adult children as being incapable of properly raising children and feel they must intervene.
  d. Some elderly people are constantly critical when their adult children are having a more successful career than the parents had.

16. Hypervigilance, disturbing dreams, and eruptions of anger are symptoms of what psychiatric disorder?
  a. Claustrophobia
  b. PTSD
  c. Borderline personality disorder
  d. Severe anxiety with panic attacks

17. Sigmund Freud and his daughter Anna developed a lengthy list of defense mechanisms, including denial, projection, rationalization, and sublimation. They proposed that the need for people to employ defense mechanisms was for which of the following reasons?

a. Because they were dishonest and did not want others to see the real person.

b. Because if they admitted the truth about themselves others would no longer accept them.

c. Because the defense mechanism allows one to avoid perceiving or accepting something very unacceptable about themselves, which they are not yet ready to address.

d. Because using defense mechanisms gives one an emotional advantage over others and makes it easier to exploit them.

18. Which of the following is NOT true?

a. Social context refers to one's environment and how this influences behavior.

b. What appears normal in one culture may appear bizarre or disgusting in another.

c. The neighborhood where one resides has no bearing on behavior.

d. Certain behaviors are acceptable in some social contexts, but the exact same behavior in a different social context might cause a person to be shunned or excluded from certain circles.

19. According to Erikson's stages of development, what is the dichotomy experienced during maturity (sixty-five years or older)?

a. Intimacy vs. isolation

b. Industry vs. inferiority

c. Ego integrity vs. despair

d. Generativity vs. stagnation

20. According to Sue & Sue's Stages of Racial/Cultural Identity Development, which stage is characterized by a period of re-thinking or challenging one's beliefs where the individual examines and appreciates positive aspects of his or her own racial/cultural group for the first time?

a. Dissonance

b. Conformity

c. Introspection

d. Resistance and immersion

21. Studies have shown that those who embrace spirituality tend to live longer and happier lives. The benefits of being a spiritual person include all of the following EXCEPT?

a. It increases the likelihood of connection with others.

b. It increases the likelihood of being artistic.

c. It increases the likelihood that the client will find purpose in their lives.

d. It increases the likelihood of self-actualization.

22. When people experience a major life-changing crisis, such as an earthquake or a terrorist attack, which of the following is NOT true?

a. Children are more resilient and, therefore, less likely to experience the negative impact as severely as adults.

b. Some immediate reactions may include disorientation, disbelief, or a sense of helplessness.

c. As the event and its aftermath is processed, more symptoms, such as insomnia or withdrawal, may begin to surface.

d. Most events of this nature are sudden and unexpected, and there is no way to prepare for them emotionally.

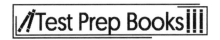

23. One's cultural background is based primarily upon all of the following EXCEPT?
    a. Where one was born
    b. At what point in time one was born
    c. Sociological practices and standards in which one was raised.
    d. Genetic predispositions inherited at birth

24. You are running a therapy group for teenage girls who have been sexually abused by a family member, and one common thread you have noted is that most of the girls experience feelings of shame and unworthiness, as well as a sense that they are different from most of their peers. Which of the following is NOT a learning goal of therapy within this group?
    a. They have been deeply betrayed by someone who was supposed to love and protect them.
    b. These feelings are normal and are experienced by most people who have been sexual assault victims.
    c. Most people who engage in therapy eventually feel better about themselves and can learn to make peace with what happened.
    d. Assessing why self-defense did not come into play so that next time they will be better prepared to fight back.

25. Which of the following is an example of indirect discrimination?
    a. An employer who tosses a resume in the trash because the name on it is commonly held by persons of the Muslim religion.
    b. A school requiring all students to come to school on Saturday for a make-up day despite having Jewish students who observe Saturday as a day of rest.
    c. A restaurant owner who refuses to serve a customer because the customer is black.
    d. A landlord who tells an interracial couple seeking an apartment that there are no vacancies, even though there are several empty units ready to be rented.

26. You are a psychiatric social worker completing a psychosocial history on a new patient admitted to the psych unit. As part of the assessment, you ask questions about sexual practices. This person indicates that she tends to fluctuate between a self-image of traditional male and female stereotypes and identifies feeling comfortable with both genders. This would be an example of which of the following?
    a. Sexual identity confusion
    b. Bi-gender sexual orientation
    c. Bi-sexual sexual orientation
    d. Transvestite sexual behavior

27. Risk-taking behavior often increases in adolescence. Which of the following is not a common theory to explain the prevalence of risk-taking behaviors among adolescents?
    a. The need for excitement and thrill outweighs any potential consequences or dangers.
    b. Risk-taking often occurs within groups to gain status and acceptance among peers.
    c. Adolescents are modeling adult behavior that has been romanticized.
    d. Adolescents engage in risk-taking behavior as a healthy outlet to channel their talents.

28. In your job as a social worker at a community senior center, you are facilitating a group on wellness in later life. One area of group focus is on spirituality. You introduce this topic because of which of the following reasons?

a. It is important that older people all have a religious community for a sense of support and belonging.
b. You believe that persons who go to church are more likely to enter the kingdom of heaven.
c. Spiritual persons tend to be more optimistic, which leads to a greater quality of life.
d. Persons who prefer not to attend church regularly tend to be angry and egocentric.

29. The learning theory of addictions is based on the premise that addictions are developed due to which of the following?

a. A need to reduce feelings of shame and poor self-esteem
b. Operant conditioning, classical conditioning, and social learning
c. An inability to be morally strong or to use will power to overcome the addiction
d. The interplay of social and cultural factors and one's genetic makeup

30. What defense mechanism occurs when a negative feeling is covered up by a false or exaggerated version of its opposite?

a. Reaction Formation
b. Displacement
c. Projection
d. Denial

31. Which of the following may be a dysfunctional family pattern?

a. Scapegoating a child
b. Affirming a child
c. Undermining a child
d. Disavowing a child

32. Which type of abuse involves the use of shame and manipulation to control a person, such as yelling, constant criticizing, or belittling, threatening, or name-calling?

a. Physical Abuse
b. Vocal Abuse
c. Psychological Abuse
d. Critical Abuse

33. What factor can cause family members or those outside the family to be judgmental toward a person suffering from mental illness?

a. Ease
b. Confusion
c. Ambiguity
d. Stigma

34. Which of the following is NOT a characteristic of a perpetrator of abuse?

a. Uses/abuses drugs or alcohol
b. Has a learning disorder
c. Tends to be controlling toward others
d. Has a history of mental illness

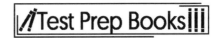

35. In Skinner's theory of operant conditioning, the term *shaping* refers to which of the following?
   a. The term *shaping* refers to placing a neutral stimuli before a reflex that occurs naturally.
   b. Changing behavior through rewarding the person each time an approximation of desired behavior occurs
   c. Exploring superstitions that might impact willingness to make behavioral changes
   d. Giving a person a reward when the desired behavior is perfected

36. In the field of personality theories, which researcher proposed that personality develops as a result of striving to become the best one can be, combined with the importance of self-perception?
   a. Eric Ericson
   b. Sigmund Freud
   c. Carl Rogers
   d. Gordon Allport

37. The process of social development as defined by Lev Vygotsky suggests that one's development in life is deeply impacted by:
   a. Income Status
   b. Birth order and gender
   c. The variety of social institutions, such as family, school, or church, to which one is exposed throughout life
   d. Physical stamina and overall health

Answer Explanations

1. C: The Genital stage starts in adolescence and lays the groundwork for future life relationships. As one enters adolescence, sexual identity and orientation begin to develop. Values regarding sexuality, views about the opposite sex, and the process of interacting with others on a more intimate level occur. These more mature elements of relationship building lay the foundation for future relationships, but not only from a sexual standpoint. Choice *A*, the Latent Stage, occurs from age six to puberty, and it is a time when the child's sexual energy becomes somewhat dormant. Choices *B* and *D* are not included in Freud's model of human development.

2. C: Developing a long-term relationship and starting a family are concepts more closely associated with stage six of Erikson's Model. This is Intimacy Versus Isolation, occurring from age eighteen through age forty. During this period, one is faced with the challenge of coming to terms with sexual preference, choosing a career path, and determining where, with whom, and how one plans to live. Long-term, future-oriented thinking is required. This phase is important, in that if not successfully mastered, the following phases—Generativity versus Stagnation and Ego Identity Versus Despair—could lead to emotional pain and anxiety in later life.

3. D: Accommodation occurs when one recognizes that previous beliefs were incorrect or no longer beneficial, based upon learning and integrating new information. Accommodation should occur throughout one's life as new information enters the consciousness and the process of assimilation occurs. If one is unable to accommodate new ideas, then it is difficult to grow emotionally and intellectually. If an individual continues to insist that a yellow legal pad and an encyclopedia is just as efficient as using a computer to complete a complex research project, accommodation has failed to occur. This forces the person to work at a snail's pace in comparison to using technology to more quickly and accurately complete the task. Choice *A* is incorrect in that schemas are a set of thoughts and ideas that fit together and present the person with a belief, or even a script, for life. Choice *B* is incorrect because assimilation refers to the process of integrating the new information gained through accommodation. Choice *C* refers to object permanence, a process in which an infant learns that even though a person or object leaves the room, that person still exists, and this understanding reduces anxiety and fear of abandonment.

4. A: Pavlov developed the theory of classical conditioning in which it has been demonstrated that pairing one stimuli with another produces specific responses in animals and humans. In his famous experiment, he noted that when feeding a dog—simultaneously pairing that feeding with the sound of a bell—the ringing of the bell eventually became associated with feeding time. Soon, a behavioral change was noted. The dog salivated to the sound of the bell, even when no food was provided. This demonstrated that people and animals can learn things though pairing one stimulus with another. Although dog training was part of his research, Choice *B* is wrong as it was not the focus of his research. Choice *C* reflects one of Erikson's stages of development, and *D* relates more to the function of behavioral theory devised by B.F. Skinner.

5. C: Taking privileges for a week is a form of punishment for negative behavior, versus a reward for positive behavior. While punishment can be an effective means for changing behavior, research indicates it is less desirable than positive reinforcement. Choices *A*, *B*, and *D* are all forms of positive reinforcement in which a person is rewarded for performing a specific behavior.

6. A: While some children who are oppositional and defiant may refuse to conform to certain standards as a means to establish control, the child described in this scenario is more likely experiencing developmental delays due to the deficits in a number of areas. At one time, the state of Illinois required children to be able to tie their own shoes before being admitted to kindergarten. Although this is a crude measure of academic readiness, it probably served as a red flag, based on the fact that the vast majority of children can perform this task by age 5. Pre-schools generally require that a three-year-old must be fully potty-trained before they will admit him or her to their program, again using a standard that the majority of children can achieve by that age. Language issues may have other causes, such as physiological symptoms, but being unable to meet these three standards is an indicator that the child is lagging behind others in attaining developmental milestones. Choices *B* and *D* refer to behavioral disorders of childhood that include symptoms of disregard/disrespect for others and sometimes include criminal behavior. Genetic deficiencies, Choice *C*, may contribute to a developmental delay, yet they could also be associated with physical issues passed genetically, such as deafness or dwarfism.

7. A: This description of states of adulthood is most commonly used in psychology and medicine. While some may question that early adulthood extends until age forty, with life spans increasing, this is a reasonable standard and is generally an acceptable conception in the fields of psychology and medicine as to how a lifetime is divided.

8. A: Parental history of mental illness is a biological feature and should serve as a red flag because some psychiatric conditions do have a genetic link, including—but not limited to—addictions and mood disorders. In addition, being raised by a parent impaired by mental illness or addictions often causes deep emotional scars that should be addressed in therapy. Income, education, and employment history are not considered biological factors; therefore, they are incorrect responses. The issues mentioned in *B*, *C*, and *D* can certainly have a biological impact, such as a scenario in which the child is deprived of good nutrition or medical care.

9. D: Sexual development is different for each person, and there is a wide range of variations in terms of achieving physical and emotional maturation. Sexuality is a very fluid and continuously changing process for most. The sexual practices one finds gratifying at age 16 may no longer be pursued at age 40. Some people do not seem to access their true sense of sexuality until mid-life. Others switch gears frequently throughout life when it comes to sexual preferences. This explains why *A* and *B* are incorrect. Choice *C* is also incorrect; in some cases it may be helpful to share one's own experience with sexual orientation, but disclosing others' sexual orientation is inappropriate.

10. A: Gerontology covers a wide range of issues related to biological, social, and psychiatric features of aging. The study of gerontology is essential as the population ages and lives longer, healthier lives. How a population ages impacts the field of economics, psychology, medicine, even architecture. For example, a two-story apartment complex in the middle of Iowa will probably not have an elevator. In Florida, where there is a large senior population, almost every apartment complex has an elevator to accommodate those in wheelchairs or those who have difficulty climbing steps.

11. D: Maslow devised his last level during his later years and referred to it as Self-Transcendence. Achievement of this goal relies on experiencing a greater sense of spiritual growth and practicing one's beliefs on a deeper level. Previously, self-actualization, Choice C, was the ultimate achievement in Maslow's hierarchy of needs. In later life, as he worked on his own spiritual evolution, he believed this went beyond the process of self-actualization and deserved to be added to his original model of human needs. Self-transcendence refers to elevating one's self to a state of spiritual enlightenment in which there is greater clarity and understanding of certain spiritual truths. Choices A and B are factors that contribute to the Self Transcendence Level, but these are not listed in Maslow's hierarchy of needs theory.

12. A: Self-image does change throughout the life cycle, and while this varies from individual to individual, age sixty represents a change in roles from being an actively engaged parent and successful member of the work force to an empty nester who will soon face retirement. In our society where youth, beauty, and wealth are revered, there is often a shortage of several of these when one enters the sixties. Even those who are financially fit will begin to experience physical changes, such as less energy, more body fat, and the onset of a variety of medical conditions that prevent one from doing some of the things that were once simple, such as lifting a three-year-old grandchild. Gracefully accepting these changes is difficult and painful. Choices B, C, and D all represent stages that consist of great change and challenging transition and often fail to correlate with a positive self-image.

13. D: Denial is first so that the person has a moment to process the loss, followed by anger at others or self for causing the loss to occur. The grieving person in desperation tries to bargain with his or her God or others in hopes of bringing back that which was lost. As reality sets in, the person grieves the loss and experiences sadness and depression. Resolution occurs when the person accepts the loss and is ready to move on, with an understanding that in spite of that which is gone, they will be all right in the long run. The other responses do not outline the order correctly.

14. C: Providing support and encouraging talking about the issue, but only at the chosen pace of the client, is the correct response. The person receiving a frightening diagnosis needs time to process thoughts and feelings. Choice A would be a form of shaming the client about the smoking addiction and does nothing to help the individual make peace with the diagnosis. Choice B is inappropriate because family is not always the client's first choice for support, and the client should decide when and with whom to share this news. Choice D puts the therapist in a sticky situation in terms of boundaries. There may be some settings in which this could be helpful, but generally this is not an expectation of either client or therapist.

15. A: At some point, the adult child is expected to provide more care and support to the parent than the parent can provide to the adult child. This is a painful process for both parent and adult child. While most adult children are willing to lend a helping hand to parents, parents sometimes feel diminished and awkward as the roles shift. When assistance is in the form of direct care, such as bathing and dressing, it can be even more difficult for the parent to accept care from their child. Choices B, C, and D may each be true in terms of causing realignments of roles, but the process of caring for aging parents, who sometimes become quite childlike and difficult in later years, is at the core of relationship realignment.

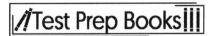

16. B: The three symptoms noted are common experiences for persons diagnosed with Post Traumatic Stress Disorder (PTSD). Along with these, PTSD survivors can be triggered into a state of anxiety or panic when exposed to stimuli associated with the trauma such as smells, sensations, or sights. Those diagnosed with PTSD may be easily started, and they can even have periods in which they feel they are re-experiencing the traumatic event. Choice *A*, claustrophobia, is a fear of small spaces. Choice *C* is incorrect, although persons with borderline personality may have a history of PTSD. Choice *D* can be a symptom of PTSD, but it is generally seen as a completely different diagnosis with a different set of criteria.

17. C: Defense mechanisms protect the ego from absorbing information it does not want to see, feel, or experience. This protective shield—which comes in many forms, such as rationalization, sublimation, or projection—helps reduce anxiety and guards against unwanted emotions like shame or guilt. Defense mechanisms can be helpful in reducing anxiety or can sometimes help one become immune to reality. Choices *A* and *B* imply that defense mechanisms are used to protect others from the truth about themselves, when this is not entirely accurate. Choice *D* suggests that defense mechanisms better allow one to exploit others. In some instances, this could apply, but for the most part, these mechanisms are acts of self-defense that keep the ego from accepting an unwanted truth.

18. C: The neighborhood in which one lives has great impact on things, such as education quality, exposure to crime, access to drugs or alcohol, and the type of role models one is exposed to. Social context shapes behavior, expectations and morals. Choices *A*, *B*, and *D* are all true and reflect various aspects of social context that can significantly influence behavioral choices, such as differences from one culture to another and how these can be impacted by different social contexts.

19. C: Erikson devised eight stages of psychosocial development. He emphasized the importance of social context, asserting that family and environment are major contributors to child development. During maturation (aged sixty-five and above), ego integrity vs. despair is the struggle. Important life tasks, such as child rearing and career, are being completed. Reviewing and evaluating how one's life was spent and success over the course of one's life provides a sense of fulfillment, while failure emerges if one is dissatisfied with accomplishments, which leads to depression or despair.

20. A: Sue & Sue's Stages of Racial/Cultural Identity Development include the following: conformity, dissonance, resistance and immersion, introspection, and integrative awareness. In the conformity stage, individuals hold a strong preference for the dominant culture and display negative views, shame, or embarrassment regarding their own racial and/or cultural groups. In the dissonance stage, individuals reconsider or challenge their beliefs. For the first time, they appreciate positive aspects of their own racial/cultural group. During the resistance and immersion stage, individuals have a pride of their racial and cultural group along with a preference for minority views and instead actively reject the views of the dominant culture. In the introspection stage, individuals become aware of the negative impact of the earlier resistance and immersion stage. At this point, they may realize that they do not actually disagree with all majority views or endorse all minority views, but find some sort of balance. Lastly, in the integrative awareness stage, individuals are able to appreciate both their own culture and differing cultures.

21. B: Spirituality tends to increase the likelihood of someone being connected to other people, the likelihood that the client might have a greater sense of purpose, and the likelihood of self-actualization. It also can provide hope to the hopeless, help reduce anxiety, aid in healing from emotional pain, and contribute toward a greater optimism. Being more artistic is not a factor connected to levels of spirituality.

22. A: Children have fewer resources for processing events of this nature because they have limited life experience and, therefore, fewer tools to help them adapt. Children are also less equipped to identify and share the emotions, memories, or thoughts they are experiencing than adults. The other responses are correct in that disorientation and disbelief are common in the beginning, and in the aftermath of disaster, other symptoms begin to emerge. Such events are indeed difficult to predict; therefore, one cannot easily prepare for trauma of this nature.

23. D: Culture is a complex and multi-faceted concept and is related to when, where, and with whom one was raised. Those in the mental health field should be constantly vigilant about a client's cultural practices because these strongly impact beliefs, ethics, and behavior. Choice *D* is the best answer because it does not constitute an aspect of cultural identity as easily as where, where, and how one was raised.

24. D: It is important to acknowledge the girl is not in any way at fault and that the act of sexual assault upon a minor is a felony. Choices *A, B,* and *C* plant a seed of hope that through sharing feelings in a safe setting. One can begin to move down the path to healing the emotional pain. It is helpful to normalize the experience to some extent so that the child realizes one in four girls are victims of some form of sexual abuse. The therapist should never blame the victim for abuse, regardless of the circumstances.

25. B: Indirect discrimination relates to laws and policies that are applied equally but have negative consequences for certain groups. The other three answers are examples of direct discrimination since the actions are based on individual biases rather than organizational decisions. In those three scenarios, people are purposefully discriminating against others. In Choice *B*, the school administrators may not have even considered the negative consequence for Jewish students.

26. B: This person's sexual orientation is bi-gender due to comfort in identification with both genders. Choice *A* is wrong because the person does not appear confused about her sexual identity. Choice *C* is incorrect as bi-sexual refers to being attracted to both genders, and that information was not really provided. Choice *D* is also incorrect. Transvestites enjoy dressing in attire of the opposite gender and engaging in stereotyped versions of the opposite gender.

27. D: Risk-taking behavior is purported to increase during adolescence by several theories including the need for excitement outweighing perceived consequences, the desire to gain status and acceptance among peers, and modeling adult behavior that may have been romanticized. Social workers should work with adolescents who engage in risk-taking behavior to find healthy outlets to channel their talents or get them involved in more positive activities.

28. C: Spirituality and religion are different concepts. Religion can be defined as an organized system of beliefs that others are expected to follow. Spirituality is a more personal process of self-growth and self-actualization. Spirituality in its purest form does not rely on an institution, religious leader, or set of rules to guide beliefs, making Choice *A* incorrect. Choice *B* is an example of a therapist overstepping boundaries and attempting to encourage others to accept his or her personal spiritual beliefs. There is no evidence to back up the statement that persons who do not attend church tend to be any angrier than anyone else.

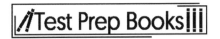

29. B: This theory of addiction is based on the interplay of classical conditioning, operant conditioning, and social learning (observation). Choice *A* is not specifically a model of addiction, but rather a supposition as to why people abuse substances. *C* refers to the Moral Model of addictions in which the person addicted to drugs or alcohol is viewed as weak-willed. Choice *D* refers to a hybrid of the *bio-psychosocial model* of addiction, which focuses on the role of the environment, such as cultural and social factors, and *genetic theory.*

30. A: Reaction formation is when a person displays an exaggerated version of the opposite emotion to what he or she is really feeling. For example, a person may display strong feelings of love toward someone, though internally and unconsciously he or she detests that person. Displacement is when the feeling someone has toward one person is displaced to another object or person, such as the dog or spouse. Projection happens when one's own feelings are viewed as actually being someone else's. Denial is the refusal to admit something exists, such as painful facts or situations.

31. A: Scapegoating a child occurs when a child is blamed for family problems and for things that are not his or her fault. This pattern of family dysfunction may happen in families where the problems are not being properly recognized or addressed, and members of the family seek to shift the blame. Affirming, undermining, or disavowing the child are not concepts connected to family dysfunction.

32. C: Psychological or emotional abuse is when the abuser uses strategies of manipulation through shame, fear, and guilt to control the other's behaviors. It also involves verbal abuse, which takes the form of yelling, constant criticisms, or belittling, threats, or name-calling. Physical abuse involves some type of physical harm. Vocal abuse is when a person damages their vocal chords. Critical abuse does not exist.

33. D: The stigma of mental illness can cause family members to become judgmental toward the individual who has been diagnosed, or he or she may have to deal with the misunderstandings of people outside the family. This is one of the reasons that dealing with a diagnosis of mental illness can be more complicated for a family than dealing with a diagnosis of physical illness. There is no ease associated with mental illness. Even though mental illness may involve some level of confusion or ambiguity, those are not terms that best answer the question.

34. B: While the use/abuse of alcohol, a history of mental illness, and a tendency to control others are all risk factors for abuse, the presence of a learning disorder is not associated with this. There are many factors that may indicate a potential abuser, but there are no foolproof ways to identify one apart from the evidence of abuse.

35. B: Changing behavior through rewards for approximation of desired behavior is the correct answer. Skinner demonstrated that behavior could be learned by rewarding actions that are similar to the desired behavior. If one wants to teach a dog to chase and catch a Frisbee thrown to the end of a field, the dog must first be rewarded for sniffing the Frisbee, then grasping the Frisbee, and then catching it when thrown four feet, then six, then ten. This process is called successive approximation. Choice *A* refers to a classical conditioning. Choice *C* refers to superstitions, meaning that one can sometimes be confused as to which behavior is soliciting the reward. Some athletes wear the same pair of "lucky" socks each game, thinking this behavior leads to the reward of winning. In reality, the behavior that leads to the win can be anything from practicing harder to playing a team that is not highly skilled; therefore, the behavior is superstitious. Choice *D* is a poor form of teaching a person to learn a new behavior because it may take much trial and error before perfection is achieved.

36. C: Carl Rogers placed much emphasis on reaching one's greatest potential and the interplay between this potential and one's perception of self. Erikson and Freud theorized that one must achieve certain developmental challenges before moving to the next level of human growth. Allport, on the other hand, believed one's destiny depended on the possession of certain clusters of personality traits. Therefore, *A, B,* and *D* are wrong. Rogers focused on the concept that humans are driven by their own need to develop into the best person they are capable of becoming.

37. C: Vygotsky believed individuals are significantly shaped by the formal and informal social groups in which they interact. These institutions teach values, how to behave in relationships, how closely one must follow rules and laws, and, in general, what is important in life. A child growing up hungry and neglected will have a very different view of life than one who is cherished and provided with love, support, and material needs. Choices *A, B,* and *D* all impact the quality of one's life, but Vygotsky leaned toward a more global explanation of social development that encompasses multiple social factors.

Assessment, Diagnosis, and Treatment Planning

Biopsychosocial History and Collateral Data

Biopsychosocial Assessment

In order for an assessment to be comprehensive, the practitioner must gather information and assess the individual *holistically*, which includes examining systems related to the biological, psychological, and social or sociocultural factors of functioning. In some cases, a spiritual component may be included. This process is based off of the *biopsychosocial framework* that describes the interaction between biological, psychological, and social factors. The key components of the biopsychosocial assessment can be broken down into five parts: Identification, Chief Complaint, Social/Environmental Issues, History, and Mental Status Exam.

Identification
Identification consists of the details or demographic information about the client that can be seen with the eye and documented accordingly. Some examples of identification information are age, gender, height, weight, and clothing.

Chief Complaint
Chief complaint is the client's version of what the over-arching problem is, in his/her own words. The client's description of the chief complaint may include factors from the past that the client views as an obstacle to optimal functioning. It could also be an issue that was previously resolved but reoccurs, thus requiring the client to develop additional coping skills.

Social/Environmental Issues
This is the evaluation of social development and physical settings. *Social development* is critical to understanding the types of support systems the client has and includes information about the client's primary family group, including parents, siblings, and extended family members.

The client's peers and social networks should also be examined. There should be a clear distinction between peers available *online* (such as through online social networks) and peers the client interacts with *face-to-face,* as online systems may provide different forms of support than in-person systems.

The client's work environment and school or vocational settings should also be noted in this portion of the assessment. The client's current housing situation and view of financial status is also included to determine the type of resources the client has. Legal issues may also be included.

History
History includes all of the events in the client's past. Clients may need to be interviewed several times in order to get a thorough picture of their history. Some information in a client's history, such as events that occurred during the stages of infancy and early childhood, may need to be gathered from collateral sources. Collateral sources are persons outside of the client, e.g., family members, police officers, friends, or other medical providers who can provide information related to the client's levels of functioning, life events, and other potential areas of significance in the client's treatment. Obtaining the client's historical information is usually a multi-stage process and can involve the following methods of data collection:

Presenting Problem

Clients should be asked to describe what brings them in for treatment. Although a client may attempt to delve into information that is well in the past, the practitioner should redirect the client to emphasize the past week or two. Emphasis is placed on the client's current situation when assessing the presenting problem.

Past Personal

When reviewing a client's history, noting biological development may determine whether or not the client hit milestones and the ensuing impact it had on his/her health. In reviewing biological development, other physical factors should also be assessed for impact on current emotional well-being, including those that may no longer persist, like a childhood illness. As much information regarding the client's entire *lifespan* (birth to present) should be gathered, with attention paid to sexual development.

Medical

During the medical component of the assessment process, information should be obtained on the client's previous or current physiological diagnoses. These diagnoses can contribute to the client's current situation.

For example, a client with frequent headaches and back pain may be unable to sleep well and therefore be experiencing the physical and psychosocial effects of sleep deprivation. Additional information on other conditions, such as pregnancy, surgeries, or disabilities, should also be explored during this time.

Mental Health

Previous mental health diagnoses, symptoms, and/or evaluations should be discussed. If a client discloses prior diagnoses or evaluations, the practitioner should determine the following:

- Whether or not the client has been hospitalized (inpatient)
- If the client has received supervised treatment in an outpatient setting (to include psychotherapeutic intervention)
- Whether the client has been prescribed medications
- If the client has undertaken other treatments related to mental health diagnoses

The client's psychological development should also be reviewed. It is important to gather details on how clients view their emotional development, including their general affect.

The client's cognitive development, in relation to information previously obtained regarding the biological development, should also be reviewed.

Substance Use

Without demonstrating judgment, practitioners should encourage clients to disclose whether or not they have used controlled substances. It is important that thorough information is gathered and symptoms related to substance abuse are assessed BEFORE rendering a primary mental health disorder diagnosis.

Should a client disclose that he or she has engaged in the use of substances, information as to the type of substance, frequency of use, and duration of exposure to the lifestyle, should be gathered. Additionally, information on what the client perceives as the positive and negative aspects of substance use should be gathered, noting whether or not the client perceives any consequences of substance abuse, such as job loss, decreased contact with family and friends, and physical appearance.

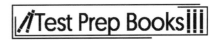

Techniques and Instruments Used to Assess Clients/Client Systems

Many psychometric instruments exist to assess and diagnose psychological functioning. Some of the most common tests include:

Beck Depression Inventory-II (BDI-II)
BDI-II is a twenty-one-question inventory used to measure presence and severity of depression symptoms in individuals aged thirteen years and older.

Bricklin Perceptual Scales (BPS)
BPS is a thirty-two-question inventory designed for children who are at least six years old. It examines the perception the child has of each parent or caregiver and is often used in custody cases.

Millon Instruments
- Millon Clinical Multiaxial Inventory III (MCMI-III): This 175-question inventory is used to determine indicators of specific psychiatric disorders in adults aged eighteen years and older.

- Millon Adolescent Clinical Inventory (MACI): This 160-question inventory is used to determine indicators of specific psychiatric disorders in adolescents aged thirteen to nineteen years.

- Millon Adolescent Personality Inventory (MAPI): This 150-question inventory is used to determine specific personality indicators in adolescents aged thirteen to eighteen years.

- Millon Behavioral Health Inventory (MBHI): This 165-question inventory is used to determine psychosocial factors that may help or hinder medical intervention in adults aged eighteen years and older.

Minnesota Multiphasic Personality Inventory (MMPI-2)
MMPI-2 is a 567-item inventory. It is one of the most widely administered objective personality tests. It is used to determine indicators of psychopathology in adults aged eighteen years and older.

Myers-Briggs Type Indicator
Myers-Briggs is a 93-question inventory widely used to help people aged fourteen years or older determine what personality traits influence their perception of the world and decision-making processes. A preference is identified within each of four different dimensions: extraverted (E) or introverted (I); sensing (S) or intuitive (I); thinking (T) or feeling (F); and judging (J) or perceiving (P).

Quality of Life Inventory (QOLI)
QOLI is a 32-question inventory that determines the perception of personal happiness and satisfaction in individuals aged seventeen years and older.

Thematic Apperception Test (TAT)
TAT is a narrative and visual test that typically requires the individual to create a story and allows the practitioner insight into the individual's underlying emotional state, desires, behavioral motives, and needs. It's used for individuals aged five years and older.

Rorschach Test

Rorschach test is a visual test that records an individual's perception and description of various inkblots. It's used to determine underlying personality or thought disorders in individuals aged five years and older.

Wechsler Adult Intelligence Scale – Fourth Edition (WAIS-IV)

WAIS-IV is a series of subtests that assesses cognitive ability in individuals aged sixteen years and older.

Information Available from Other Sources

When working with clients, social workers need to compile a complete and accurate assessment of the client's background. Assessments may include information from a variety of sources. Primary sources of information are those provided directly by the client. This may include the intake form they complete, direct responses to questions asked by the social worker (such as during an interview or counseling session), documented medical history provided straight from the client, journal entries or other personal communications of the client, or body language exhibited in person. Secondary sources of information are taken from a source other than the client.

A medical history provided by the client's doctor, rather than by the client, is considered a secondary source. Records from the client's place of employment, schools, and public data such as home ownership or jail information are also examples of secondary sources of information. Social workers may choose to interview or provide group services to a client's family and friends. Any information that is shared about the client by people close to him or her is considered secondary information. Additionally, if the social worker chooses to conduct literature reviews or searches of evidence-based research to shape an intervention, they are seeking secondary sources.

When requesting or seeking secondary information, such as from employment records or from interviews with family members, social workers must carefully consider the legal, ethical, and moral consequences of their actions. Whenever applicable, consent to seek and use secondary source information should be provided by the client. When this is not possible, such as with a client who is physically or mentally unable to provide valid consent, social workers should use empathy, compassion, a high standard of ethics, and discretion when searching for information about the client. The client should be treated with dignity and respect during this process. All information should be gathered with the sole intention of providing help and support in the client's best interest.

Obtaining Sensitive Information

Interviews are a critical component of social work practice wherein clients provide verbal reports, accounts, or narratives that serve as the main source of information and data collected during the assessment process.

The basis of the interview is a verbal report that involves introductions between the practitioner and client. In some practice settings, the verbal report may be supplemented by an *information sheet* that provides client demographics and a brief overview of the *presenting problem*. Presenting problems are prevailing circumstances, symptoms, or difficulties that the client believes is a problem requiring psychotherapeutic assistance.

Principle: Practitioners Need to Establish Rapport with the Client

Providing a description of the services provided and what the client can expect during sessions is the practitioner's first opportunity to build rapport with the client. Rapport development impacts the thoroughness of the information provided from the client. If the level of rapport is limited, the client may not feel comfortable enough to provide sufficient information. The level of rapport also affects the type of impression the client wishes to make on the practitioner. Consequently, it is linked to the client's perception of self-awareness. Some key points to remember are as follows:

- The social worker's own personal characteristics (gender, race, age, etc.) may affect the level of client interaction, based on the client's cultural background.

- Clients may adjust their responses to questions based on how they perceive the social worker's characteristics.

- The social worker's demographics may also have an impact on how the client feels about disclosing sensitive information, such as domestic violence, sexual conduct, or child abuse.

Principle: The Basics of Social Work Practice Should be Used When an Interview is Conducted

Once the introductions have been made and an overview of services and interview processes provided, the client should be asked to explain why they came in for treatment.

Empowering clients to share their concerns and emphasizing the point of hearing things from their perspective provides the practitioner with an opportunity to gauge a client and start "where the client is" in the initial phases of the assessment process.

Technique

The use of encouraging, neutral phrases will help move the conversation forward and encourage the client to share, e.g., "What brings you in to see me today?"

While being encouraging to the client, it is important that practitioners are genuine and not phony. Practitioners should avoid overly complimentary statements, such as "I'm so glad you came in today!" If the client senses the interest is insincere, they may not wish to share.

Principle: The Practitioner Should Start Where the Client is.

After engaging the client, they should be allowed to open up, "vent," or speak freely for approximately fifteen minutes.

Technique

While the client is delving into any emotions, the practitioner should utilize active listening to keep the client engaged. Additionally, it is important to observe the client's *non-verbal cues* (posture, gestures, voice tone and pitch, and facial expressions) that lend to the emotional state. Once the client shares primary concerns, the practitioner can focus on what is important to the client.

The practitioner should observe the client's emotional state, allowing them to feel those emotions freely while providing the account of the problem. Demonstrating empathy is important when responding to the client's emotions. The emotion observed should be acknowledged. For example, if a client is crying, the practitioner can state, "You seem saddened about this," to demonstrate empathy. This practice can also hone in on an important area of the client's life that may be addressed later.

Once the client has been allowed to speak freely, the practitioner should utilize exploratory interviewing skills to delve into the specifics of topics that seemed particularly troubling for the client during the disclosure of the presenting problem.

After the client has revealed the presenting problem and the emotional state has been observed, the client should be asked to delve further into details about current life circumstances. This will provide an opportunity for the practitioner to gain additional information related to the context of the client's problem. It also allows the practitioner to uncover particularly troubling areas that can be explored later. Moreover, it may reveal certain boundaries for the client who is unwilling or unready to discuss certain details of their life.

Principle: It is Important to Engage the Client Verbally While Simultaneously Observing Non-Verbal Cues

The practitioner should ask questions to provide clarification and deeper insight into the client's problems and level of functioning.

Question Techniques

Open-ended questions may provide more detail and allow the client to expand into other areas that can be explored later.

Closed-ended questions are ideal for fact-finding from a client.

Clarification questions should be asked whenever necessary. This may be done through active listening and reflective sharing on the social worker's part, to foster comprehensive communication and further build rapport.

Note Taking Techniques

If the client has questions as to why notes are taken, the reasoning behind it should be explained, and a copy should be offered to provide the client to make them feel more comfortable and involved in the interview process.

Observation of client behaviors during the interview may be indicative of how the client behaves or reacts in settings outside of the session. Conversely, clients may act outside of their norm, due to the perceived pressure from the interview process. The aforementioned questions and non-verbal observations are essential to determine factors of the client's personality and the context of presenting issues.

Practitioners should also be aware that their interactions affect client behaviors and responses during the interview process. For example, the client may mimic rigid body language (folded arms, crossed legs, minimal eye contact) from the practitioner and become defensive in speech pattern, pitch, or tone.

Active Listening and Observation

Active listening is crucial to the relationship and rapport building stage with clients. Social workers must be fully engaged in the listening process and not distracted by thoughts of what will come next or intervention planning. The worker must not only hear the audible language the client is offering but must also look at the non-verbal behaviors and the underlying meaning in the words and expressions of the client. Nonverbal behaviors include body language, facial expressions, voice quality, and physical reactions of the client. Other aspects of active listening include head nodding, eye contact, and using

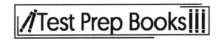

phrases of understanding and clarity such as, "What I hear you saying is . . ." and "You (may) wish to . . ." Workers may verify they understand the client's message by paraphrasing and asking for validation that it is correct (i.e., "What I hear you saying is . . .").

Indicators of Sexual Dysfunction

Sexual dysfunction can be related to physical or psychological causes and symptoms—or both. A medical examination can determine if the cause is physical and can usually provide treatment options that include medication or lifestyle changes. If the cause is psychological, such as a result of abuse, depression, or stress, then psychotherapeutic intervention may also be needed. Indicators of sexual dysfunction include:

- Erectile dysfunction in men
- Vaginal dryness or pain in women
- Pain during intercourse or arousal
- Lack of interest in sexual behavior (physically, mentally, or emotionally)
- Fear of sexual interaction
- Inability or difficulty reaching orgasm
- Inability to become aroused or difficulty maintaining arousal
- Negative emotions associated with sexual behavior (i.e. guilt, fear, shame, regret)

Symptoms of Neurologic and Organic Disorders

Neurological and organic processes control the nervous system, and, consequently, all of the physical sensations, muscle contractions, perceptions, sensory experiences, and other biological mechanisms. Therefore, if something goes wrong in these processes, the symptoms that present can vary vastly. These symptoms include:

- Pain: muscle pain, joint pain, nerve pain, tingling or burning in an area

- Physical dysfunction: muscle paralysis, muscle tremors, muscle spasms, involuntary muscle tics, imbalance, fainting, vertigo, slurred speech, loss of tongue control

- Abnormal sensations: tingling, burning, hot or cold bursts on the skin, inability to feel cold or heat, incorrect indicators for cold and heat (i.e., touching something warm only to have it feel cool), numbness, "creepy-crawly" feelings on the skin

- Sensory dysfunction: sudden partial or complete blindness, abnormal smell and taste perception, hallucination, ringing in the ears

- Cognitive changes: loss of memory, difficulty in comprehending language or speech, inability to form sentences, difficulty recognizing familiar objects or faces

Assessment and Diagnosis

Problem Formulation

The problem system refers to factors that are relevant to the client's presenting problem, which may include other people or environmental elements the client deems relevant to the situation. It is important that questions be asked to determine what the client's perception of the presenting problem is.

Additionally, the practitioner should determine if there are other legal, medical, or physical issues related to the problem. For a comprehensive assessment, the client should also be asked how long the problem has been present and if there are any triggers he/she believes contribute to the problem. Identification of external supports and access to resources is also key when examining and discussing the problem system.

The presenting problem is generally revealed in the client's statement about why he or she has come in for treatment. If collateral sources are used, information can also be gathered from one or more of the collateral sources who have insight as to why the client is in need of assistance.

Disclosure of the presenting problem allows the social worker to determine the prevailing concerns deemed important by the client.

Social workers can gain a sense of how distressed the client is about the problem or situation and what client expectations are for treatment.

The manner in which the client describes the presenting problem can also provide insight as to how emotionally tied the client is to the problem and whether or not the client came in under his/her own volition.

It is important to determine the true root causes of the presenting problem. Although a client may come in and voice a concern, it may not be the root cause of the issue. Rather, this concern may simply be an item the client feels comfortable discussing. For example, a client who is experiencing sexual issues may initially speak about anxiety before disclosing the actual problem. This may require an investment of time to allow the client to become comfortable trusting the practitioner.

The history of the problem is important to address because it clarifies any factors contributing to the presenting problem, as well as any deeper underlying issues. Gathering background information on the problem history is also helpful for developing interventions. There are three key areas to address when reviewing the problem history: onset, progression, and severity:

Onset
Problem onset addresses when the problem started. It usually includes triggers or events that led up to the start of the problem; these events may also be contributing factors.

Progression
Assessment of the progression of the problem requires determining the frequency of the problem. The practitioner should ask questions to determine if the problem is intermittent (how often and for how long), if it is acute or chronic, and if there are multiple problems that may or may not appear in a pattern or recurring cluster.

Severity
Practitioners should determine how severe the client feels the problem is, what factors contribute to making the problem more severe, and how the situation impacts the client's adaptive functioning. This may be determined by addressing the following questions:

- Does the problem affect the client at work?

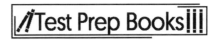

- Is there difficulty performing personal care because of the problem?

- The practitioner should ascertain whether or not the client has access to resources that can provide adequate care (running water, shelter, and clothing).

- The client's living situation should be explored, if there are difficulties with personal care activities.

- The practitioner should also ask if there are others for whom the client is responsible, like children or elderly parents/relatives.

- Has the problem caused the client to withdraw from preferred activities?

- Has the client used alcohol or other controlled substances to alleviate or escape the problem? If so, for how long and to what degree?

Psychosocial Stressors

Psychosocial stressors related to the problem should also be addressed by examining what the stressors are and addressing how they may influence the presenting problem.

A Likert Scale can be designed to assess the client's perception of how certain stressors are influential.

A *Life Events Scale* can also be utilized to assess the impact of psychosocial stressors. This scale has more than 40 life changes including divorce, death of immediate family members, marriage, work termination, and retirement, and provides a quantitative level of stress associated with such major events.

Problem ABCs

The *ABCs of a problem* refer to the Antecedent, Behavior, and Consequences linked to a client's perceived problem. The discovery of these items allows the client to define the problem specifically and examine factors affecting emotional well-being.

Antecedents to a problem may be prefaced by the involvement of certain individuals in the client's life. It is important to gather understanding on how the client was involved with these individuals and how the client felt affected. Environmental antecedents may also be present.

The client may disclose interactions that lead to problematic *behaviors*, based on the aforementioned information in the evaluation of the antecedent. When addressing the behavior, it is important that practitioners gather information on what is said before, during, and after the maladaptive behavior takes place.

The *consequences* to a presenting problem are comprised of both cognitive, or personal (internal), and environmental (external) interactions or reactions to the behavior. The client and other identified participants linked to the problem will reveal their belief sets and values based on the role played in either sustaining the behavior or attempting to decrease it.

The client's coping skills should be evaluated to determine the type of mechanism that he or she implements when the problem is present and whether or not it is an appropriate coping mechanism for the situation.

If the client presents with a heightened emotional reaction, as a consequence to the problem, it could parlay into another problem and create more complex issues for the client.

At this juncture, the information previously gathered on the client's legal and medical history is beneficial for practitioners to incorporate into the assessment process as it may have a significant impact on the factors shaping the client's problem and the resulting consequences.

Involving Clients/Client Systems in Problem Identification

Accurately identifying an individual's problem helps the practitioner tailor an appropriate intervention. This process includes defining the issue and why it's an issue in the individual's life. It's important to note that the problem is separate from the individual in order to allow the individual to look at the issue objectively without directing blame or shame. Problem identification can be accomplished by administering written or verbal assessments, interviewing the individual's social system or support, and holistically examining the individual's personal situation.

Mental Status Examination

A mental status exam is a concise, complete evaluation of the client's current mental functioning level in regard to *cognitive and behavioral aspects* (rapport-building, mood, thought content, hygiene). There are mini-mental status examinations available that allow practitioners to provide a snapshot of the client's overall level of functioning with limited resources and time available. Mental status examinations are usually conducted regularly and discreetly through questioning and noting non-verbal indicators (such as appearance), in order for the practitioner to best guide the session.

Practitioners should document a mental status examination as part of the individual's personal file in order to complete an accurate assessment with all client information. This examination also serves as a baseline for the development and implementation of ensuing therapies, treatments, and interventions. The mental status typically includes details about the individual, such as appearance, grooming, facial expressions and general body language, cognition, orientation, manner of speech, indicators of the influence of any controlled substances, mood, impulse control, judgment, thinking style, memory, intellectual functioning, perception of reality, presence of hallucinations or delusions, and interest in the session.

Incorporating Psychological and Educational Tests into Assessment

Psychological and educational tests play a critical role in understanding client backgrounds, belief systems, and perspectives as part of the overall assessment. They also indicate any current or potential psychological, social, or physical needs that the client may have. These pieces of information shape the way social workers develop and tailor interventions for a specific client; they also allow social workers to maintain the highest level of safety for the patient as well as themselves. Psychological testing usually includes an interview component, in which the social worker may conduct the initial intake assessment, ask the client personal and family-related questions, and notice body language and other physical behaviors. Answers to interview questions and body language observations are incorporated into assessments by indicating potential risk or protective factors, individual capacity to accept and receive services, and strengths and challenges that the social worker can incorporate into the client's treatment plan. Clients are also often tested for their communication, comprehension, reasoning, and logic skills in order to determine which methods of intervention will be best received. For example, a client that is unable to communicate verbally may not benefit from simply listening to the social worker providing counseling; a non-verbal, interactive approach will need to be developed for such a client. Clients may also take personality and behavior tests, which allow the social worker to incorporate aspects of the client's beliefs, attitudes, perspectives, and reactions into the assessment.

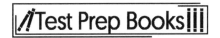

Psychosocial Stress

Psychosocial stress occurs when an individual perceives a real or imagined threat and feels unable to cope with it. Unchecked, stress can lead to physiological and mental health problems such as heart disease, depression, and anxiety. Indicators of psychosocial stress include:

- High blood pressure
- Regular feelings of sadness, irritability, or anxiousness
- Withdrawal from social events
- Sweating
- Feeling faint or dizzy
- Feeling jittery or antsy
- Muscle and joint pain and stiffness
- Teeth clenching and grinding; chronic jaw pain
- Headaches
- Feeling constantly overwhelmed or unable to complete routine tasks
- Chronic fatigue or sleep problems
- Inability to concentrate

Exploitation Across the Lifespan

Exploitation is taking advantage of someone in a vulnerable position for personal gain.

Financial exploitation of older adults occurs when caretakers, family members, or other individuals take advantage of the elderly member's finances. Indicators of financial exploitation are missing identification, money, credit cards, documents, or valuable possessions; large or frequent checks made out to cash; frequent or expensive gifts for caregiver; older adult's unawareness of income or bills; and blank checks, cash withdrawals, or money wires/transfers.

Sexual exploitation of children occurs when an individual takes advantage of a minor by trading sexual acts or pornography for basic needs. Indication of sexual exploitation are spending time with older individuals or an older "boyfriend" or "girlfriend"; spending time in inappropriate locations such as hotels or bars; signs of emotional or physical abuse or neglect; uncertainty of where one's self is (as they have moved around to various geographic locations); missing from home or not attending school; fearful or anxious around others; signs of being groomed (someone building a connection with the child, either online or in-person, in order to gain trust and ultimately abuse and/or exploit the child). Individuals who are being groomed might be secretive about their behavior, might possess unexplained money or items, and may have access to alcohol and/or drugs.

Girls are disproportionately affected by sexual exploitation and trafficking. The majority of children and adolescents are exploited by someone they know.

Traumatic Stress and Violence

In normal circumstances, an individual is typically able to return to a calm state after a stressor passes. Traumatic stress and violence, however, cause long-term effects, and the patient may not be able to recover to a normal state. Indicators of traumatic stress and violence include:

- Unexplained anger or outbursts
- Substance use and abuse
- Uncontrolled behaviors such as binge eating, compulsive shopping, gambling, hoarding, or sex addiction
- Attachment issues
- Chronic and intense feelings of shame, regret, guilt, and/or fear
- Obsessive thoughts or behaviors related to the traumatic event
- Eating disorders
- Self-harm, self-injury, or other self-destructive behaviors
- Sleep problems such as insomnia or sleeping too much
- Intense anxiety, especially in social or crowded situations
- Children may become fearful, clingy, aggressive, or withdrawn, or they may regress in developmental behavior

Methods Used to Assess Trauma

Trauma occurs when a client experiences a deeply disturbing experience that yields an intense emotional response. Traumatic events may interfere with a client's baseline level of functioning. It is important for the social work practitioner to have an understanding of the detrimental effects, both visible and invisible, that traumatization can have on a client.

The practitioner should have an understanding of the client's baseline level of functioning. This information may be gathered first-hand from the client or through collateral sources, if the client is unable or unwilling to provide that information.

The practitioner should have an understanding of how to guide the client gently through describing the traumatic experience and the emotions related to it. In doing so, the practitioner should have an understanding of the widespread, lasting, effects that trauma can have, as well as the multiple recovery and treatment options. This knowledge also helps prevent re-traumatizing the client.

An adult client may present with traumatic stressors due to one or more events that occurred during childhood. Symptoms of anxiety, depression, or other mood disorders that are actually related to the traumatic event(s) may present in session and daily functioning. A practitioner should be aware that symptoms of trauma could manifest in places and interactions outside of the client, such as within the family system, with peers, and at work.

Risk Assessment Methods

The practitioner conducts risk assessment to determine any influence that could result in harm or increased risk of harm to the individual. Assessing risk can be an ongoing process, as it's important to always have updated, accurate information. Risk-assessment methods will also vary depending on the circumstance (i.e. criminal justice, child abuse or neglect, community care). Some common methodology themes in risk assessment include the following:

Universal Risk Screening
General screening for certain risky behaviors (e.g., violent behavior, substance abuse problems, self-harm) that may result in additional screenings, referral for treatment, or stronger outcomes such as institutionalization (in the instance of high suicide risk, for example). This screening often takes place in initial consultations or as part of the individual's intake forms and may be administered on an ongoing basis (e.g., at every session) to remain current.

Unstructured Methods
These typically include clinical assessments without any specific, prepared structure. While high-level professionals often make judgments during this process, outcomes can sometimes be considered biased and unreliable.

Actuarial Methods
These include highly logical, regimented tests and scales used to predict the likelihood of certain behavior patterns in a specified time frame. While scientific and evaluative in nature, some argue that these methods may place undue blame on individuals or be too inflexible to allow for the likely interplay of many influencing factors in an individual's presenting issue.

Structured Professional Judgment
This combination of the previous two methods is generally the most accepted. It uses structured tools appropriate for the scope of the case, but allows for the judgment and flexibility of the practitioner to decide what information is useful and to note any external information that may not be caught by standardized assessments.

Client's Danger to Self and Others

Practitioners should always be alert to indicators that individuals may pose a threat to themselves or others. These indicators may be obvious or discreet and may include:

- Substance use and abuse
- Sudden apathy towards others or society
- Sudden lack of personal care or grooming
- Isolation
- Apparent personality change
- Drastic mood shifts
- Marked change in mood. Both depressed mood and a positive change in mood can be associated with suicidal thoughts or plans. A sudden positive change may indicate that the individual has made a decision and is no longer experiencing personal turmoil.
- Verbalization of feelings such as extreme self-loathing, desire to be dead, being a burden to others, or volatility toward others.

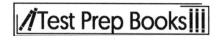

Risk Factors for Danger to Self and Others

A client who presents as a danger to self or others should be assessed through a biopsychosocial lens. In addition, tailoring crisis management techniques to the immediate problem can help de-escalate the situation. Open-ended questions should be used to gather as much information from the client as possible. It is also important to consult collateral information from any nearby family members to document other pertinent information about the client.

- The client should be asked if there are plans to harm anyone. If the client states yes, the practitioner should determine what the plan entails.

- Any and all threats made should be taken seriously and reported to the proper authorities. Colleagues may be consulted to determine the validity of a threat, if the practitioner is unclear on the client's intent.

- Identifying the critical event and antecedent that preceded it is important. The client should be asked to provide as much information on this as they are willing, in order for the practitioner to gain a better perspective of the client's point of view.

- Determining whether or not the client has engaged in self-injurious behaviors (SIB) is also important. Here are a few examples of SIB:

    o Excessive use of alcohol or other substances

    o Cutting

    o Banging one's head against a hard object

    o Ignoring necessary medical advice (not taking prescribed pills, leaving a hospital against medical advice)

- The practitioner should also evaluate the social and cultural factors that contribute to how the client reacts to stressful situations, including the following:

    o History of violence

    o Stability of relationships (school, work, and home)

    o Social isolation or withdrawal from others

    o Limited access to social resources

- Any recent life stressors that would lead to the client carrying through with a plan to harm self or others

- Assessing the client's current thought process is important. Do they present with confusion, clarity of the situation, or irrational thinking?

- If the client has a clear, concrete plan of action, then the risk for harm to self or others should be considered high.

Risk Factors Related to Suicide

- Previous attempts at committing suicide
- History of cutting
- Multiple hospitalizations related to self-injurious or reckless behavior, such as those noted below:
- Drug overdose
- Alcohol poisoning
- Inhalation of carbon monoxide
- Statement of a plan to commit suicide/suicidal ideations and access to the means to complete it
- Ownership or access to a lethal firearm
- Stated plan to cut one's wrists "the right way"
- Warnings or statements that suicide is planned
- Other factors related to suicide risk
- Age—middle-aged adults present highest suicide risk over other age groups
- Gender—males more likely to commit suicide than females
- Adolescents—high suicide risk, especially those heavily-entrenched in social media groups as a means of support and socialization
- Presence of a mental health disorder
- Life stressors from work or school
- Family history of suicide
- Family discord or other relationship trauma (divorce, break-up, widowed)
- Excessive drug or alcohol use
- Chronic illness
- Job loss

Assessing the Client's/Client System's Strengths, Resources, and Challenges

Once the client has identified the existing problem and systems, the client's *internal support systems* should be assessed, which includes examining the client's strengths and coping abilities. As with other facets of the assessment process, the client can provide a verbal report answering an open-ended question about what they view as current strengths and weaknesses.

Additionally, the social work practitioner can ask the client to provide a narrative related to a recent experience (it does not necessarily have to be linked to the presenting problem), in order to showcase strengths and weaknesses. Using finding questions can guide the client to describe their reaction to events comprehensively, to identify what favorable actions were taken, and to research what alternative actions could be taken. The social work practitioner may then summarize back to the client the strengths they heard in the narrative. This ensures that the client feels heard and understood.

The social work practitioner may also use scales to assess the client's strengths and weaknesses. A *dual perspective worksheet* may be utilized to identify the supports and obstacles perceived by the client in current social interactions. The worksheet helps create a visual map of the areas of strength the client can rely on as a means of improving areas of functioning, while simultaneously allowing the client to see areas that could use additional improvement. The social work practitioner can create a treatment plan with the client to develop or enhance coping skills, focusing on strengthening weaker areas and utilizing stronger ones.

Indicators of Motivation, Resistance, and Readiness to Change

Motivation and resistance impact a client's readiness to change behavior. These are two crucial components to examine when developing an intervention plan. High motivation is indicated by self-confidence and self-efficacy, as the client believes they are capable of change. High motivation is also characterized by a client's desire to correct an identified problem, work toward a goal, and reliably show up for sessions. High motivation also shows in the client's belief that implementing a change will improve their overall quality of life.

Resistance can refer to any behavior that indicates the client does not want to work with the social worker or improve their personal situation. Resistance may be indicated by a client's refusal to show up on time, or at all, for sessions. A client involuntarily coming to sessions (such as by a court order) may state that there is no tangible problem to work on, or the client may state they feel no changes are occurring. Social workers should examine resistance holistically to ensure they are not contributing to it. For example, clients may exhibit resistance to counseling sessions if they do not feel comfortable with the social worker, if they do not understand the social worker, or if they are expected to work on issues they do not yet feel ready to address.

Readiness to change occurs in six stages: pre-contemplation (where an individual does not believe a need for change exists, or is not self-aware), contemplation (where an individual recognizes a problem but is not ready to address it), preparation (where an individual recognizes a problem and sets the stage for change), action (where an individual takes active, involved steps to stop a problem), maintenance (where the individual commits to the desired behaviors), and termination (where the individual is able to regularly sustain the desired behaviors without relapse).

Assessing Motivation, Resistance, and Readiness to Change

Motivation and resistance pertain to the individual's readiness to acknowledge and change behaviors. The more the individual feels ready to make a change, the higher the motivation and the lower the resistance. Some indicators of high motivation and low resistance include:

- Awareness and open acknowledgment of the presenting issue
- Willingness to list pros and cons of behavior change
- Willingness to make small steps toward and document outcomes of behavior change
- Acknowledgment that changing behavior is in the individual's best interest

Some indicators of low motivation and high resistance include:

- Lack of recognition of a present problem
- Hostility or apathy towards the practitioner (which may be revealed by skipping sessions)
- Discussion of a presenting issue without openness to changing associated behaviors

Practitioners can increase the client's motivation by discussing changes positively in terms that demonstrate benefit to the client's life, allowing the client to set his or her own goals and providing assistance only for those specific goals, highlighting the tools the client possesses to make changes, and acknowledging and respecting the client's fears about change.

Assessing the Client's/Client System's Communication Skills

An individual can communicate verbally and non-verbally through body language or silence. Interviews, two-way casual conversations, and written or verbal standardized assessments can help the practitioner determine the individual's communication skills. Role-playing a specific situation can help the practitioner determine how an individual communicates in certain contexts. Assessing the individual's personal, family, social, or cultural context can also provide valuable insight to communication skills and help validate an assessment.

Assessing the Client's/Client System's Coping Abilities

Ego strength is the ability of the individual to be resilient in the face of stressors. Generally, individuals with high ego strength will be able to return to a normal emotional state after experiencing crisis. They will be able to appropriately process it and cope with the demand of doing so. Positive or high ego strength is marked by:

- The ability to acknowledge mood shifts without getting overwhelmed
- The ability to cope positively with loss and setbacks
- Realizing painful or sad feelings will decrease in intensity over time
- Taking personal responsibility for actions and reactions
- Self-discipline in the face of temptation or addictive urges
- Setting and respecting firm limits and boundaries
- Avoiding people who are negative influences
- Learning from mistakes rather than blaming oneself or someone else

Consequently, the absence of these indicators may reveal areas around which to tailor intervention or treatment. These indicators may be determined through verbal discussion or standardized assessments.

Strengths and Challenges of the Client

A client's personal and system strengths are aspects that support and promote an effective intervention and recovery. Individual client strengths may include a desire for positive change, willingness to collaborate with the social worker in developing an intervention, an interest in personal growth, resiliency, the presence of positive coping mechanisms, reliable transportation to and from counseling sessions, a way to pay for services, and any other physical, psychological, emotional, or financial behavior that promotes a continuous journey toward a positive resolution for the client. The client's system refers to their personal support system (such as family, friends, and professional colleagues) and the environment in which the client lives and works. Strengths in the client's system include aspects like close friends and family who support intervention procedures, employers that allow time off or sponsored insurance for receiving care, and colleagues that support the client's goals during the work day.

Client challenges include any personal aspect that may be a barrier to an effective intervention. Challenges may include a client who does not desire to change, who is not willingly attending social services, who feels their situation is hopeless, or who does not have the means to reliably attend intervention services (whether due to financial reasons, lack of child care, lack of transportation, and so on). Challenges in the client's system may include a non-supportive family unit (that does not support receiving social services, or that is unwilling to examine the family role in the client's issues), a lack of

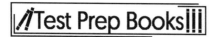

close friendships or relationships, the inability to leave work for sessions, or cultural norms or beliefs that stigmatize receiving counseling services.

Methods to Assess Ego Strengths

Ego strength is the ability of the individual to be resilient in the face of stressors. Generally, individuals with high ego strength will be able to return to a normal emotional state after experiencing crisis. They will be able to appropriately process it and cope with the demand of doing so. Positive or high ego strength is marked by:

- The ability to acknowledge mood shifts without getting overwhelmed
- The ability to cope positively with loss and setbacks
- Realizing painful or sad feelings will decrease in intensity over time
- Taking personal responsibility for actions and reactions
- Self-discipline in the face of temptation or addictive urges
- Setting and respecting firm limits and boundaries
- Avoiding people who are negative influences
- Learning from mistakes rather than blaming oneself or someone else

Consequently, the absence of these indicators may reveal areas around which to tailor intervention or treatment. These indicators may be determined through verbal discussion or standardized assessments.

Diagnostic and Statistical Manual of the American Psychiatric Association

The current *Diagnostic and Statistical Manual of the American Psychiatric Association* (APA) utilized for the classification of mental disorders is the *DSM-5*. It is an update to the APA's previous classification and diagnostic tool from 2013, the *DSM-IV-TR*. The *DSM-5* serves as an authority for psychiatric/mental health diagnosis and functions as a tool for practitioners to make treatment recommendations. The *DSM-5* is organized in accordance with the developmental lifespan.

While the *DSM-5* provides classifications and symptoms of mental disorders, causation is not discussed. There are several notable changes to the *DSM-5*:

- the exclusion of Asperger syndrome as a distinct disorder on the autism spectrum
- the loss of some subtype variations for schizophrenia
- the renaming of gender identity disorder to gender dysphoria
- the restructuring of criterion for posttraumatic stress disorder (PTSD) to incorporate application to combat veterans and first responders
- the omission of the bereavement exclusion for depressive disorders

Complete Listing of DSM-5 Chapters
- Neurodevelopmental Disorders
- Schizophrenia Spectrum and other Psychotic Disorders
- Bipolar and Related Disorders
- Depressive Disorders
- Anxiety Disorders
- Obsessive Compulsive and Related Disorders
- Trauma and Stressor Related Disorders
- Dissociative Disorders

- Somatic Symptom Disorders
- Feeding and Eating Disorders
- Elimination Disorders
- Sleep-Wake Disorders
- Sexual Dysfunctions
- Gender Dysphoria
- Disruptive, Impulse Control and Conduct Disorders
- Substance Use and Addictive Disorders
- Neurocognitive Disorders
- Paraphilic Disorders
- Other Disorders

Mental and Emotional Illness Throughout the Lifespan

Mental and emotional illness can present in a number of ways and vary depending on the illness, the person, and the circumstances. Some symptoms of mental and emotional illness include:

- Chronic feelings of sadness
- Inability to focus
- Extreme mood variation
- Loss of interest in activities one used to enjoy
- Lack of sexual interest or desire
- Intense, and sometimes unexplainable, feelings of guilt, shame, regret, fear, or worry
- Chronic fatigue
- Sleep problems, such as insomnia or sleeping too much
- Feeling overwhelmed by daily routines or tasks
- Substance abuse
- Compulsive or obsessive thoughts or behaviors
- Hallucination
- Thoughts of suicide
- Thoughts of harming oneself or others
- Excessive weight gain or weight loss
- Unexplained anger or irritability
- Detachment from loved ones
- Medically unexplained physical symptoms (psychosomatic) such as headaches, jaw pain, stomach pain, or joint stiffness.

Effect of Aging on Biopsychosocial Functioning

The *biopsychosocial model* proposes multiple causes from three main groups (biological, psychological, and social/environmental) that can contribute to mental health disorders. *Biological factors* are related to the body's physiological response and may present in the form of fluctuations in heartbeat, sweating, shortness of breath, digestive issues, or issues with brain function.

Biological factors are also linked to genetics. One may have pre-disposed vulnerabilities to mental health disorders, based on inherited traits or a history of mental health disorders within one's family. Although biological factors may heighten one's vulnerability to mental health issues such as stress and anxiety, they are not enough to substantiate a mental health diagnosis.

Psychological factors refer to cognitive processes, such as thoughts, beliefs, one's view of an experience, and one's view of self. Thought process and shape the view of self, which, in turn, shapes the sense of stability and control across environments and has a direct impact on how a person functions. Specifically, cognitive process or psychological factors determine whether a person perceives a situation as threatening or non-threatening and reacts accordingly.

Social or *environmental factors* are present in one's immediate physical surroundings and social systems such as work, school, home, and peer group. A person's social environment is significantly influenced by the aforementioned biological and psychological environments. For example, his or her level of stress may be directly and simultaneously affected by conditions in the workplace and by a peer group. The stress may present with physiological symptoms (such as muscle pain), negatively contributing to one's overall health and wellness.

Biopsychosocial Responses to Illness and Disability

Receiving a diagnosis of a serious physical illness is life changing in many ways. Along with the many physiological impacts of the illness, such as pain and tiredness, there are many psychological and social factors that influence a person's ability to cope with the new diagnosis. Parenting, careers, and intimate relationships are just a few areas that may be impacted.

One's lifelong aspirations are challenged and may have to be adjusted with the reality of a foreshortened future. Some illnesses may bring feelings of guilt or shame, if related to unsafe sexual behaviors, drug use, smoking, overeating, or other unhealthy behaviors. Depression is a common response to a diagnosis of illness, which may reduce motivation to comply with treatment. It could also cause the person to withdraw at a time when support is important or reduce one's confidence in asking others for needed assistance.

Many illnesses have an emotional component and symptoms can be triggered or exacerbated by stress. In addition to counseling or the use of anti-depressant medication, taking an active role in treatment and finding a support group of others dealing with the same illness has been proven helpful. Marriage and family therapy may be useful as well since serious illness impacts all the people who are close to the patient.

Psychotropic and Non-Psychotropic Prescriptions and Over-the-Counter Medications

Psychotropic prescription medications are used to treat disorders such as schizophrenia, psychosis, depression, anxiety, bipolar disorder, attention deficit disorder, and a variety of mood disorders. Common antipsychotics include the brand names Abilify, Risperdal, and Seroquel. Possible side effects of antipsychotic medications include fatigue, weight gain, nausea, vomiting, anxiety, and gastrointestinal discomfort. Common mood stabilizers include the brand name Depakote and a variety of lithium-based medications. Possible side effects of mood stabilizers include gastrointestinal discomfort, weight gain, and fatigue. Common antidepressants include brand names Celexa, Lexapro, Zoloft, Prozac, Elavil, Tofranil, and Parnate. Possible side effects of antidepressants include nausea, weight gain, sexual dysfunction, sleep disorders, and gastrointestinal discomfort. Common antianxiety medications include brand names Ativan, Xanax, Valium, Lexapro, and Buspar. Possible side effects of antianxiety medications include fatigue, nausea, and gastrointestinal discomfort. Other psychotropic prescription medications include Vyvanse, which manages attention deficit disorders and hyperactivity, and Lyrica, which prevents seizures.

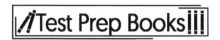

Non-psychotropic prescription medications are used to treat non-psychological disorders, such as hormonal disorders. The most common non-psychotropic prescription medications include the brand names Lipitor and Crestor (which lower cholesterol levels), Synthroid (which manages hypothyroidism), Ventolin (which manages asthma), and Nexium (which manages acid reflux). The side effects of these medications vary based on pre-existing conditions, but can include appetite dysfunction, nausea and vomiting, gastrointestinal discomfort, sleep problems, jitters, dry mouth, and fatigue.

The most commonly used over-the-counter medications include cough, cold, pain relief, and fever-reducing medications. These include the brand names Tylenol, Motrin, Aleve, Advil, Mucinex, Sudafed, and Claritin. Major side effects are typically only associated with over-the-counter cough and cold medications and can include extreme drowsiness. Other commonly used over-the-counter medications include those that treat acid reflux, constipation, and diarrhea.

Indicators of Somatization

Somatization refers to physical and physiological manifestations of mental, emotional, and psychological conditions. Somatization most commonly occurs when a client does not have coping tools or capacity to manage mental, emotional, or psychological stressors. There may or may not be physical or physiological indicators of the symptoms that the client says they feel; however, the symptoms feel extremely real to the client. If a client visits a medical doctor reporting physical or physiological symptoms for which the doctor can find no tangible cause, this may be an indicator that the client is experiencing a somatoform disorder. Common somatoform symptoms include pain, muscle stiffness, nausea, fatigue, gastrointestinal disorders and discomfort, the experience of losing a function or sense, and hypochondriasis. When investigated from a biopsychosocial perspective, these symptoms often correspond with anxiety, stress, or trauma. Pediatric patients often report somatoform symptoms if they feel neglected, scared, or in need of attention. Therapeutic interventions often involve cognitive behavioral therapy, including introspective practices, the development of healthy coping mechanisms, and the development of problem solving skills. Therapy may extend to the family unit in pediatric cases, as a shift in parenting style or the provision of parenting support can often help alleviate the pediatric patient's symptoms.

Indicators of Feigning Illness

Feigning illness refers to individuals acting, for deceptive purposes, as though they have symptoms of a physiological, psychological, or social disorder. They may feign illness for an external purpose, such as gaining a reward or avoiding punishment. For example, it is possible that a client who is undergoing a divorce feigns symptoms of spousal abuse to gain more from the proceedings. A client who is charged with homicide may feign a mental illness in order to change the outcome of their sentencing. Feigning illness can also take place for internal reasons. For example, a client may be struggling with a personal situation, such as a lack of employment or lack of a romantic relationship. They may feign symptoms they present as the cause for their problems. It can be difficult to concretely pinpoint when someone is feigning illness, and it is important not to undermine clients or accuse them of falsifying symptoms that could be real from their perspective. Clients who are truly feigning illnesses may have trouble maintaining the symptoms or relaying them accurately over long periods of time, may have visible circumstances that would indicate that having an illness would be beneficial for their situation (such as someone who is trying to claim disability work benefits), or their client systems may report that the client shows no symptoms outside of intervention sessions.

Basic Medical Terminology

Basic medical terminology can help the practitioner determine the relationship between an individual's physiological and psychological health. It can also help practitioners work seamlessly in multidisciplinary teams with health care professionals such as psychiatrists and nurses. There are ten primary biological systems in the human body, and learning certain prefixes and suffixes can help one understand which systems are related to common medical conditions and terminology.

Cardiovascular System

The cardiovascular system circulates blood through the body via the heart. It uses arteries to bring oxygen and nutrients to the organs of the body and veins to take away waste from the organs. Related terms include:

- Cardi-/Cardio-: heart
- Angi-: vessel
- Veno-: vein
- Hem-/Hemo-: blood
- Thromb-: clot
- Atherosclerosis: hardening of the blood vessels
- Angina pectoris: chest pain
- Arrhythmia/dysrhythmia: abnormal heart rhythms (e.g., too fast or too slow)
- Ischemia: insufficient blood flow to the heart, which can lead to angina or heart attack

Digestive System

The digestive system removes nutrients from consumable energy sources through the mouth, esophagus, stomach, and intestines. It removes wastes from the body through the intestines and bladder. Related terms include:

- Gastr-/Gastro: stomach
- Hep-/Hepato-: liver
- Chol-: gall
- Cyst-/Cysto-: bladder, sac
- Emes-: vomit
- Gastroesophageal Reflux Disease (GERD): a condition where stomach acid reverses into the esophagus and causes severe burning and inflammation
- Cirrhosis: progressive liver disease, often caused by alcoholism
- Crohn's Disease: a chronic, painful bowel or intestinal disease marked by constant inflammation
- Peritonitis: inflammation of the abdomen

Endocrine System

The endocrine system uses hormones to regulate complex functions like growth, reproduction, and metabolism. Related terms include:

- Thyro-: thyroid
- Aden-: gland
- Hypo/hyperthyroidism: a condition where the thyroid makes too little or too much thyroid hormone, resulting in metabolic and energy issues

Integumentary System

The integumentary system consists of skin, hair, and nails to protect the internal organs from external damage. Related terms include:

- Adip-: fat
- Lip-: fat
- Cutaneo-: skin
- Derm-: skin
- Melan-: black, dark
- Seb-: sebum, oily
- Melanoma: a type of skin cancer
- Dermatitis: inflammation of the skin
- Kaposi Sarcoma: usually fatal skin tumor

Lymphatic System

The lymphatic system is a network of vessels that promote the body's ability to fight infection and disease. Related terms include:

- Blast-/-blast: bud or germ
- Lymph-: clear fluid
- Phag-: eat
- Lymphoma: a malignant condition of lymph tissue
- Metastasis: the spreading of cancerous cells, usually through lymph

Muscular/Skeletal System

The muscular/skeletal system enables the body's physical structure and movement. Related terms include:

- Oste-: bone
- Chondr-: cartilage
- Arth-: joint
- Myel-: bone marrow
- Ten-: tendon
- Burs-: bursa
- Myo-: muscle
- Arthritis: loss of mobility and cartilage in joints
- Osteoporosis: loss of calcium in bones resulting in structural weakness

Nervous System

The nervous system is responsible for communication between the brain and the muscles, resulting in physiological action and tangible sensation. Related terms include:

- Ceph-: head
- Myel-/Myelo-: spinal cord
- Neur-/Neuro-: nerve
- Multiple Sclerosis: a disease where nerve fibers lose their insulation and ability to communicate with muscles, often leading to paralysis or other sensory problems

- Epilepsy: seizures or convulsions
- Aphasia: loss of speech

Renal System

The renal system comprises primarily the kidneys, which filter waste from the blood. Related terms include:

- Neph-: kidney
- Ren-: kidney
- Ur-/-uria: urine
- Pyel-: renal ducts
- Nephrosis: diseased kidneys
- Nephrolith: kidney stone
- Urethritis: inflamed urethra, which affects the expulsion of urine
- Enuresis: uncontrollable bladder and urine expulsion

Reproductive System

The reproductive system includes sexual organs responsible for conception and maturation of a fetus. Related terms include:

- Orchid-: testes
- Test-: testes
- Andr-: male
- Hyst-: uterus
- Colp-: vagina
- Men-: menstruation
- Mammo-: breast
- Masto-: breast
- -pareunia: intercourse
- Prostate-Specific Antigen: a protein which, in high levels, may indicate prostate cancer in males
- Endometriosis: excessive, hardened uterine tissue that can cause abdominal bleeding and painful menstruation in females
- Pelvic inflammatory disease: inflamed uterine tubes in females
- Dyspareunia: painful sexual intercourse

Respiratory System

The respiratory system brings oxygen into the body and releases carbon dioxide out of the body through the lungs. Related terms include:

- Rhin-/Rhino-: nose
- Laryn-: larynx
- Trach-: trachea
- Bronch-: lung
- Pne-/Pneu-: breathing, lungs
- Pulmo-: lung
- Ephysema/Chronic Obstructive Pulmonary Disease (COPD): a lung condition where the progressive deterioration of the membranes results in the inability to exchange oxygen

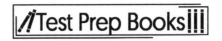

- Cystic fibrosis: a genetic disease resulting in abnormal mucous production, lung infections, and lung scarring
- Pneumoconiosis: any lung disease in which pollutants become trapped or lodged in the lungs

Indicators of Behavioral Dysfunction

Ideas about what is normal versus what is abnormal with regard to behavior are society-dependent. People tend to equate *normal* with "good" and *abnormal* with "bad," which means that any behavior labeled as abnormal can potentially be stigmatizing. Use of person-centered language is one way to reduce stigma attached to abnormal behavior or behavior health issues (e.g., saying "a person with schizophrenia," rather than "a schizophrenic.")

The "Four Ds" of Abnormality assist health practitioners when trying to identify a psychiatric condition in their clients. Deviance marks a withdrawal from society's concept of appropriate behavior. Deviant behavior is a departure from the "norm." The *DSM-5* contains some criteria for diagnosing deviance. The second "D" is dysfunction. Dysfunction is behavior that interferes with daily living. Dysfunction is a type a problem that may be serious enough to be considered a disorder. The third "D" is distress. Distress is related to a client's dysfunction. That is, to what degree does the dysfunction cause the client distress? A client can experience minor dysfunction and major distress, or major dysfunction and minor distress. The fourth "D" is danger. Danger is characterized by danger to self or to others. There are different degrees of danger specific to various types of disorders. *Duration* is sometimes considered a fifth "D," as it may be important to note whether the symptoms of a disorder are fleeting or permanent.

Placement Options Based on Assessed Level of Care

A client's need for care can fall on a wide spectrum. Some clients may comfortably live in their own residence but attend regularly scheduled meetings with a social worker to receive care. Other clients, after being appropriately assessed, may require institutional care where they can receive medical and therapeutic support as often as is needed. Institutional care may be a long-term or short-term solution for a client. The level of care required for a client is assessed by examining a number of self-sufficiency factors, such as the presence of any formally diagnosed developmental disabilities, physical disabilities, or mental disorders. Additionally, the client's ability to communicate needs, IQ level, ability to complete self-care tasks (such as dressing, toileting, grooming, et cetera) alone or with assistance, and risk of voluntary or involuntary harm to self or others will also be taken into consideration. Based on the client's health and caretaking needs, they may receive outpatient services (such as regular therapeutic appointments), inpatient services (such as a behavioral program that lasts for a predetermined period of time), assisted living in a facility such as a nursing home, or in-home support (such as a home health nurse). Regardless of where a client falls on the care spectrum, services for mental wellness and adjusting to this new context of life will likely be beneficial to care.

Organizational Functioning

In order to ensure an organization is achieving and maintaining its mission, goals, and objectives, it should undergo regular assessments to review performance and outcomes. Often, external audits (such as those from an independent group or a regulating body) are designed to assess organizational functioning. They are normally performed at regular intervals as preventative quality measures, and they may be performed more frequently if any noncompliance issues arise or if a social work institution is not meeting established performance benchmarks. Internal audits performed by workers in the organization can help gauge the organization's performance and whether there are any areas that should be remedied before an external audit. Noncompliance or lack of performance by an organization can result in fines, penalties, or micromanagement from a regulating agency.

Depending on the size of the social work institution, the type of social work that is performed, and the time and resources that are available for performing evaluations, the organization may also be assessed for factors that go beyond auditing compliance lists. These aspects may include how well its main processes work (through quality focused assessments such as value mapping and waste analysis) and the types of resources that are available in the institution (such as workers' credentials, types of services offered, and technological capabilities). Almost all social work organizations will be assessed for the outcomes it produces. This includes simple data outcomes, such as the total number of clients served in a region, to more complex outcomes, such as how many client interventions led to a defined, successful outcome.

Data Collection and Analysis Methods

Qualitative data can be collected through interviews, observations, anecdotes, and surveys, and by reviewing literature and other relevant documents. Qualitative data collection methods are often subjective and cannot be generalized to larger samples or populations. Quantitative data can be collected from experiments, recordings of certain events and timed intervals, surveys in which an answer choice must be selected for each question, data management systems, and numerical reports. Quantitative data methods are often objective and abstract, and they can be generalized to explain relationships between variables in large populations.

To analyze data, researchers must ensure all collected data are relevant to the questions being posed, are accurate, come from a credible, unbiased source, and are complete. Often, all "cleaned" data sets are entered into a computer-based data management system software from which analyses and inferences can be calculated. Clean data sets can be accurately described for relationships between variables and to make simple observations. They can also be used to answer related hypotheses, or propose new ideas and inferences based on visible relationships. Often, these can be applied to explain behaviors, phenomenon, or other questions related to large population.

Treatment Planning

Methods to Involve Clients in Intervention Planning

Practitioners should always treat the individual as the expert on the individual's life, and while practitioners should gather relevant external and collateral information, they should make all efforts not to allow these sources to supersede information provided by the individual. Practitioners should involve the individual as much as possible in problem identification and resolution planning by asking about details about the individual's life, any presenting issues and what might be causing them, what kinds of changes the individual would like to make, how these changes might enrich quality of life, and real and perceived fears.

All of these details should be acknowledged, respected, valued, and referred to when planning and implementing interventions. Practitioners should also tailor interventions to highlight and utilize established strengths and resources of the individual.

Cultural Considerations in the Creation of an Intervention Plan

An intervention's success depends in part on whether the intervention plan is aligned with the individual's cultural experience. All individuals are part of cultures with specific traditions, habits, and norms. These can vary by race, ethnicity, immigration status, income level, geographical location, or social status. It's important to take culture into context in order to show respect for the individual's way of life, tailor interventions to be easily understood, create trust and cooperation, and avoid wasting time or resources. Cultural contexts can be understood through researching the community, reading literature or periodicals from the area, and networking with people in the setting.

Intervention/Treatment Modalities

When utilizing a holistic approach for client assessment and treatment planning, practitioners should utilize evidence-based research to support the selected interventions and treatment modalities. The interventions and treatment modalities selected will be based on a number of things, including the client's current level of functioning (based on the biopsychosocial assessment), level of care needed, presenting symptoms, and the practitioner's background. Here are some things a practitioner will want to consider when constructing interventions or treatment modalities:

- Are the selected interventions evidence-based?
- Do the selected interventions arise from a strengths-based perspective specifically tailored around the client's strengths, interests, and needs?
- Do the associated risks with the selected interventions outweigh the possible positive outcomes?
- Is the selected intervention culturally-sensitive and culturally-appropriate?
- Did the client participate in the construction of the intervention selection and/or consent to it?
- Does the practitioner feel comfortable and well-versed in the selected intervention to increase the levels of intensity as needed and provide a continuity of care for the selected modalities?
- Does the selected intervention coincide with the client's financial ability to pay?

Intervention, Treatment, and Service Plans

Creating SMART objectives allows for data-driven and measurable intervention plans. When creating objectives, practitioners should be able to measure the desired behavior that is exhibited, the number of times the desired behavior is exhibited over a period of time, the conditions in which the desired behavior must be exhibited, and progress from the undesired behavior to the desired behavior through baseline evaluation and evaluation at pre-determined intervals.

Theories of Trauma-Informed Care

Trauma-informed care refers to providing interventions in a way that accounts for the possibility that a client has had traumatic experiences. The definition of trauma will be relative to the client, but common experiences include major loss, assault, abuse, manipulation, neglect, major injury or accident, and major life change. If these events occur during vulnerable periods in a client's life (such as early childhood), symptoms associated with trauma may be more pervasive or exacerbated. Personal trauma often drives mental health and behavioral conditions, so understanding a client's history and the influence of any experienced trauma is a critical component of providing effective care. Experiences of multiple or repeated trauma are associated with higher rates of substance abuse and other health problems. These can present with additional coinciding and related risk factors, such as poverty, infectious disease, homelessness, or lack of personal support.

The trauma-informed model of care encourages all practitioners who work with clients experiencing mental or physical health issues to recognize the influence of traumatic experiences. This model helps practitioners assess the level of risk assumed by clients, and provides preventative interventions to help mitigate risks at different trauma levels. The client's perspective of how the traumatic event occurred (i.e., unexpectedly or expectedly, from a stranger or loved one), the time during the lifespan in which the event occurred, and other cultural, social, or personal factors determine the level of risk faced by the client. Reactions to traumatic events may manifest less subtly than obvious problems such as substance abuse. They can present as anxiety, pain, muscular tension, elevated heart rates or cortisol levels, depression, headaches, and so on. Therefore, allowing room for the consideration of prior trauma when working with all clients broadens the scope of interventions that practitioners choose to employ.

Approaches to Trauma-Informed Care

Trauma-informed care systems ensure that trauma and its effects are understood by health services providers and that signs and symptoms of trauma are recognized even when not explicitly stated by the client. Trauma-informed care means that trauma-informed practices are integrated into all procedures of the care system. Incorporating these aspects into care involves ensuring a sense of safety and security for the client and the client's family. Trauma-informed care also ensures that the client feels they can trust the social worker and that all procedures are communicated and transparent. It provides a network of support, empowers the client to collaborate with their health care providers to develop a suitable intervention, and encourages the client to ask questions and voice concerns at any time. Trauma-informed care also accounts for each client's specific personal history, cultural and social norms, and other unique factors. Interventions encourage respect, self-efficacy, hope for future outcomes, and identify that various behaviors correlate as coping mechanisms to specific instances of trauma. Trauma-informed care is a model that is encouraged with any social services client, but it is especially beneficial for survivors of abuse, those experiencing eating disorders or addiction, or those who grew up in poverty or violence.

Immigration, Refugee, or Undocumented Status on Service Delivery

Immigrants, refugees, and undocumented individuals often have the highest need for social services but also have the most barriers to effectively receiving support. Immigrants often face the stress of leaving their home country and assimilating into a completely new culture, economy, and lifestyle. While a social worker can help navigate these changes to set the foundation for a new life, immigrants often experience language barriers or simply may not realize such services exist for their use. Social workers may need to actively advertise their assistance and understand the background and culture of the immigrant in order to help.

Refugees often have the same stresses and barriers that immigrants have, but often they have also left violent or destructive situations in their home country. They may be happy to be safe, but they may also have deep feelings of sadness, especially if their families were affected (such as through death of a loved one or the necessity of leaving family members behind). While many immigrants come on work visas, refugees may have no means to make money and may need help navigating welfare benefits. There may also be feelings of discomfort in receiving these benefits. Social workers should be especially sympathetic to the diverse reasons behind an individual's refugee status.

Undocumented individuals may feel scared to seek out social services, fearing reprisal or deportation, even though social services can be an avenue to help undocumented families change their status to documented. Social workers who hope to help these groups should focus on building trust and creating spaces of security and safety.

Crisis Plans

Any client who visits a social worker may experience a personal crisis at any time. A crisis is defined as any instance where the client is unable to cope with an event in a healthy, resolution-seeking manner. While all social workers should have a general plan for developing with unexpected client crises (such as calling for backup support or an emergency contact), a tailored plan should be developed during the initial sessions with the client based on what the client's needs are. The client should feel invited to collaborate in developing this plan to promote a sense of responsibility, accountability, empowerment, and engagement. Developing a crisis plan may include discussing what possible stress and crisis triggers are for the client, and discussing what the client feels like is the best solution for diffusing a crisis situation (such as employing trusted family members, utilizing a security item, managing therapeutic medications, and so on). This plan should be reviewed at regular intervals with the client to ensure it is still valid and does not need revisions to account for new triggers or resolved behaviors. Finally, should a crisis arise, social workers should be as transparent as possible about implementing the crisis plan. They should clearly communicate the steps they are taking as they take them, and invite the client to engage in the plan as well (if it is possible). Social workers should be mindful to note the context and present situation of the crisis, so that they can provide the best support in that moment. If the social worker tries to push the client too far in taking responsibility during a crisis or is too overbearing when the client would like to practice self-sufficiency, the crisis intervention may backfire and create a long-term barrier between the client and the social worker.

Discharge, Aftercare, and Follow-Up Planning

An important part of treatment planning is discharge planning. There are numerous reasons that services for a client may end. Clients may feel that they no longer need the services, that they are not compatible with the social work practitioner providing the services, that an increased level of care is needed that is beyond the scope of the practitioner, or they may have successfully met goals for treatment.

Discharge planning should begin with the onset of the initial assessment for the client. The practitioner should not delay discharge planning, as discharge may occur at any time. Making the client aware of the choices for discharge and the discharge planning process empowers the client during treatment. It also provides continuity of care for the client.

The main purpose of discharge planning is to develop a plan of care that goes beyond the current treatment sessions to promote success once services have concluded. In the event the client is going to a higher level of care or to a different professional, effective discharge planning is useful in disseminating pertinent information about the client to assist in continuity of care and effective treatment. In this sense, the current practitioner should prepare to become a collateral resource linked to the client's level of care for the next professional.

In addition to benefitting the other practitioners the client may meet with, effective discharge planning is a benefit to the client as well. If services have been completed successfully and the client has met the stated goals, then discharge planning ensures the client has a plan to sustain a stable level of function and maintain the successes achieved. This is particularly useful with clients who suffer from substance use or other addictive behaviors, as effective discharge planning can prevent relapse.

Upon the conclusion of the client discharging from services, a discharge summary should be created and placed in the client's file. The *discharge summary* should include the following information:

- Reason for discharge
- Description of treatment goals and the degree to which they were met
- Client's response to the interventions
- Description of the client's levels of functioning
- Baseline
- Progress during treatment
- Functioning at discharge
- Recommendations for follow-up care
- Links to community resources
- Appointment dates for other providers (if available)
- Provision of additional contacts, client supports
- Description of potential risks post-discharge
- Contact information for post-discharge support and crisis intervention

Follow-Up Techniques in Social Work

At the final session, the social worker and client can schedule a follow-up session at a predetermined time to evaluate the client's continued progress after termination. Another option is to propose a time to meet and alert the client that the worker will contact the client to schedule a follow up. The follow-up session enables the social worker the opportunity to determine how well the client has progressed and to determine the effectiveness of the intervention(s) used during sessions.

Techniques Used to Evaluate a Client's Progress

Treatment evaluation is a necessary part of direct practice. Social workers should strive to exercise best practice techniques by using evidence-based practice evaluation. It is beneficial for clients to see the progress they have made, while simultaneously providing information to funders and insurance companies that typically require documentation and outcome measures for reimbursement of services. Other benefits include providing indicators that interventions should be modified or that treatment is complete and termination is warranted. Several factors are important in the evaluation of a client's progress, including identifying specific issues to be addressed; creating appropriate goals, objectives, and tasks; using effective and relevant techniques and tools to measure success; and routinely documenting progress.

Client progress may be measured using a quantitative or qualitative approach used in research. Quantitative measures relate to the rate of occurrence or severity of a behavior or problem. When performing quantitative evaluation, first establish a baseline, which is a measurement of the target problem, prior to intervention. Qualitative measures are more subjective and reflective of the client's experience (information is gathered largely from observation and different forms of interviewing) and provide a view of whether progress is being made.

Methods, Techniques, and Instruments Used to Evaluate Social Work Practice

Evaluation is an important component of any field of study, as it allows practitioners to understand which processes are working well and providing results. Evaluation also allows one to identify areas of opportunity and areas for improvement. The process often utilizes data and consumer feedback, and it focuses on processes in place and specific desired outcomes of the practice.

Social workers should continuously evaluate their practice. This evaluation begins with what exactly they would like to evaluate. An evaluation typically focuses on processes (such as clinical intake, client satisfaction, time spent with clients, frequency of sessions, type of intervention) and outcomes (such as were specific goals met for a client, how many clients return after being discharged). Many health care organizations provide evaluation tools for social workers, such as benchmark reports that provide client satisfaction responses or practice outcomes. Additionally, social workers can employ pre-tests before an intervention to serve as a baseline data set, and they can employ a post-test to measure changes from the baseline. Social workers can also administer surveys, Likert scale questionnaires, or specific intervention evaluation assessments to the client or client system. These tools can measure quantitative results as well as provide an option for anecdotal or testimonial information. Entrance and exit interviews with the client or the client system can also provide a wealth of evaluation information. When evaluating clients face-to-face or through a survey, it's important to create an environment that fosters comfort, open dialogue, and honesty. Clients may feel pressured to provide positive evaluations if they are answering directly to the social worker, or if they feel as though a satisfaction survey they are completing can be traced back to them. This can bias the evaluation process and produce skewed results.

Objective and Subjective Data

Both objective and subjective data are used during the assessment and treatment processes. The client provides their perspective on what happened and the correlated feelings and experiences felt, which is the *subjective data*. Subsequently, the social work practitioner uses the information and may ask finding questions to better understand where the client is emotionally, while teasing out facts related to the client's situation. These facts are *objective data*.

The information from both the subjective and objective data is combined to formulate a concise, yet comprehensive, assessment for the client. In some note-taking practices, the identification of the subjective and objective data, along with assessment formation, is required. This style of documentation is known as the *SOAP method*, an acronym that stands for Subjective, Objective, Assessment, and Plan. Another note-taking style that focuses on the subjective and objective data is the BIRP documentation method. *BIRP* stands for Behavior, Intervention, Response, and Plan. It is not as commonly used as SOAP.

Methods to Interpret and Communicate Policies and Procedures

Social workers have direct contact with clients and are in strategically critical positions to develop, implement, evaluate, and communicate policies and procedures. Policies and procedures are necessary to allow clients and employees to be aware of treatment and agency goals, objectives, resources, and limitations. Policies can sometimes be a barrier to client services, so social workers must be aware of this possibility and point out these barriers when necessary.

Factors in policy and procedure development:

- Front line workers should be involved in policy and procedure development, since they are in the best position to determine and evaluate how clients are affected.

- Policies should be clearly written and communicated to clients/workers with copies available for distribution. Workers should receive periodic training on current policies and procedures.

- Polices should be in the best interest of clients, but also protect the agency and staff.

Factors to consider when evaluating the effectiveness of policies and procedures:

- The origins of the policy and/or procedure, including values and the related ideology
- Client reactions, thoughts, and feelings about the policy
- Alignment with social work ethics and values
- Intentional and unintentional consequences and benefits
- Regular re-evaluation to ensure policies and procedures are still relevant and in the best interests of clients, workers, and the agency

Research Design and Methods

Basic and applied research are two separate categories of systematic investigation. Basic research aims to expand knowledge, although the new knowledge may not have any immediate application in the real world. Basic research can often lead to new ideas and theories. Basic research can explore, explain, or describe existing or potential ideas, with the end goal of simply understanding or creating new information. Applied research is conducted with the specific aim of answering a question or solving a problem. It is often used by business entities, scholars, and non-profit organizations to gather and analyze data relating to a very specific inquiry.

Basic and applied research designs can be qualitative (where qualities of interest are examined) or quantitative (where measurements of data are examined to statistically explain relationships between variables). Qualitative data methods include performing case studies on a specific entity, observation, interviews, and developing and confirming narratives about a phenomenon. These techniques are commonly employed in social work cases and interventions, where human behavior, family history, relationship history, environmental interactions, and other subjective variables are examined and manipulated to support a client's health outcome. Quantitative methods measure two or more variables and concretely examine the relationship between them. Correlational design is a quantitative method that examines two or more variables to determine the influence one variable has on other variables (such as the relationship between age and IQ). Causal comparative design examines groups with similar features and differences to understand factors that may influence the similarities and differences. Experimental design establishes one control group as a baseline and conducts an experiment on another group to quantify the influence of the experimental factor. Control and experimental groups may be

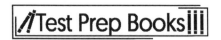

randomly assigned or assigned with a purpose (such as employing a sample of 21-year-olds in order to examine a specific behavior in this age range). Some designs use both quantitative and qualitative methods; these are called mixed research designs.

Assessing Reliability and Validity in Social Work Research

Reliability is used to describe whether a measurement method produces the same results over a long period of time and across different users. The reliability of a measurement method is analyzed through inter-rater reliability (if multiple researchers can use the method the same way), test-retest reliability (when measurements stay the same even when the method is used multiple times by the same person), parallel forms reliability (measuring the same results even when slight variations in the method exist), and internal consistency reliability (how consistent responses to the measure are). A strong measurement method performs well across all four of these reliability techniques.

Validity is used to describe how well a measurement method works to collect the data it is designed to collect. Face validity is used to describe how well a measurement method appears to be collecting desired information to the participant who is using the method. This is believed to influence participants into responding accurately. Construct validity is used to describe how well a specific variable is measured (as opposed to other measures that may be present). Criterion validity is used to infer performance. Formative validity is used to study outcomes and determine how to improve a measure or program. Sampling validity is used to describe how complete a sample is in order to eliminate bias.

Measurement methods can have high reliability and low validity, and vice versa. A strong research metric will be high in both reliability and validity.

Practice Questions

1. Which of the following is NOT a critical part of client interview?
    a. Building rapport
    b. Verifying payment
    c. Starting where the client is
    d. Use of encouraging, neutral questions

2. What types of questions can limit insight into the client's problems during an interview?
    a. Open-ended questions
    b. Clarifying questions
    c. Note taking
    d. Closed-ended questions

3. Which of the following does NOT affect client behaviors and responses during the interview?
    a. Practitioner's clothing
    b. Practitioner's speech pattern
    c. Practitioner's eye contact
    d. Practitioner's pitch of speech

4. The client's chief complaint may include all of the following EXCEPT?
    a. Factors from the past that influence current level of functioning
    b. A previously resolved issue
    c. Collateral resources that describe or validate the problem
    d. Client's description of the over-arching problem or issue

5. An example of information included in the social part of the assessment is?
    a. Demographic information pertaining to the client
    b. Factors influencing the current level of functioning
    c. Interaction with peers, work, and home environment
    d. Previous or current diagnoses

6. What is the first item to focus on during the client interview?
    a. What the client wants to discuss first
    b. Historical influences that contribute to the presenting problem
    c. Family dynamics and social supports (or lack thereof)
    d. Medical diagnoses that complicate the presenting problem

7. In addition to past personal issues, the following factors are also important to review when gathering a client's history EXCEPT?
    a. Previous or current physiological health diagnoses
    b. Employment history and related financial status
    c. Review of psychological development
    d. Past experiences with substance abuse

8. Which of the following is NOT a collateral source?
   a. Family members
   b. Police Officers
   c. Client
   d. Other medical providers

9. The following statements about standardized instruments are true EXCEPT?
   a. Examples of standardized instruments include police reports and physician's reports.
   b. Standardized instruments are crucial to providing a uniformed, reliable method of providing a comprehensive screening.
   c. Standardized instruments can be used to facilitate ongoing clinical evaluation.
   d. Standardized instruments are tools to measure client behaviors, knowledge, and other affects.

10. When reviewing the problem history, which of the following is not one of the three key areas?
   a. Progression
   b. Severity
   c. Performance
   d. Onset

11. The ABCs of a problem can be described as what?
   a. Antithesis, Behavior, Coordinate
   b. Articulate, Behavior, Consequence
   c. Antecedent, Behavior, Consequence
   d. Antecedent, Boredom, Collaboration

12. What is the primary difference between atypical and typical antipsychotics?
   a. Atypical antipsychotics were developed decades after typical antipsychotics and generally have fewer side effects.
   b. Typical antipsychotics were developed decades after atypical antipsychotics and generally have fewer side effects.
   c. Atypical antipsychotics were developed decades after typical antipsychotics and generally have more side effects.
   d. Typical antipsychotics were developed decades after atypical antipsychotics and generally have more side effects.

13. Controlled observation can be best defined as which of the following?
   a. Picking up on non-verbal cues in the surrounding environment for a holistic assessment
   b. Recalling interactions with the client to fill in gaps of information
   c. Purposely targeting a client's behaviors in a pre-determined setting
   d. Looking at facial expressions and mannerisms to gain insight on communicative deficits

14. Observing the antecedents, behaviors, and consequences is known as what?
   a. Functional analysis
   b. Formal observation
   c. Formal analysis
   d. Controlled Observation

15. The intake form contains all of the following information about the client, EXCEPT which of the following?
   a. Client's household
   b. Client's age
   c. Client's food allergies
   d. Client's gender

16. A genogram is most useful for what?
   a. Determining the occurrence of behaviors
   b. Establishing peer support systems
   c. Pinpointing significant life events
   d. Understanding life events and familial patterns

17. All of the following items are used in the flow of an ecomap, EXCEPT?
   a. Solid lines
   b. Dotted lines
   c. Triangles
   d. Arrows

18. All of the following are the best methods to assess a client's strengths and weaknesses, EXCEPT?
   a. A verbal report with open-ended questions
   b. An intake form with specific, closed-ended questions for accuracy
   c. Parroting back responses during the social work interview
   d. Using finding questions during the interview

19. Which statement is NOT true about indicators of motivation?
   a. Indicators of motivation are very basic and transparent.
   b. A client's level of engagement with the practitioner is an indicator.
   c. A client involuntarily coming for mandated treatment consistently indicates high motivation.
   d. Time progression will reflect the level of motivation.

20. Clients who are resistant to treatment will do all of the following, EXCEPT:
   a. Provide rationalizations for behaviors
   b. Appear disengaged
   c. Arrive late or cancel frequently
   d. Request assistance outside of business hours

21. Rationalization, intellectual capacity, creativity, and drive are all examples of what?
   a. Interpersonal skills
   b. Cognitive skills
   c. Coping skills
   d. Internal supports

22. Problem solving, self-confidence, the ability to empathize, and relationship sustainability are all examples of what?
   a. Internal supports
   b. Cognitive skills
   c. Coping Skills
   d. Extrinsic factors

23. Self-regulation, the ability to multi-task, temperament, and optimism are all examples of what?
   a. Internal supports
   b. Problem-solving skills
   c. Coping skills
   d. Extrinsic supports

24. Stress can manifest itself in the following symptoms: cognitive, emotional, _____, and behavioral.
   a. Irrational
   b. Vocational
   c. Physical
   d. Mutable

25. During a mental status exam (MSE), assessing how well the client pays attention is an example of what main element of the MSE?
   a. Psychomotor behavior
   b. Mood and affect
   c. Cognition
   d. Thought patterns

26. During a mental status exam (MSE), assessing the client's cooperation is an example of what main element of the MSE?
   a. General appearance
   b. Mood and affect
   c. Speech
   d. Level of consciousness

27. Which of the following statements is NOT true about the assessment process?
   a. It should focus on person in environment (PIE).
   b. Practitioner's beliefs are not influential.
   c. Resources available to the client should be highlighted.
   d. Obtaining an accurate view of the problem is essential to treatment.

28. Perception of family relationships, mental functioning, occupation, and social class are elements that help guide which of the following?
   a. The assessment process
   b. Formal observation
   c. Diagnosis
   d. Life span development

29. Which of the following is NOT an example of ego strength?
   a. Divulging medications being taken
   b. Moving forward after a loss
   c. Empathizing with others without minimizing the pain
   d. Being aware of and accepting one's own limitations

30. Factors linked to the body's physiological response are known as what?
    a. Psychological factors
    b. Biological factors
    c. Social factors
    d. Environmental factors

31. A client's view of an experience and/or self is an example of which of the following?
    a. Psychological factors
    b. Physiological factors
    c. Social factors
    d. Person-in-environment

32. Factors that are present in one's immediate physical surroundings and social systems are known as?
    a. Physiological factors
    b. Psychological factors
    c. Biological factors
    d. Social factors

33. Which of the following statements is NOT true about co-occurring disorders?
    a. Co-occurring disorders may also be known as dual diagnoses.
    b. Co-occurring disorders are less prevalent in clients with a history of substance abuse.
    c. Co-occurring disorders may be difficult to diagnose due to symptom presentation.
    d. Symptoms possibly appear related to another disorder.

34. Mistrust of others, fear of going home, presence of marks, and frequent vomiting are indicators of what?
    a. Physical neglect
    b. Physical abuse
    c. Sexual abuse
    d. Psychological abuse

35. Excessive desires to be a people pleaser, low self-esteem, and fluctuation between aggression and passiveness are indicators of what?
    a. Physiological malfunction
    b. Cognitive deficits
    c. Sexual abuse
    d. Psychological abuse

36. Excessive sleepiness, untreated medical problems, excessive hunger, and reports that no one is around to provide care are indicators of what?
    a. Physical neglect
    b. Biological assessment flaws
    c. Sexual neglect
    d. Starvation

37. The Bricklin Perceptual Scales are typically utilized in what type of cases?
    a. Custodial cases
    b. Homicide cases
    c. Suicide cases
    d. Substance abuse cases

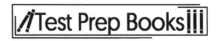

38. The methods used to develop an intervention/treatment plan are problem definition, problem causation, _____, and obstacle/risk identification.
    a. Objective development
    b. Risk assessment
    c. Solution identification
    d. Information gathering

39. Interventions matched to client problems are based on _____ and empirical data gathered by the social worker.
    a. Biopsychosocial assessment information
    b. Behavioral approach
    c. Problem causation
    d. Solution identification

40. The discharge summary should include the following information, EXCEPT:
    a. Reason for discharge
    b. Change of address
    c. Description of treatment goals
    d. Description of the client's level of functioning

41. When should discharge planning take place?
    a. At the halfway mark of the contracted sessions for treatment
    b. At the conclusion of the sessions
    c. At the onset of services
    d. Whenever the client indicates he/she is ready

42. Which of the following is NOT a characteristic of a good treatment goal?
    a. Subjective
    b. Specific
    c. Measurable
    d. Achievable

43. When the client provides his or her perspective on what happened and the correlated feelings and experiences felt, it is known as what?
    a. Measurable data
    b. Objective data
    c. Subjective data
    d. Planning data

44. When the social work practitioner uses information and asks finding questions to better understand where the client is emotionally, while distinguishing the facts related to the situation, he or she is using what?
    a. Controlled data
    b. Objective data
    c. Subjective data
    d. Qualitative data

45. How many main sections make up the DSM-5?
    a. One
    b. Two
    c. Three
    d. Four

46. Jane wakes up every morning with a headache, jaw pain, and neck pain. She struggles to get out of bed, and even basic household tasks seem to take all of her energy. She has trouble getting to work on time, and even when she has an important deadline, she doesn't seem to care or be able to concentrate. She always feels cranky and sometimes finds herself crying over things that never used to bother her. At her office health fair, a vendor took Jane's blood pressure and found it to be 150/90. What might Jane's symptoms indicate?
    a. Psychosocial stress
    b. Gout
    c. Alzheimer's disease
    d. Generalized Anxiety Disorder

47. An individual with schizophrenia may be prescribed which of the following medications?
    a. Vyvanse
    b. Ritalin
    c. Nexium
    d. Abilify

48. What does a genogram visually depict?
    a. History of all prescribed medications and dosages
    b. Social interactions over a specific period of time
    c. Risk of carrying certain genetic diseases
    d. Stress triggers

49. Which of the examples listed depicts obtaining information from a collateral source?
    a. An initial verbal consultation conducted with a potential client
    b. A self-report assessment filled out by the client
    c. An official medical report brought by the client to their first session
    d. The client draws a picture illustrating their current mental state during a session

50. Which of these is NOT a commonly used psychometric in social work?
    a. Myers-Briggs Type Indicator
    b. Beck Depression Inventory
    c. Wechsler Adult Intelligence Scale – Fourth Edition
    d. Miller Analogies Test

51. Social workers typically examine a client's personal history holistically through what kind of lens?
    a. Clinical
    b. Biopsychosocial
    c. Psychosomatic
    d. Environmental

Answer Explanations

1. B: Verifying payment is not a critical part of the client interview. Payment may occur before the interview process or may be pre-determined based on the work setting. Choice A, building rapport, happens at all stages of the client interview and is an important characteristic of interviews. Choice C, starting where the client is, is another important feature of the interview and is part of empowering the client by hearing things from his or her perspective. Choice D, the use of encouraging, neutral questions, is also part of empowering the client and moves the conversation forward, encouraging the client to share.

2. D: Closed-ended questions can limit insight into the client's problems during the interview because they deter answer explanations. Open-ended questions (Choice A) encourage discussion and help the social worker gain insight into the client's problems. Choice B, clarifying questions, can also help the social worker gain insight because he or she provides alternate explanations to problems, as well as validate that the client is being heard. Choice C, note taking, is an effective way for the social worker to record information during the interview.

3. A: Practitioner's clothing does not affect client behaviors and responses during the interview. Practitioner's speech patterns, eye contact, and pitch of speech (Choices B, C, and D) may all affect a client's behaviors and responses during the interview process because the client may mimic the rigid body language of the practitioner and become defensive.

4. C: This question asks the test taker to determine which of the four answer choices is not included in a client's chief complaint. Let's look at what may be included in a client's chief complaint. The text says the following:

Chief complaint is the client's version of what the over-arching problem is, in his/her own words (Choice D). The client's description of the chief complaint may include factors from the past that the client views as an obstacle to optimal functioning (Choice A). It could also be an issue that was previously resolved but reoccurs (Choice B), thus requiring the client to develop additional coping skills.

We can see that Choices A, B, and D are all represented describing the client's chief complaint. Thus, Choice C is the only option not included in a client's chief complaint, which is the collateral resources that describe or validate the problem.

5. C: Interaction with peers, work, and home environment are examples of information included in the social part of the assessment. Choice A, demographics, is incorrect because this does not give insight into the client's social life and is part of the identification stage of the assessment. Choice B is incorrect because the client's current level of functioning is assessed during the mental status exam. Choice D is incorrect because previous or current diagnoses would be information given during the medical component of the assessment process.

6. A: The first item to focus on during the client interview is what the client wants to discuss first. The client should be empowered to guide the focus of discussion. Choices B, historical influences that contribute to the presenting problem, C, family dynamics and social supports, and D, medical diagnoses that complicate the presenting problem, are all good to focus on, but should not be forced at the beginning of the interview by the social worker.

7. B: Employment history and related financial status are not commonly explored during the gathering of historical data. Choices A, previous or current physiological health diagnoses, C, review of psychological development, and D, past experiences with substance abuse, should all be explored when gathering a client's history.

8. C: The question asks which of the answer choices is NOT a collateral source. Let's look at the answers that do qualify as collateral sources:

Collateral sources are persons outside of the client like family members (Choice A), police officers (Choice B), friends, or other medical providers (Choice D) who can provide information related to the client's levels of functioning, life events, and other potential areas of significance in the client's treatment. Choice C is the only answer choice that is NOT considered a collateral source.

9. A: The question asks which statement concerning standardized instruments is not true. Let's look at the following statements that are true:

Standardized instruments are crucial to providing a uniformed, reliable method of comprehensive screening (Choice B). Standardized instruments can also be used to facilitate ongoing clinical evaluation of clients in social work practice (Choice C). Finally, standardized instruments are defined as tools to measure client behaviors, knowledge, or other affects (Choice D).

Police reports and physician's reports are not examples of standardized instruments, which means Choice A is the answer that is not true concerning standardized instruments.

10. C: Performance is not one of the three key areas when reviewing the problem history. Progression (A), severity (B), and onset (C), are the three key areas of the problem history. The history of the problem is important to address because it provides clarification on the factors contributing to what the client describes as the presenting problem, as well as the actual problem. Gathering background information on the problem history is also helpful for developing interventions.

11. C: The ABCs of a problem refer to the Antecedent, Behavior, and Consequences linked to a client's perceived problem. The discovery of these items allows the client to specifically define the problem and examine factors affecting emotional well-being. Antecedents to a problem may be prefaced by the involvement of certain individuals in the client's life. The client may disclose interactions that led to his or her problematic behaviors, based on the aforementioned information in the evaluation of the antecedent. The consequences to a presenting problem are comprised of both internal (cognitive or personal) and external (environmental) interactions or reactions to the behavior.

12. A: Atypical antipsychotics were developed decades after typical antipsychotics and generally have fewer side effects. Atypical antipsychotics were developed in the 1990s and have been shown to have less severe side effects. Typical antipsychotics were developed in the 1950s. They can be used if atypical antipsychotics don't work for the client, but they usually have severe side effects.

13. C: Controlled observation can best be defined as purposely targeting a client's behaviors in a pre-determined setting. A client may be observed in a setting such as a school environment or home to allow the social work practitioner to get a better understanding of how the client functions in his or her natural environment.

14. A: Observing the antecedents, behaviors, and consequences is known as functional analysis. Choice B, formal observation, is a method that includes functional analysis, but also includes other methods where specific data is collected on the client in a pre-determined setting. Choice C is also incorrect. Choice D, controlled observation, is purposely targeting a client's behavior in a pre-determined setting.

15. C: The intake form does not contain information about the client's food allergies. The assessment form includes identifying information about the client's household (A), age (B), and gender (D), as well as a brief description of the problem in the client's own words. Clients are generally asked to complete an assessment form prior to the first session. The social work practitioner may review this form before or after meeting with the client to gain additional insight into the client's needs.

16. D: A genogram is most useful for understanding life events and familial patterns. A genogram is not useful for Choice A, determining the occurrence of behaviors. While the genogram can provide insight into the perceived relationship between the client and family and existing support systems, it does not establish peer support systems (Choice B), nor does it pinpoint significant life events (Choice C)—it is only useful for understanding them.

17. C: The question asks which item is NOT used in the flow of an ecomap. Let's look at the items that are used in the flow of an ecomap:

When the client constructs the map of social relationships, the client connection between the self and relationships is demonstrated with Choice A, a solid line. Choice B, the dotted line, would indicate a fractured relationship. Arrows may be used to add more detail to the relationship status and help the client and social worker understand the overall function of the relationships.

Triangles, Choice C, are not used in the flow of an ecomap.

18. B: The question asks which method is NOT the best way to assess a client's strengths and weaknesses. Let's look at the methods that are considered the best to way to assess a client's strengths and weaknesses:

The client is encouraged to provide a verbal report answering an open-ended question about what aspects he/she views as current strengths and weaknesses (Choice A). The social worker may parrot back to the client the strengths heard in the narrative and response (Choice C). Finally, practitioners are encouraged to use finding questions and phrases to guide the client to share personal reactions to the event, discuss what favorable actions were taken, and examine what alternative actions could have been taken (Choice D).

Intake forms with specific, close-ended questions for accuracy are not the best method to assess client's strengths and weaknesses (Choice B).

19. C: The question asks which statement is NOT true about indicators of motivation. Let's look at the choices that are true concerning indicators of motivation:

Indicators of motivation are very basic and transparent (Choice A). As time progresses, the client's level of engagement with the practitioner is an indicator of motivation as well (Choices B and D).

A client involuntarily coming for mandated treatment does not consistently indicate high motivation (Choice C).

20. D: The question asks when clients are resistant to treatment, what will they NOT do? First, let's look at the things they will do:

Clients who are resistant may provide rationalizations for behaviors, rather than trying to address them (Choice *A*). Additionally, a resistant client may appear disengaged during sessions or explicitly state that he or she will not take the recommended actions for an intervention (Choice *B*). Finally, resistant clients may frequently arrive late, cancel, or be a no-show for sessions (Choice *C*).

Clients who are resistant to treatment will not likely request assistance outside of business hours (Choice *D*).

21. B: Cognitive skills include rationalization, intellectual capacity, creativity, and drive. Choice A, interpersonal skills, are skills someone would use to get along and interact with others. Choice C, coping skills, are skills a person uses in order to deal with stressful events or situations. Choice D, internal supports, is what the client uses to deal with situations, such as strengths and coping abilities.

22. A: Problem solving, self-confidence, the ability to empathize, and relationship sustainability are all examples of internal supports. Choice B, cognitive skills, involve a person's rationalization, intellectual capacity, creativity, and drive. Choice C, coping skills, are the methods one uses to deal with stressful situations. Choice D, extrinsic factors, refers to factors that exist external to the client and are reviewed in social work assessment and diagnosis.

23. C: Self-regulation, the ability to multi-task, temperament, and optimism are all examples of coping skills. Choice A, internal supports, are the inner resources the client uses to cope. Problem-solving skills, Choice B, involve working through a problem in order to achieve a solution. Extrinsic supports, Choice D, involve support outside of the client.

24. C: Stress can manifest itself in the following symptoms: cognitive, emotional, physical, and behavioral. Stress may result from a threat to the client's functioning, both real and imagined. Some common factors contributing to biopsychosocial stress are natural disasters or disruption of relationships, such as divorce, death, break-ups, or moving.

25. C: During a mental status exam (MSE), assessing how well the client pays attention is an example of cognition. Attention, level of concentration, memory, orientation, and judgment are examples of cognition during an MSE. Choice A, psychomotor behavior, involves eye contact, a handshake, posture, movement and coordination. Mood and affect (Choice B) involve cooperation, appropriateness, stability, and demeanor, while thought patterns (Choice D) include flow of thought and the ability to be present and engage in relevant conversation.

26. B: During a mental status exam (MSE), assessing the client's cooperation is an example of mood and affect. Cooperation, appropriateness, stability, and demeanor (e.g., flat, bubbly, warm, or restricted) are examples of mood and affect examined during an MSE. Choice A, general appearance, is determined by race, age, sex, body build, personal hygiene, and grooming. Choice *C* is incorrect because its attributes include syntax, rhythm, voice quality, and phrases used. Choice D, level of consciousness, includes alertness and presence of fatigue or lethargy.

27. B: The question asks which statement is NOT true concerning the assessment process. Let's look at the statements that are true:

The assessment process focuses on the person-in-environment (PIE) and is an ongoing part of client treatment that involves review of the client's situation (Choice A). The assessment process should also highlight resources available to the client, in order to address presenting problems (Choice C). Finally, it is suggested that obtaining an accurate definition or view of the problem is essential to guiding the appropriate treatment plan and diagnosis (Choice D).

The practitioner's beliefs are influential in the assessment process; however, Choice B states that they are not, which makes Choice B the answer.

28. C: Perception of family relationships, mental functioning, occupation, and social class are elements that help guide diagnosis. Finding questions about what is going on in the client's life and desired outcomes from therapy may help guide the diagnostic process. Choice A, the assessment process, focuses on the person-in-environment (PIE) and is an ongoing part of client treatment that involves review of the client's situation. Choice B, formal observation, is where specific data is collected on the client in a pre-determined setting. Choice D, life span development, refers to physical and cognitive alterations throughout a client's lifespan.

29. A: Divulging medications being taken is not an example of ego strength. Ego strength is exhibited when a client demonstrates the ability to utilize a skill or set of characteristics that deal with highly demanding, stressful situations. Choice B, moving forward after a loss, Choice C, empathizing with others without minimizing the pain, and Choice D, being aware of and accepting one's own limitations, are examples of ego strength.

30. B: Factors linked to the body's physiological response are known as biological factors. These factors may present in the form of fluctuations in heartbeat, sweating, shortness of breath, digestive issues, and/or brain functioning. Choice A, psychological factors, refer to cognitive processes, such as thoughts, beliefs, one's view of an experience, and one's view of self. Choice C, social factors, and Choice D, environmental factors, are present in one's immediate physical surroundings and social systems such as work, school, home and peer group.

31. A: A client's view of an experience and/or self is an example of psychological factors. Psychological factors refer to cognitive processes, such as thoughts, beliefs, one's view of an experience, and one's view of self. Choice B, physiological factors, present in the form of fluctuations of heartbeat, sweating, shortness of breath, digestive issues, and brain functioning. Choice C, social factors, are present in one's immediate physical surroundings and social systems, like work, school, home and peer group. Choice D, person-in-environment, means learning about an individual based on the context of environmental situations in which the individual lives and acts.

32. D: Factors that are present in one's immediate physical surroundings and social systems are known as social factors. Social or environmental factors are present in one's social systems, such as work, school, home, and peer group. Physiological factors, Choice A, present in the form of sweating, shortness of breath, or digestive issues. Psychological factors, Choice B, refer to cognitive processes like thoughts or beliefs. Biological factors, Choice C, are known as the factors connected to the body's physiological response and are linked to genetics.

33. B: The question asks which of the statements is NOT true concerning co-occurring disorders? Let's look at the statements that are true:

Co-occurring disorders may also be known as dual diagnoses (Choice *A*). It may be difficult to diagnose substance abuse due to symptom presentation, which may appear related to other disorders (Choices *C* and *D*).

Co-occurring disorders are less prevalent in clients with a history of substance abuse; Choice *B* states that co-occurring disorders are less prevalent in clients with a history of substance abuse, which makes Choice *B* the question that is "not true."

34. B: Mistrust of others, fear of going home, presence of marks, and frequent vomiting are indicators of physical abuse. Indicators of Choice A, physical neglect, may be the appearance of being malnourished, excessive sleepiness, or untreated medical problems. Victims experiencing Choice C, sexual abuse, may have mistrust or fear of those who bear resemblance to the abuser or may have severe alterations in behavior such as depression, anxiety, or fearfulness. Choice D, psychological abuse, is indicated by extreme fluctuations between aggression and passiveness, manifestation of emotional stress, people-pleasing, or developmental delays.

35. D: These symptoms are indicators of psychological abuse. Psychological abuse may be one of the more difficult types of abuse for a social worker to detect. Choice A, physiological malfunction, has nothing to do with people-pleasing or low self-esteem. Cognitive deficits, Choice B, are also unrelated to the question and have to do with an intellectual disability beginning in childhood. Choice C, sexual abuse, is indicated by severe alterations in behavior such as depression, anxiety, or fearfulness, especially around the abuser or those who resemble the abuser, such as other adults.

36. A: These symptoms are indicators of physical neglect. Physical neglect can be the appearance of always being hungry, excessive sleepiness, or untreated medical problems. Other indicators of physical neglect are parents of caregivers demonstrating lack of interest or suffering from chronic illness. Usually, the home is an unsafe environment for victims who experience physical neglect.

37. A: Custodial cases. The Bricklin Perceptual Scales are typically administered to children six years of age and older in custody cases to determine the child's perception of each caregiver.

38. C: Solution identification is the third method used to develop an intervention/treatment plan. This is where the practitioner works with the client to suggest solutions towards which to work. Three goals included in this solution are (a) objectives developed for the goal, (b) developed objectives that are SMART (specific, measurable, achievable, relevant, and time-specific), and (c) activities developed in an effort to assist the client in achieving goals.

39. A: The components of the biopsychosocial assessment drive the data pertinent to designing interventions that match the client's problems, such as client strengths and risk factors. In turn, these strengths and risk factors help guide the practitioner in the selection of a theoretical model to apply (in an effort to enhance client functioning and improve the client's overall well-being).

40. B: The discharge summary should not include change of address. The discharge summary should include Choice A, reason for discharge, Choice C, description of treatment goals, and Choice D, description of the client's level of functioning. Discharge summaries should also include recommendations for follow-up care. The main purpose of discharge planning is to develop a plan of care that goes beyond the current treatment sessions to promote success once services have concluded. The current practitioner should prepare to become a collateral resource linked to the client's level of care for the next professional.

41. C: Discharge planning should take place at the onset of services. The practitioner should not delay discharge planning until several sessions have occurred as discharge may occur at any time. Further, it is within the best interests of the client to engage in concurrent planning. Making the client aware of the choices for discharge and the discharge planning process empowers the client during treatment. Choices *A, B,* and *D* are true for when the services might come to an end, which is at any time. However, they are not the correct times to plan the client's discharge.

42. A: *Subjective* is not a characteristic of a good treatment goal. Choices B, C, and D make up the acronym regarding SMART goals: Specific (B), Measurable (C), Achievable (D), Relevant, and Time-specific. The client and practitioner must both agree on the measurability of a goal with specificity. Measurable terms used in writing the goals should focus on the type of behavior the client wants to achieve. The type of language used to plan and the objectives themselves should be relevant to the client. Objectives should be both short and long-term. Short-term objectives should only be a few weeks in length. The time-frame for completion should align with the nature of the objective.

43. C: Subjective data is when the client provides his or her perspective on what happened and the correlated feelings and experiences felt. The social worker may use the information to tease out facts related to the client's situation, which is known as objective data, Choice B. Measurable data (Choice A) and planning data (Choice D) are not relevant to the context of the question.

44. B: Objective data is correct. The social worker collects objective data to determine the facts in a client's situation. Subjective data (Choice C) is when the client provides his or her perspective on what happened and the experiences felt. Controlled data (Choice A) and qualitative data (Choice D) are not relevant to the context of the question.

45. C: The DSM-5 has three sections—one that explains an overview of the changes, one that lists the classes of and criteria for disorders, and one that covers areas for future research.

46. A: Psychosocial stress. Gout is a kind of arthritis characterized by joint pain and inflammation. Alzheimer's disease is a neurological condition characterized by memory loss and confusion. Generalized anxiety disorder is characterized by persistent and excessive worrying and fear.

47. D: Abilify. Abilify is an atypical anti-psychotic used to treat symptoms of schizophrenia. Vyvanse and Ritalin are stimulants typically used to treat attention-deficit/hyperactivity disorders. Nexium is a proton-pump inhibitor used to treat reflux diseases.

48. B: Social interactions over a specific period of time. The other three answers do not fit the function or purpose of a genogram, which is used to show how a person's social (often familial) relationships affect attachment, behavioral patterns, and relationship dynamics.

49. C: An official medical report brought by the client to their first session. The other three examples show primary sources of information, as all of the information available is provided directly by the client. While the client is still the one physically giving the medical history report to the practitioner, it's considered a collateral source because it was officially documented and then obtained from a secondary source (the client's healthcare provider).

50. D: The Millers Analogy Test is a standardized test used for admissions in high IQ societies. The Myers-Briggs Type Indicator, the Beck Depression Inventory, and the Wechsler Adult Intelligence Scale are all commonly used psychometrics in social work.

51. B: Biopsychosocial. While social workers look at an individual's clinical, psychosomatic, and environmental history, these are small components that make up a full spectrum of influences in the individual's history. The biopsychosocial lens allows the social worker to look at biological, psychological, and social factors together to make reliable diagnoses and plan treatments.

Psychotherapy, Clinical Interventions, and Case Management

Therapeutic Relationship

Components of the Social Worker-Client Relationship

The relationship between the social worker and the client or client system is influenced by a number of components. These include the type of emotion that is shown by the parties during sessions, the general attitude toward the working relationship (e.g., positive, supportive), and the value each party places on the working relationship. The social worker should ensure that empathy, sympathy, and acceptance of the client and client system are shown during sessions to help foster a positive relationship. These aspects can be further supported by the social worker's initiative to build rapport with the client, such as through allowing the client to openly express feelings, work at a pace that feels comfortable, and encouraging them to shape and make decisions related to the intervention.

Additionally, a number of external tools may be a vital part of the social worker/client relationship. These include tools and documents that provide information related to the client's personality and behavior, and can help the social worker shape the intervention for the client. These might include items such as assessments, medical history, family history, current living situation, socioeconomic situation, and personal goals for the intervention.

Building and Maintaining a Helping Relationship

As the principal conduit for client change and acceptance, the social worker/client relationship is primary to the problem solving and therapy process. If the social worker cannot develop a positive relationship with the client, the change process is hindered. The worker/client relationship should be based on trust, empathy, and acceptance by both parties in order to facilitate growth. Some clients may have difficulty building trust with the social worker, and the social worker may need to be patient with the client in order to make treatment goal progress. If the social worker cannot develop an appropriate trusting, empathetic, and accepting relationship with the client, the social worker should seek supervision. In some cases, the social worker will need to transfer the client because it will be very challenging for the client to make progress if trust does not exist. Social workers should be alert for countertransference issues in the relationship with the client and address these issues promptly if they occur.

Principles of Relationship Building

Rapport building begins during the initial contact the social worker has with the client, a crucial time for establishing trust and harmony. After building rapport, the client and the social worker can begin working on client issues and continue developing the relationship on deeper levels. The relationship that the client has with the social worker is representative of the relationships the client has in other areas of life; the social worker needs to engage with the client within this framework to effect the greatest change.

Termination of the relationship occurs when the client and the social worker have reached treatment goals. Even though the relationship is terminated, the client may feel warmly toward the social worker, and congruence and empathy may still be part of the relationship. Some clients may require maintenance sessions to continue stability, but when termination is the next clear stage in the relationship, psychotherapy sessions should end.

Power and Transparency in the Social Worker-Client Relationship

Throughout their careers and in specific interventions, social workers should always remain aware of the power differential that is likely to exist between themselves and their clients. As the main person guiding the intervention, social workers inherently have more power in the relationship. Additionally, social workers may have more education, more independence, a clean legal record, better finances, or some other privilege that may make the client feel uncomfortable, ashamed, or defensive (especially when the client is involuntarily in the session, such as court-ordered cases). Awareness is one fundamental component of ensuring that this power dynamic doesn't have a negative effect. Transparency is another fundamental component, as it allows the client to feel like an equal who is involved in the problem-solving process. Social workers can foster transparency in the working relationship by openly discussing areas of privilege they may have, sharing as much information as they can about the problem-solving process and how it may be of benefit to the client, and empowering the client to take as much of the process as possible into their own control (such as through independent decision making). When possible, the social worker should avoid hiding information or being unclear about why certain processed of interventions are being pursued.

Social Worker's Role in the Problem-Solving Process

The problem solving therapeutic model serves to teach clients how to manage stressors that come in life. Often clients do not possess skills that allow them to effectively navigate negative events or emotions without increasing personal harm. The goal of the problem-solving model is to teach clients the skills necessary to deal with negative life events, negative emotions, and stressful situations. In particular, goals of this model should be to assist clients in identifying which particular situations may trigger unpleasant emotions, understanding the range of emotions one might feel, planning how to effectively deal with situations when they arise, and even recognizing and accepting that some situations are not able to be solved.

The social worker, however, may be an instructional guide to facilitate problem solving for the client. Because problem-solving skills are one of the primary methods of resolving issues, and often are skills that clients lack, the social worker may need to model them for the client so that the client can then develop their own skills. Social workers need to maintain empathy and congruence with the client during the problem solving process, and even though they may have verbally instructed or modeled problem-solving methods, they need to maintain rapport in the relationship.

Roles and Responsibilities of the Social Worker and Client in the Intervention Process

Clarifying the roles and responsibilities of the social worker, the client, and the client system in the intervention process can reduce the chance of miscommunication, misunderstanding, and interventions not working as intended. This clarification process can be developed during the intake process and initial sessions by actively listening to what the client hopes to achieve, and working together to develop a step-by-step intervention methodology. When possible, the stages, objectives, and milestones of the intervention should be documented in order to have an available reference point, drive accountability, and reduce any confusion around the expectations of all involved parties.

The problem-solving approach to interventions is a commonly used framework to cover these points. This is a seven-stage model that encourages active listening and engagement techniques (such as eye contact and other receptive body language); fostering trust and collaboration with the client (such as by showing genuine interest in the client as a person, rather than just in the context of the issues at hand); working together to identify the problem to be addressed and possible solutions, introducing allies in the resolution processes (such as clinical providers, a yoga or meditation teacher, or other experts that could help the client); developing a documented resolution plan and actively engaging all parties to follow it (such as through accountability cues, positive reinforcement, and celebrating small victories); and support for sustaining the desired behaviors until the client is capable of terminating the intervention. While one can be hopeful that the client and client systems will be cooperative and willing in this framework, that is not always the case. Clients may show distrust, anxiety, fear, or apathy, especially in the beginning. Often, the most important role of the social worker is building trust with the client and the client system. The social worker should continue to encourage a trusting, collaborative relationship until the time of service termination.

Acceptance and Empathy in the Social Worker-Client Relationship

Empathy is being able to relate to client circumstances and direction without the social worker actually experiencing it themselves. Sympathy differs from empathy in that sympathy is compassion for the client without having experienced the client's state of being. Empathy involves "being with" the client in their time and frame of mind. It involves connecting to the client on a visceral level while still maintaining some objectivity. Because empathy is the framework on which social work practice is built, it is imperative that social workers be empathetic with their clients. Those who cannot be empathetic should seek additional supervision or counsel in order to do their work effectively, or refer the client to another worker.

Diversity in the Social Worker-Client Relationship

Attitudes and Beliefs
Social workers should be culturally aware in their attitudes and beliefs. This requires a keen awareness of their own cultural background and gaining awareness of any personal biases, stereotypes, and values that they hold. Practitioners should also accept different worldviews, be sensitive to differences, and refer minority clients to a practitioner from the client's culture when it would benefit the client.

Knowledge
Practitioners should have the appropriate knowledge of different cultures. Specifically, practitioners must understand the client's culture and should not jump to conclusions about the client's way of being. Throughout their careers, social workers should be willing to gain a greater depth of knowledge of various cultural groups and update this knowledge as necessary. This includes understanding how issues like racism, sexism, and homophobia can negatively affect minority clients. Practitioners should understand how different therapeutic theories carry values that may be detrimental for some clients. Social workers should also understand how institutional barriers can affect the willingness of minority clients to use mental health services.

Cultural Skills
Social workers should be well-versed in cultural skills. They must be able to apply interviewing and counseling techniques with clients and should be able to employ specialized skills and interventions that might be effective with specific minority populations. Practitioners should be able to communicate

effectively and understand the verbal and nonverbal language of a client. They also should take a systematic perspective in their practice, work collaboratively with community leaders, and advocate for clients when it's in their best interests.

When working with clients from diverse backgrounds, practitioners should be able to shift their professional strategies. Below are techniques and strategies social workers should keep in mind when working with clients of different cultures.

Various Cultural and Racial Backgrounds
- Have appropriate attitudes and beliefs, gain knowledge about the client's background, and learn new skills as needed.

- Encourage the client to speak in his or her native language and arrange for an interpreter when necessary.

- Assess the client's cultural identity and how important it is to the client.

- Check accuracy of any interpretations of the client's nonverbal cues.

- Make use of alternate modes of communication, such as writing, typing, translation services, and the use of art.

- Assess the impact of sociopolitical issues on the client.

- Encourage the client to bring culturally significant and personally relevant items.

- Vary the helping environment to make it conducive to effective work with the client.

Various Religious Backgrounds
- Determine the client's religious background in the beginning sessions.
- Check personal biases and gain information about the client's religion.
- Ask the client how important religion is in his or her life.
- Assess the client's level of faith development.
- Avoid making assumptions about the religion.
- Become familiar with the client's religious beliefs, important holidays, and faith traditions.
- Understand that religion can deeply affect the client unconsciously.

Client's Developmental Level on the Social Worker-Client Relationship

A client's development level will vary from client to client, and it may even vary for the same client over the full course of an intervention. Therefore, the social worker should make no assumptions about the client's ability to cope, the way the intervention will be accepted and utilized, or any other aspect of the working relationship. These factors should be assessed upon intake and at regular intervals thereafter, the frequency of which may vary on a case-by-case basis.

Assessments should holistically take into account the client development, including age, psychological factors, emotional factors, social factors, acute personal conditions (such as an impending divorce or recent refugee status) that may temporarily impact the client's functioning, and any other scope of development that may be appropriate for the client's need. For example, a client who has a history of violent behavior and a history of playing physical sports with extreme contact may find it beneficial to

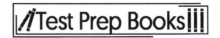

undergo neurological development assessments. By viewing the client through a holistic perspective, social workers can ensure interventions are appropriate across all domains of development; if so, the interventions are more likely to be effective and received positively by the client.

Domestic, Intimate Partner, and Other Violence on the Helping Relationship

Any type of abuse in a client's life can impart symptoms of trauma to the client. These symptoms may be subtle in nature, or they may be relatively obvious to the social worker. Obvious indicators of abuse include physical marks, chronic muscular or stomach pain (as a result of trauma or stress), consistently dressing in high-coverage clothing, even in cases where it seems abnormal (such as a hot day), or particular body language when the abuser is in the room or attending a session. Most abusive relationships occur as a manifestation of dysfunctional power and control tactics. If the client is an abuser, it may be difficult for him or her to be guided by a social worker, as there may be an experience of a loss of control or power. Abuse victims may feel distrustful or fearful of the social worker and the helping relationship; they also may be uncomfortable discussing their abuser in a negative light. This can be a setback to the intervention process, and social workers may need to spend extra time fostering rapport and building a trusting relationship with these types of clients.

Verbal and Nonverbal Communication Techniques

Social workers use verbal and nonverbal communication techniques to engage clients in completing treatment goals. Verbal communication is vital to the social worker/client relationship, and social workers should be skilled at greetings, summarization, reflection, and the conveyance of new information to the client. The client may misconstrue a social worker's body language if it does not represent openness and trust. Likewise, the social worker needs to be adept at analyzing the client's body language in order to move forward. Clients use both verbal and nonverbal communication to convey their story to the social worker, and communication techniques used by the social worker can be modeled to teach the client improved communication. Clients should be instructed to recognize their own communication techniques in the context of the relationship with the social worker. Clients who are withdrawn or isolated may need especially sensitive communication with the social worker in order to better communicate verbally and nonverbally.

In order to build a strong helping relationship with the client, the worker must learn to use effective verbal and nonverbal techniques. These skills are necessary throughout the treatment process, but especially during assessment and engagement.

Congruence in Communication

Social workers need to be congruent—in agreement and harmony—with client feedback and encourage clients' self-direction. Social workers and clients begin treatment by enhancing congruence in communication so that mutually agreed upon goals may be developed for the client. The social worker should be invested in the therapeutic relationship and able to participate in a way that assists the client in becoming more self-aware. If a social worker is not congruent with the client, then treatment progress may be hindered and the client should be referred to another worker who is a more appropriate fit.

Obtaining and Providing Feedback

There are several ways social workers can receive feedback. It can come in the form of evaluation by another social worker during supervision, or from a client during treatment. Obtaining feedback is an important means to improve a social worker's skill and ensure effective treatment for clients. Feedback from clients may be formal or informal. Clients may offer unsolicited feedback verbally or non-verbally during treatment, using words, body language, or tone of voice. Social workers must be sensitive to the messages clients are expressing to decipher how to interpret feedback that may not be clear.

When seeking feedback from a client, the social worker should ensure the method is appropriate to the skills, resources, and abilities of the client (i.e., in writing, by mail, text, in person, etc.)

Factors to consider when obtaining feedback from clients:

- Social workers may consider a client's progress toward a goal or lack thereof as a type of feedback. If treatment is not progressing as expected, the worker should evaluate and make adjustments as necessary.

- Always be clear why the information is needed and ensure client confidentiality to the fullest extent possible.

- Feedback can be sought at different times throughout the treatment process to ensure reliability and consistency.

- Workers should seek feedback regardless of whether it is expected to be negative or positive. All feedback should be viewed as a learning tool to enhance treatment and worker skill.

Factors to consider when receiving feedback during supervision/consultation:

- Social workers can benefit from feedback during supervision or consultation, especially with difficult clients/cases or at significant times in treatment, such as termination.

- When discussing cases, client confidentiality should be protected as much as possible, and client consent to release information should be acquired.

The Intervention Process

Interviewing Techniques

Interviewing is common in social work. An interview should always be focused and have a purpose—this is often to gather data, diagnose, and provide therapy. An interview can be used to discuss behavior patterns, ensure the practitioner and the individual are discussing the same presenting issues, bring attention to presenting issues, or provide new perspectives on presenting issues. Interviews are generally verbal, although the practitioner should be mindful of observing non-verbal communication. While the questions of the interview should be planned, the practitioner should be able to tailor the questions based on the individual's needs.

There are several communication techniques beneficial to the social work practice other than the basic interview process used to gather general demographic and presenting problem information. Here are several:

Furthering

A technique that reinforces the idea that the worker is listening to the client and encourages further information to be gathered. This technique includes nodding of the head, facial expressions, or encouragement responses such as "yes" or "I understand." It also includes accent responses, whereby workers repeat or parrot back a few words of a client's last response.

Close/Open-Ended Questions

Depending on the timing or information the worker is seeking to elicit from the client, one of these types of questions may be used. Close-ended questions, such as "How old are you?" will typically elicit a short answer. Conversely, open-ended questions, such as "What are your feelings about school?" allow for longer, more-involved responses.

Clarifying and Paraphrasing

This is when social workers ask a client for clarification to ensure they understand the client's message. Clarifying also includes encouraging clients to speak more concretely and in less abstract terms to provide clearer messages. When paraphrasing, workers should convey a message back to the client to ensure an understanding of the client's meaning.

Summarizing

This is similar to paraphrasing, but summarizing includes more information. It's frequently used to help focus the session and allow the worker to summarize the overall messages, problems, or goals of the client.

Active Listening

Using facial expressions, body language, and postures to show the worker is engaged and listening to the client. Workers should display eye contact and natural but engaged body movements and gestures. An example would be sitting slightly forward with a non-rigid posture. As with all communication techniques, social workers should be aware of cultural differences in what is appropriate, especially related to direct eye contact and posturing.

Methods of Summarizing Communication

Social workers may paraphrase and echo clients' verbal statements to acknowledge their feelings. Summarizing may involve reflecting back the statements made by the client to clarify what the client has said. Social workers also must summarize communication in order to provide sufficient records of the session. Further, during the end of the session, the social worker may wish to clarify goals and homework assigned for the next week so that the client is clear on the changes that need to take place.

Methods of Facilitating Communication

Social workers may facilitate communication with the client by verbally encouraging communication or by addressing the client with constructive information concerning the case. Social workers need to recall information concerning the client from session to session in order to facilitate communication and move forward with the client. Clarifying what the client has said, and the client's feelings, helps not only to ensure the social worker clearly understands what is being communicated, but also lets the client know that the social worker is engaged and actively listening. Development of trust with the client may facilitate additional communication, and social workers should be sensitive to the trust-building process because it is the cornerstone of the helping relationship. Social workers may provide clients with homework outside of a session that facilitates communication during the next session.

Mandated clients, including court ordered clients or clients ordered to counseling from child protective services, may face challenges in communicating with the social worker because they do not choose to be in treatment. Developing trust with these clients to facilitate communication is especially important for progress to be made. It's helpful to acknowledge the client's feelings and possible frustration about the mandated treatment. Clients who require out-of-home placement need clear communication with the social worker to clarify what is happening and make appropriate psychological adjustments to their circumstances.

Using Bias-Free Language in Interviewing

When interviewing a client, a social worker must be careful to eliminate all personal bias from their language. This relates to all subtle negative phrasing related to race, ethnicity, socioeconomic status, gender, gender identity, life choices, disability, or psychological disorders. The job of the social worker is to support the client without bias, always promoting the client's self-identity. Phrases or expressions that demean or stereotype a particular group of people should never be used. Similarly, labeling someone can be hurtful, especially in cases where that label has a negative connotation or stigma attached to it. Sometimes it may even be appropriate for the social worker to ask the client how they wish to be identified or addressed. Inclusive and affirming language should be used when talking about all groups of people, and especially when talking to or about the client. Terms that are known to be offensive or degrading should always be avoided.

The Phases of Intervention and Treatment

The treatment intervention process consists of four stages. There is some crossover between stages, and the activities of each stage may occur at other times during the process. For instance, the assessment and evaluation phases of intervention are ongoing throughout treatment. Here are the four stages:

Engagement and Assessment

During this stage, the worker focuses on relationship and rapport building with the client. The worker gathers data, assesses the client's history and systems, and identifies problems and challenges.

Goal Identification and Intervention Planning

This stage consists of the client and worker collaborating to identify goals to be accomplished. Plan of care/treatment is developed and the contract is implemented.

Implementation

The caseworker implements selected interventions and tasks. The client works toward identified goals. During this stage, the plan is frequently reviewed by the worker in collaboration with the client to assess progress toward goals. Adjustments are made by either party if necessary.

Termination and Evaluation

The social worker should begin the termination phase at the onset of services, since the client may abruptly terminate services for various reasons. It is within best practice guidelines and the best interest of both social worker and client to be prepared for service termination. The social worker should inform the client about the termination guidelines once services begin. Moreover, goal attainment is assessed and evaluation of interventions occurs. The social worker should also review the plan for maintenance of acquired skills while follow-up procedures are discussed and implemented.

Problem-Solving Models and Approaches

When working with clients to develop problem-solving skills, workers must first engage and prepare clients by discussing the benefits of improving such skills and encouraging clients to commit to the problem-solving process during the goal setting/contracting phase.

Steps in the problem-solving process:

Assess, Define, and Clarify the Problem

As with goal setting, social workers should assist clients in clearly determining and defining the specific problem. Workers should focus on the current problem and ensure clients do not become distracted by other past or current difficulties. Examine specific aspects of the problem, including behaviors and the needs of those involved.

Determine Possible Solutions

Social workers should lead discussion among participants to determine possible solutions and encourage client(s) to refrain from limiting options at this point. The purpose is for clients to gain practice in solution development. In the case of family work, all capable members should be allowed to offer solutions and should feel safe to do so without fear or criticism from other members.

Examine Options and Select/Implement a Solution

Workers should assist clients in examining the benefits and drawbacks of each possible solution and choose an option that best meets the needs of those involved.

Evaluate and Adjust

Social workers should help clients to determine the success of the solution. Client(s) can use a practical form of tracking solution effectiveness (charts, logs, etc.). If it is determined the solution is not working, the client can return to the solution-generating stage.

Client's Role in the Problem-Solving Process

Whenever possible, social workers should invite their clients to take a collaborative perspective in designing interventions, establishing objectives, and developing program goals. This allows the client to feel empowered and engaged as an active member of the problem-solving process. These factors are associated with higher incidences of positive outcomes, as they encourage clients to feel accountable for their behaviors, actions, and personal changes.

Collaboration should begin at the intake process. This is a period in which the social worker can make assessments, but they can also get information directly from clients about why they are in the session and what they hope to achieve. The social worker can also ask clients the steps they believe they need to take to reach their desired outcomes. While clients may or may not provide useful or feasible answers, this process still sets the tone that allows clients to feel acknowledged and involved in their own care.

In the intake session or in the sessions that immediately follow, the social worker can invite the client to develop SMART objectives to reach their goals. This may also include establishing accountability tools, documenting plans of action to address potential barriers and how to overcome them, and any other support protocols that clients may need for their individual situations. Depending on the client's specific

131

case, this process may take one session or may take much longer. Social workers should continuously show patience, compassion, and a welcoming desire to engage the client in the process.

Engaging and Motivating Clients/Client Systems

When determining a client's motivation, the engagement and assessment stage is crucial. When clients voluntarily seek services and/or are facing a crisis, the commitment and motivation will likely be high. Non-voluntary clients are identified as those who are seeking assistance based on pressure outside of the legal system (i.e., a woman gives her spouse an ultimatum to get help or she will leave). When working with non-voluntary or involuntary clients who are mandated legally to seek treatment, the social worker must help determine client-identified problems. This should be in addition or complementary to the presenting problem. The worker and client collaboratively should create a treatment plan that addresses both types of issues.

Additionally, the worker must help the client overcome any negative feelings of anger or mistrust about treatment. With all clients, appropriate relationship building between the worker and client is a necessary part of engagement and motivation. Clients must feel they are in a safe, empathetic environment. They also should experience a sufficient level of trust for the social worker in order for treatment to be effective. To create an effective treatment relationship, the social worker must project an attitude free of judgment, recognize the client's individual attributes, strengths, and abilities, and encourage the client's right to be an active participant in his or her own treatment.

Engaging and Working with Involuntary Clients/Client Systems

When working with involuntary clients, motivation levels can be improved by helping the client realize they have options. Even if services are mandated by a government agency, the client can choose to accept the consequences of not participating. Therefore, agreeing to adhere to the mandate is still a choice. When setting goals and treatment planning, ensure that the client's identified problems are included along with the mandated goals. Attempts to protect a client's right to self-determination should be practiced as much as possible (e.g., encouraging a client's participation in goal setting, problem identification, and priority setting, etc.).

Limit-Setting Techniques

Although it may be difficult for social workers to develop the ability to set limits with clients, it is necessary for treatment to be effective. Many clients struggle with the ability to follow rules and maintain healthy boundaries. In addition to ensuring the treatment process progresses smoothly, when workers set limits, clients also learn to develop helpful life skills. This is especially important with involuntary clients receiving legally mandated services that cannot be modified or negotiated. Other reasons for limit setting are ensuring the maintenance of an appropriate client-worker relationship, refusing a client request to give misinformation to a legal institution/employer, and saying no if a client asks for monetary loans.

Role-Play Techniques

Role-play is a type of modeling, also called behavior reversal. This technique enables clients to view the different ways a person may handle a challenging situation. It also allows a client to view a non-tangible behavior in a more tangible way. When clients practice skills and develop new and more productive

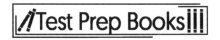

methods of coping, they are able to take an active role in treatment, increasing their sense of empowerment and self-determination.

Role Modeling Techniques

Role modeling, which offers the client a real life view of desired target behaviors, can be an important tool to learn new skills. The social worker can request that clients demonstrate the behavior before modeling it, thereby allowing the worker to assess a client's current skills and abilities. Social workers can demonstrate a coping model showing the skill or desired behaviors, including difficulties, anxieties, or challenges. The worker can also demonstrate a mastery model, which shows confidence and competence with the desired behaviors. Each method has benefits and drawbacks. In coping mode, the client and worker can process the interaction and identify improvements or changes that can be made to the desired behaviors or actions. There are several types of modeling:

- Symbolic Modeling: client watches a visual representation of the modeled behavior (i.e., video, TV, images)
- Live Modeling: client watches while a person performs the behavior
- Participant Modeling or Guided Participation: client observes model performing behavior and then performs the behavior and/or interacts with the model
- Covert Modeling: client visualizes the desired behavior

Harm Reduction for Self and Others

Clients who are in immediate danger of self-harm should be referred to a local emergency room or hospital immediately. Clients who are a danger for self-harm may develop a no-harm contract with the social worker, even though this may not be legally binding. Clients who engage in self-harm may find relief in applying ice to the area of harm, snapping a rubber band, or using colored markers instead of sharp objects. Social workers also need to engage clients in changing distorted thinking related to harm reduction. Clients who are at risk for harm to others may need to be hospitalized or placed in protective custody. Social workers who are aware that the client is at risk of harming a specific victim have a duty to warn the potential victim and report this threat to the appropriate authorities. This mandate originated with the Tarasoff case involving a client who was not reported to the prospective victim and then proceeded to kill her. This is a mandatory legal requirement when a client threatens a specific victim.

Teaching Coping and Other Self-Care Skills to Clients

Social workers may act in the role of teacher to instruct clients about coping and other skills. Coping skills may include relaxation techniques, deep breathing, time out, and improved communication skills. Common diagnoses that often require the instruction of coping skills include stress reduction, anxiety, and major depression. Clients may be able to utilize coping and acceptance skills for these diagnoses because they are frequently chronic, and clients will need to cope with them on an almost daily basis. Clients often need to learn a plethora of new skills to manage their issues and complex problems, and they and the social worker should collaborate on coping and other skills to manage these circumstances. Social workers can partialize and brainstorm with clients concerning coping and other treatment skills. Clients sometimes need detailed instructions in order to succeed with treatment goals. Clients need to be engaged in therapy outside of sessions and learn how to cope when the social worker is not present, so assigning clients homework between sessions is a method of skills building. While the social worker may offer suggestions to the client for coping and other skills, the client is ultimately the most effective arbiter of their own treatment.

Self-Monitoring Techniques

Client self-monitoring can be a useful technique for turning subjective qualitative information into more quantifiable data. Clients may engage in self-assessment techniques and practices that include journaling, questionnaires, and evaluations. Clients collect data about goals, objectives, and the targeted behavior. This technique collects important information about client progress, but it also adds to clients' feelings of empowerment and self-determination as they become collaborators in treatment. Clients can either track information related to thoughts or behaviors or can use more formal charting techniques. Social workers should assist clients with defining and identifying which type of information to track and then demonstrate how to use the selected tracking technique. Self-monitoring methods serve several purposes. As clients become more invested in treatment, their awareness of strengths and areas in need of improvement may also increase. This will enable the client to monitor behaviors as they occur, allowing for the development of insight related to behavioral change.

Conflict Resolution

Social workers may engage in conflict resolution with clients by acting as a mediator or advocate. Mediators work with clients to intervene in the conflict and develop helpful solutions that reflect all parties involved. For example, the social worker may act as a mediator in family or couples therapy conflicts. Social workers may also work with clients on developing their own conflict resolution skills through methods such as reflection, role-playing, and empty chair techniques. Social workers may also encourage clients to practice the use of *metacommunication*, which is communication about the behaviors and reactions of their regular and possibly dysfunctional method of interactions or communication. Sometimes the client is in conflict with the social worker and transference issues must be resolved before progress can be made. Social workers and clients need to be in collaboration concerning treatment goals and modalities so that conflict is reduced.

In some cases, agencies contract with mediation services outside the agency to assist clients in resolving conflicts. Professional mediators are trained in mediation techniques and are paid by the agency for their services. They can be the final step of resolution when the agency cannot resolve client conflict. Child protective services agencies sometimes use professional mediators to reduce or eliminate conflict in cases involving juveniles.

Crisis Intervention and Treatment Approaches

A crisis can occur whenever a client is in physical danger or extreme emotional need. For example, suicidal threats or ideation qualify as a crisis situation. When a crisis arises, the very first concern is always safety. It is important to get the client into a safe situation, protected from themselves or others. After safety is established, it is then possible to assess the level of need and what should happen next in order to best assist the client.

Another important strategy is de-escalation. When there is a crisis, extreme emotions are usually involved. If possible, a client should be guided through relaxation techniques to help calm them down. Oftentimes, a calm and neutral party who can facilitate a conversation or listen to the client empathetically, but without feeding the emotion, will automatically de-escalate the situation. Confrontation or matching the client's emotions will escalate the situation. Allowing the client to communicate the situation fully may help them to become less emotional and more focused on the facts. At this point the client may be able to focus on the next steps and specific tasks that need to be done. If possible, help the client to regain emotional control so that extreme options such as restraints are unnecessary.

In cases where a client is suicidal, it is important to establish if there is a suicide plan or means of committing suicide in place. These two things will determine the severity of suicidal ideation and how at-risk the client is. If it is determined that a client is at imminent risk of suicide, they should be admitted to the hospital or a mental health facility for their own protection.

Creating crisis plans ahead of time, in collaboration with clients, may assist them in preventing crisis situations or more quickly regaining control when the crisis arises. If clients have been part of the planning process, they may feel empowered, even when their emotions are overwhelming them. Part of the plan should be to identify the potential triggers or warning signs, and have immediate steps that can be taken to avoid a crisis. This could be engaging in relaxation strategies, or calling a supportive friend, family member, or clinician.

Anger Management Techniques

Anger management is a fairly common treatment goal for clients, so social workers need to be familiar with anger management techniques. Clients may manage anger by counting to ten before responding to a situation, taking a time out from the situation to reduce intensity, or practicing deep breathing techniques. Clients may also benefit from vigorous physical exercise to reduce anger. If clients are involved in vigorous exercise, they may need to consult with a physician for approval. Clients may also engage in thought stopping techniques to alleviate anger. Thought stopping sometimes involves the use of guided imagery, such as a stop sign, to reduce moments of intense emotion or thinking.

Stress Management Techniques

Social workers will often encounter clients with stress related problems and should be well versed in stress management techniques to offer clients suggestions for this issue. Social workers may engage clients to practice relaxation techniques in order to manage stressors. Clients may engage in physical exercise at their physician's discretion to relieve stress. Deep breathing exercises are also beneficial in relieving stress. Clients may work to change fallacious thinking patterns and distorted perceptions to reduce stress through treatment such as cognitive behavior therapy or rational emotive therapy. Clients may be stressed concerning basic living needs and social workers can link clients to services in the community to assist them with these issues. If clients are at the safety and physical stages of the hierarchy of needs, these stressors should be addressed before other issues are included in the therapeutic process.

Out-of-Home Displacement

Out-of-home displacement is considered one of the most stressful adjustments a person can experience in their lifetime. It often leads to homelessness, an inability to work, and permanent loss of meaningful personal items. Out-of-home displacement also usually results from a distressing event to begin with (such as a natural disaster, a divorce, immigration from a poor situation in another country, flight from a war zone or other humanitarian crisis, job loss, and so on). Alongside the long-term consequences, individuals can face considerable internal and external struggle as a result of out-of-home displacement.

The intensity of struggle is correlated with four distinct factors: how far the individual is displaced, the type of housing (or lack thereof) to which they are displaced, how many times the individual has to move, and how long the individual has to stay in displacement housing. Another important variable is whether or not separation from family members, close friends, or other important community members occurs. Clients may deal with general psychological distress, post-traumatic stress disorder, acute or long-term poverty, adjustment stress disorder, and unhealthy coping mechanisms, such as substance abuse.

Children are more profoundly affected and become vulnerable to future risks of obesity, substance abuse, and chronic disease. It is also important to note, however, that while many clients who experience home loss or displacement experience health and wellness issues that impact them in the long term, a fair number also self-report feeling an increased sense of resiliency and self-efficacy, a strong sense of community and gratitude for receiving aid from others, and hope for the future as their situation begins to improve.

Policies and Procedures that Minimize Risk for Individuals, Families, Groups, Organizations, and Communities

Often, the clients and client systems that require the services of a social worker are already in a vulnerable place. Therefore, minimizing additional risk to individuals, families, groups, and their associated organizations and communities (such as places of employment and recreation) is an important component of providing care. To ensure policies and procedures minimize additional stress, burden, discomfort, or suffering on the part of the client and client systems, practices should employ the constructs of the National Association of Social Work's Code of Ethics in their policies and procedures.

Practices should utilize a sense of transparency, empowerment, and respect in all service procedures. These factors support clients and their systems in playing an active role, when possible, in the services they receive. Policies and procedure should ensure that all services offered have the overarching goal of benefiting clients or client systems, maintain the dignity and self-respect of the client and client systems, and emphasize the importance of cultivating healthy human relationships and the effects those have on recovery.

As social workers implement interventions and treatment, they should always keep lines of communication open with their clients, foster and nurture trust, and continue their educational efforts to ensure they are delivering the highest quality of care at each session. All client intake work should include an informed consent process, and it should engage the client in developing portions of the intervention plan. Social workers should treat all clients of all backgrounds with open-mindedness, without judgment, and with the client's desired intervention outcomes at the center of all interactions.

Social workers may work with clients of different cultures, and social workers should respect the opinions and boundaries that these differences bring to treatment. If a social worker runs into a situation that falls outside the scope of the practice, such as the requirement of clinical intervention for a client, there should be policies in place to address such a situation, and social workers should feel comfortable referring to avenues of care outside of their scope.

Psychotherapies

Social workers need skills in a broad spectrum of areas, including case management, advocacy, and political change. Social workers need also be versed in psychotherapy modalities so as to enhance client engagement in the change process. Psychotherapy modalities originated with the "talk therapy" based on Sigmund Freud's work, and include, but are not limited to, cognitive behavioral, narrative, psychodynamic, solution focused, and behavioral therapies. It is up to social workers to decide which psychotherapies are most effective for their clients and should be pursued. Agencies may favor a particular type of psychotherapy that the social worker should learn. Insurers may favor psychotherapy modalities and social workers need to consider this in their work with clients.

Psychoanalytic and Psychodynamic Approaches

Psychodynamic approaches engage clients in discovering how their unconscious drives affect their conscious lives. Unconscious drives include sexual and aggression drives that may be unknown to the client on a conscious level. Clients engage in stream of consciousness discussion with the therapist, and the therapist acts mostly as a listener. There is also a focus on dream interpretation in psychodynamic approaches, in which clients are encouraged to discuss their dream states with the social worker. Psychodynamic approaches originate with Freud's "talking cure," in which Freud encouraged clients to attend sessions several times a week.

There are several psychoanalytic organizations in the United States devoted to psychodynamic training. These schools usually have multiyear programs to train new psychoanalysts. While psychodynamic approaches may not encompass the entirety of a client's experience, they are a useful approach for certain clients and may be integrated into psychotherapeutic treatment along with other approaches.

Carl Jung's Psychoanalytic Theory

Jung's theory is similar to Freud's psychoanalytic theory, with differences related to the purpose of the libido, the unconscious, and behavioral motives. Libido is a psychic energy that motivates individuals.

Jung theorized two parts to the unconscious:

- Personal unconscious: contains information not accessible to the conscious mind
- Collective unconscious (transpersonal): the memories from a person's ancestors that the individual has from birth

Jung identified this collective unconscious into four main archetypes.

- Persona: the artificial self that an individual shows to the world to hide who they really are
- Anima/Animas: the masculine qualities that women express to society and the feminine qualities that men express to society
- Shadow: similar to Freud's id, signifies raw needs and desires
- Self: the unconscious and conscious mind come together to form a unified whole, occurs as a consequence of individuation

Cognitive and Behavioral Interventions

Cognitive Approaches

Cognitive approaches to the social work process involve changing the way the client thinks in order to facilitate progress and problem solving skills. Cognitive approaches tend to be evidence based and favored by insurance carriers, as they are efficacious for a variety of client issues, including substance use and personality disorders. Cognitive approaches focus on changing maladaptive thinking and cognitive distortions, and thus may help clients engage in behavior change. Cognitive distortions involve fallacious thinking patterns engaged in by the client, such as black-and-white thinking. Types of cognitive approaches may include cognitive behavior therapy, rational emotive behavior therapy, and solution focused brief therapy. There are many modalities of cognitive therapies and social workers should become familiar with—and implement—them when necessary.

Behavioral Approaches

Behavioral approaches, which originated with Skinner and Pavlov, include methods of changing and motivating client behaviors toward reaching constructive goals. The underlying concept is that if clients can change behavior, they may also alter the way they think. Skinner and Pavlov believed that all behavior is learned, and they believed in conditioning. Tokens may be awarded for positive behavioral changes in the client; this occurs in what is called a token economy. Cognitive behavioral therapies, which focus on both the cognition and the behavior of the client, are considered evidence based and are favored by managed care insurers.

Strengths-Based and Empowerment Strategies and Interventions

Empowerment is a strengths based modality, and the goal is that all clients should feel empowered based on their personal identities. Clients need to feel in control of most of their lives and circumstances, and this is what empowerment permits. Working from a strengths based perspective empowers clients to facilitate change in their own lives. Social workers may seek to empower clients by focusing on strengths and bolstering clients' social constructs. Clients may need to be empowered from a racial, ethnic, religious, gender, or age perspective because they have suffered discrimination in these areas. Social workers may act as political advocates in these realms to combat social oppression affecting clients. The social worker should take into account the differences each client possesses due to their personal race, religion or circumstance, and use these differences as strengths.

Goal-Setting Techniques

Goal setting is a necessary factor in both the treatment and evaluation of direct practice. Social workers should work collaboratively with clients to determine goals. To be effective, goals need to be specific, measurable, achievable, realistic, and timely. They also should be directly related to the target problem. During the assessment process, begin identifying possible goals for treatment. Depending on the identified issues, goals may focus on desired behavioral, cognitive, or emotional changes.

Reciprocal goals are complimentary goals agreed upon by members of a system related to the same target problem (i.e., a father's goal is to offer more compliments to his son, while son agrees to increase verbal acknowledgement to father's positive feedback).

Shared goals are when members of a system choose the same goal that addresses an identified problem (i.e., spouses each agree to communicate needs more frequently).

Contracts

Once goals are determined, a contract is the next step to engage the client in services. Contracts can be formal or informal, and written or verbal depending on the policies of the agency and the nature of treatment. A contract between client and worker provides a set of expectations and guidelines for treatment. Clients should be made aware the contract is a commitment by both parties, but not a legal document. Components of the contract include goals, assignments of tasks, timeframes, frequency of sessions, methods for determining progress, and how updates or revisions of the contract can occur.

Other items that can be included are lengths of sessions, financial arrangements, and procedures for cancelling appointments.

Partializing Techniques

Partializing means to break down into smaller steps. Clients sometimes need partializing techniques to address complex problems, which may involve trauma, grief, or even personality disorders. A social worker can partialize with the client by encouraging the client's suggestions about solving the problem or making a written list. Partializing assists the client in reaching treatment goals in a more organized and efficient fashion. Case management of the client's goals may also include partializing techniques so that the client does not encounter stressors in addition to the problem solving process. Clients with complex cases may benefit from partializing techniques because they can focus on one step at a time and avoid becoming overwhelmed with treatment goals. Clients may learn partializing techniques from the social worker and then learn to implement them in their own lives so that they can partialize issues that they encounter at home.

Assertiveness Training

Assertiveness training is an intervention that can be used in multiple settings with an assortment of interpersonal difficulties. This type of training helps individuals learn to express their emotions, thoughts, and desires, even when difficult, while not infringing on the rights of others. There are ways in which individuals can assert themselves, including saying no to a request, having a difference of opinion with another person, asking others to change their behavior, and starting conversations. Social workers must respect cultural differences when working with clients to develop assertiveness skills. For example, some cultures feel it is inappropriate for women or children to assert themselves. Role-play is an effective technique to help clients develop assertiveness skills.

Task-Centered Approaches

Task Centered Practice is comprised of a practical, evidence-based intervention that lasts for six to twelve sessions (short term). Task Centered Practice can help resolve problems related to daily living tasks, i.e., lack of basic needs, interpersonal/social relationships, role performance, and decision-making skills. This method is client-driven, with the social worker as a guide or collaborator. A specific problem is identified with an associated goal to be accomplished. Afterward, the social worker assists the client in identifying and conquering smaller tasks to resolve the problem. Subsequently, the assessment phase is vital to this process as both client and social worker identify issues, strengths, and resources, and work together to define goals/tasks. The Task Centered Practice model also places emphasis on contracting, carefully planned task implementation, evaluation, and termination.

Psychoeducation Methods

Psychoeducation refers to any form of training or instruction that is provided to clients and the client system as a part of understanding mental health or psychological issues and treatments. Its goal is to support clients experiencing mental illnesses, their families, and their networks while eliminating the stigma that has been associated with mental health issues for decades. Psychoeducation methods include explaining potential causes for specific mental health issues, understanding the challenges of specific mental health issues, explaining how support systems can acknowledge and cope with not only a client's mental health condition but also their own caregiving stress, and teaching coping skills, building resiliency, and overcoming obstacles in ways that are accessible. This form of education can occur in group settings, seminars or webinars, and in individual or family sessions. It can also through newsletters, other media, and formal courses. It may be offered in-home, online, in hospitals or other healthcare facilities, in community centers, or at conference venues. It is not considered treatment, but it is a beneficial complement to clinical care. It promotes positive and inclusive language, eliminates shame and fear around mental illnesses, creates educational value, fosters network support and understanding, and acknowledges a variety of feelings and responses to mental health conditions. Psychoeducation techniques are associated with reduced inpatient and hospitalization rates for clients with mental health conditions. Psychoeducation is correlated with clients' self-reported feelings of acceptance and increased family support. Family and friends self-report a better understanding of their loved one who may have a mental health condition, a better understanding of their role in providing positive support and care, the ability to draw healthy boundaries for themselves, and relief from learning and utilizing self-care techniques that reduce caregiver stress.

Group Work Techniques and Approaches

Group work can be defined as a goal-directed intervention with small groups of people. The intention of this work is to improve the socioemotional and psychoeducation needs of the individual members of the group through the group process. There are two types of groups in social work: therapeutic and task groups. Task groups are created to perform a specific task or purpose. These groups differ in the amount and type of self-disclosure, confidentiality, and communication patterns. There are several types of treatment groups, including support, educational, and therapy groups. Groups can also be long-term or short-term, depending on the type and purpose.

Groups can be open or closed. Open groups are ongoing and allow for new members to enter at any time. Open groups are typically used for support and life transitions. There are challenges to this type of group, since the members are at different stages in the group process. The frequently changing membership can be disruptive to the group process because members may not feel as emotionally safe to share with others. Closed groups are time-limited, and new members can only join during the beginning stage. The advantages to this type of group is more engagement and better trust by the members, since the group process is more stable. A disadvantage is that if several members leave the group, the group process may not be as effective. There are several variations by theorists that describe the stages of group development. A general method of categorizing the group process is the beginning, middle, and end stages. Each stage is classified by different activities, processes, and tasks:

Beginning Stage
Social workers determine the group's purpose, members, objectives, and other logistical tasks (time, location, etc.). Group formation occurs at this stage as new members come together. The social worker fosters a safe and trusting environment by establishing acceptable group norms. As group members become more comfortable, conflicts arise as power and control behaviors emerge. Group roles and alliances begin to form. The worker's role is to help guide the group through these challenges and process any conflicts that arise within the group.

Middle Stage
This stage is where most group work is done. Members share information, openly address issues, and work through conflicts. Some groups do not make it to this stage for several reasons, including member dynamics and a lack of investment of the group members. Group cohesion or the connectedness of the members is extremely important at this stage. The role of the worker is to help members focus on methods and the meaning of communication, working through group differences and confronting

members when necessary. Workers should also help develop more intensive levels of cohesiveness while building on member individuality.

End Stage

Group members come to resolutions on the issues addressed during the group process. Members may have strong reactions to termination, especially if there was a high level of cohesion developed during the group process. The social worker should lead the group in discussing feelings about termination and be aware of negative reactions that may surface. When these types of emotions occur, social workers should address any challenges that arise with members. The social worker should also help group members identify and reflect on the skills learned in the group process and how those skills can benefit the members with future challenges.

Working with Individuals in the Group Context

It is the role of the social worker to encourage all members to participate in the group process. The worker can solicit feedback from each member of the group throughout the group process. Clients typically take on various roles during group treatment. Roles can be defined as functions the individual members of the group are fulfilling or performing that facilitate the group process. Some roles include that of a clown, scapegoat, mediator, etc. The worker must be aware of the roles of each individual and how those roles are affecting the group so interventions can be made when necessary.

Family Therapy Models, Interventions, and Approaches

One of the main goals of family therapy is to allow each family member to function at his or her best while maintaining the functionality of the family unit. When working with families, the social worker must do the following:

- Examine and consider all systems affecting a family and each individual member to determine problems, solutions, and strengths, and must also consider the functionality of the family subsystems.

- Respect cultural, socio-economic, and non-traditional family systems and not automatically define those systems as dysfunctional if they are not the norm. The overall and individual family functioning should be accounted for.

- Work to engage the family in the treatment, while considering the specific traits of the family (i.e., culture, history, family structure, race, dynamics, etc.).

- Assist in identifying and changing dysfunctional patterns, boundaries, and family problems.

Important Concepts

Boundaries: Healthy boundaries around and within the family must exist for families to function effectively. The boundaries must be clear and appropriate.

Emotional Proximity and Distance: the type of boundaries that exist within a family system

Enmeshed: Boundaries are unclear and pliable. Families that have very open boundaries within the family unit may have very fixed boundaries between outside forces and the family.

Disengaged: Boundaries are rigid with little interaction and emotional engagement. Families that are disengaged within the family system tend to have very open boundaries around the family unit.

Family Hierarchy: The power structure within the family. For families to function effectively, there must be a clear delineation of authority. There must be an individual or individuals who hold the power and authority in a family system. In a traditional family, this should ideally be located within the parental system.

Homeostasis: Family systems should maintain homeostasis or remain regular and stable. When life events become too stressful and the family can no longer function as it normally would, the state of homeostasis is threatened. This is usually when many families seek help.

Alliances: Partnerships or collaborations between certain members of a family. When alliances exist between some members of a family, it can lead to dysfunction (i.e., parent and child have an alliance that undermines the parental subsystem).

Couples Interventions and Treatment Approaches

Many couples enter treatment after experiencing long-standing problems and may seek help because all other options have failed. One of the goals of couple's therapy is to help clients develop effective communication and problem-solving skills so they can solve problems throughout and after treatment. Other goals include helping the couple form a more objective view of their relationship, modifying dysfunctional behavior/patterns, increasing emotional expression, and recognizing strengths. Workers should create an environment to help the couple understand treatment goals, feel safe in expressing their feelings, and reconnect by developing trust in each other. Interventions for couples are often centered on goals geared toward preventing conflicting verbal communication and improving empathy, respect, and intimacy in a relationship. Therapeutic interventions, along with exercises, are designed to help couples learn to treat each other as partners and not rivals. Cognitive Behavioral Therapy is also used in working with couples. It uses cognitive restructuring techniques to help change distorted thinking and modify behavior.

Permanency Planning

Juvenile clients who are in danger within their families of origin and/or in foster care may benefit from permanency planning. Clients whose parents have terminated parental rights may be adopted into their foster home or put up for adoption by the state. While the first goal of social workers is to reunite juveniles with their family of origin, this is not always possible due to harmful circumstances in the home. Native American juvenile clients, for instance, are bound by the Indian Child Welfare Act (ICWA) when making considerations for permanency planning. ICWA regulations favor the placement of the child with Native families so that the child does not lose contact with their heritage.

Adults who are at risk of abuse and neglect may require permanency planning. Vulnerable adults may be reported to Adult Protective Services agencies. Adult foster care has become more popular in the last few decades and may be an option for at-risk adults. Group homes are another form of permanency planning for vulnerable adults, but the quality of these homes varies. The social worker should make careful screening of these facilities.

Mindfulness and Complementary Therapeutic Approaches

Complementary therapeutic approaches, such as mindfulness, meditation, yoga, exercise, spending time in nature, music therapy, and art therapy can provide emotional, physical, and mental relief for clients who are struggling to cope with adverse events. Mindfulness is the act of paying purposeful attention to specific or general events without attaching feelings, judgment, or reason to the events. It can be practiced during a specific time set aside for it, it can be incorporated in increments, or it can be an ongoing behavior throughout one's day. This practice allows clients a way of introspecting and reducing external stimuli, and it is an evidence-based method of stress reduction.

Meditation, another evidence-based method of stress reduction, can include mindfulness as a component. Meditation encourages the practitioner to focus on thoughts and repetitive mental patterns in order to clear them, relax the mind, and improve physiological indicators of stress (such as deeper and slower breathing rates, lowered heart rates, and reduced muscular tension).

Yoga incorporates meditation, focused breathing exercises, and movements to promote mental clarity and strength, improved circulation and respiration, reduce muscular tension, and connect with one's mind and body. Under the guidance of well-trained instructors or a certified yoga therapist, clients can take group or private sessions that are tailored to and address common counseling issues, such as trauma, grief, post-traumatic stress disorder, aging, physical changes, and so on.

Different forms of exercise can have a therapeutic effect, including strength and resiliency building (both mentally and physically), stress reduction, and the management of chronic disease indicators (such as excess weight or blood lipid levels). Group exercise can also be a way to build community and support through a shared, wellness-oriented interest. Finally, exercise programs often support clients in the practice of setting and achieving goals. While this may start off as a primarily physical practice, a number of mental and emotional benefits (such as improved moods and higher self-esteem), introspection, and behavior change often follow suit. Other types of recreational activity, such as creating art, listening to musical sounds and vibrations, and spending time in nature are associated with positive changes at the cellular level.

Follow-Up Techniques

At the final session, the social worker and client can schedule a follow-up session at a predetermined time to evaluate the client's continued progress after termination. Another option is to propose a time to meet and alert the client that the worker will contact the client to schedule a follow up. The follow-up session enables the social worker the opportunity to determine how well the client has progressed and to determine the effectiveness of the intervention(s) used during sessions.

Time Management Approaches

Social workers can effectively manage their time through a number of organizational methods. These may include daily prioritization of tasks for the day (such as urgent tasks versus tasks that can wait until the next day), ensuring that all meeting and phone calls with colleagues are scheduled with objectives in mind (such as with the use of a meeting agenda), breaking more tedious tasks into chunks, and planning in a way that works best for one's personality. For example, one person may enjoy making weekly color-coded schedules of tasks with gaps available throughout the week for unexpected assignments that come up; another may prefer to manage tasks daily in a simple list style, with flexible room built in per day. While no schedule can be absolutely rigid, as unforeseen circumstances are guaranteed to arise from time to time, a schedule that is guarded and respected by the social worker fosters effective time management. It is important to decline non-urgent tasks or responsibilities if one's schedule is booked, while ensuring there is space in one's schedule to assist with unanticipated emergencies.

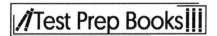
Community Organizing and Social Planning Methods

The social change process is one in which interested groups (i.e., community members, lawmakers, businesses, government agencies, community organizations) can work together to create change or solve an identified community or societal problem. Collaborative social planning increases the chances of positive change and allows community members to take ownership of the change and resulting policies. It also encourages the community to become more energized and more likely to make positive changes in the future. The role of the social worker as a leader in this process includes the following:

- Community engagement
- Problem identification
- Organization and engagement of community members
- Identification of resources, challenges, and solutions
- Creation and implementation of a plan
- Evaluation and follow-up

Measurable Objectives for Client Intervention, Treatment, and Service Plans

Goals in intervention plans should be SMART—Specific, Measurable, Achievable, Relevant, and Time-specific. Devoting specific attention to the measurability of a goal requires mutual agreement between the client and practitioner.

Key recommendations are noted, here:

- Measurable terms used in writing the goals should be based on the criteria of the type of desired behavior or action to be demonstrated (and how often), in order to achieve the proposed solution(s).

- Positive, action-oriented language should be utilized when describing the methods that an objective will be measured by. For example, the client should "plan" or "attend" a social gathering. Success of the stated objective will be "demonstrated" or "evidenced" by actually attending or planning a social gathering of some kind. The use of action-oriented language with specific targets assists the practitioner in more effective data collection.

- Objectives should be both short and long-term.

- Short-term objectives should only be a few weeks in length.

- Long-term objectives should be broken down into incremental, small chunks so as not to overwhelm the client and make progress towards success readily visible. The time-frame for completion should align with the nature of the objective. Often, many short-term objectives can make up one long-term objective or goal (for example, the short-term objective of developing a twice-weekly exercise habit leads to a long-term objective of losing five pounds).

Primary, Secondary, and Tertiary Prevention Strategies

Emphasis on Prevention in Social Work

During the past few decades, the social work profession has increasingly moved toward a prevention-focused service distribution model. This movement has resulted in the development of a three-stage model of prevention in social work practice. These three stages are primary prevention, secondary prevention, and tertiary prevention. Each stage assesses the severity of the problem impacting individuals or groups and provides appropriate and evidence-based social work interventions.

Primary Prevention

The *primary prevention* stage includes actions that practitioners take before a problem occurs for the client to address the potential causes of the problem. These actions are specifically aimed at getting rid of a problem's root cause, such as advocating against unfair policies or laws before they are voted upon or take effect. This type of prevention focuses on meeting the needs of the population at an almost universal level.

Secondary Prevention

The *secondary prevention* stage occurs when a problem has already started to impact a person or group. Actions to be taken involve attempts to stop specific social problems before they spread and cause further harm. These actions are designed to help any individuals or groups that are beginning to show symptoms of increased problem severity.

Tertiary Prevention

The *tertiary prevention* stage occurs when both previous stages have failed to address the problem. These actions are designed to decrease a problem's severity through remedial service provision that will decrease its lasting effects and duration. This stage is more intense than the previous stages and focuses on individuals that are most impacted by the problem.

Visualizing the Three Stages of Prevention

These stages can be visualized as three parts of a pyramid. The wide base of the pyramid represents primary prevention, as these are more universal services that reach the broadest portion of the population. The middle of the pyramid represents secondary prevention, more prevention services applied to a smaller portion of the population. The top of the pyramid represents tertiary prevention, with the highest degree of prevention services for the smallest percentage of the population.

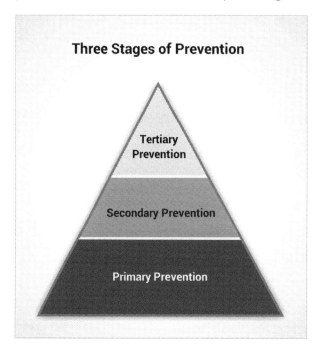

Client Readiness for Termination

When clients have made significant progress on the treatment plan, goals, and objectives, the worker can begin planning for termination. Depending on the identified goals and objectives, a standardized assessment can be used to determine how much progress has been made. Social worker practices vary depending on what level of goal attainment should be completed before termination (i.e., some, most, all). Other options can be offered to the client for continued work and learning such as groups, workshops, and reading materials. In many instances, services are terminated due to limitations by insurance or other funding sources. It is extremely important in these circumstances that the worker assists the client in locating additional resources that can be used following service termination. When preparing clients for termination, workers should discuss the following topics with the client:

- Initial reasons for requesting help
- What skills the client initially lacked that led to initiating services
- Skills developed as a result of treatment and how those new skills will help the client with future challenges
- Ways the client will continue to build on new skills development
- Social worker and client feelings about termination

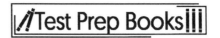

Service Delivery and Management of Cases

Policies, Procedures, Regulations, and Legislation on Social Work Practice and Service Delivery

Immigrants, refugees, and undocumented individuals often have the highest need for social services but also have the most barriers to effectively receiving support. Immigrants often face the stress of leaving their home country and assimilating into a completely new culture, economy, and lifestyle. While a social worker can help navigate these changes to set the foundation for a new life, immigrants often experience language barriers or simply may not realize such services exist for their use. Social workers may need to actively advertise their assistance and understand the background and culture of the immigrant in order to help.

Refugees often have the same stresses and barriers that immigrants have, but often they have also left violent or destructive situations in their home country. They may be happy to be safe, but they may also have deep feelings of sadness, especially if their families were affected (such as through death of a loved one or the necessity of leaving family members behind). While many immigrants come on work visas, refugees may have no means to make money and may need help navigating welfare benefits. There may also be feelings of discomfort in receiving these benefits. Social workers should be especially sympathetic to the diverse reasons behind an individual's refugee status.

Undocumented individuals may feel scared to seek out social services, fearing reprisal or deportation, even though social services can be an avenue to help undocumented families change their status to documented. Social workers who hope to help these groups should focus on building trust and creating spaces of security and safety.

Impact of the Political Environment on Policy-Making

Social welfare legislation can have a dramatic effect on social work practice. Some legislation may help solve social problems that social workers encounter and other legislation may create more problems, challenges, and barriers through which social workers must help clients navigate. To be effective, social workers must be knowledgeable about legislative measures that affect clients. Another possible role of a social worker is that of legislative advocate, which is working to change, modify, or create legislation for the benefit of a group of people.

Significant Social Welfare Legislation:

- Civil Rights Act of 1964
- Older Americans Act of 1965
- The Child Abuse and Prevention Act of 1974
- Adoption Assistance and Child Welfare Act of 1980
- Americans with Disabilities Act of 1990
- The Family Medical Leave Act of 1993
- The Health Insurance Portability and Accountability Act of 1996 (HIPAA)
- The Patient Protection and Affordable Care Act of 2010

Advocacy for Policies, Services, and Resources to Meet Client Needs

Social workers must help clients understand their needs versus the services and resources available to them. Workers must be knowledgeable of the services available at their agency and in the communities in which their clients live. It is the role of the worker to assist clients in obtaining resources, but also to help clients understand their options and their right to choose or refuse which resources to access. Clients should receive assistance in identifying the pros and cons of each resource. They should also be involved in identifying and seeking resources as much as possible to foster the development of self-determination and empowerment.

Methods of Service Delivery

Social workers may be employed in a variety of agencies. Some organizations, such as hospitals or government entities, employ diverse professionals. Other types of organizations, such as direct service non-profits or private practice agencies, maintain predominantly social services staff. Agency policies directly and significantly impact the working environment, the services provided, and, as a result, the effectiveness of the care clients receive. All agencies should have a mission statement that gives the agency purpose and serves as an umbrella for the agency's smaller goals and objectives. Agency policies must be in the best interest of the client and must support the ethical guidelines to which social workers adhere. They must also be clearly written and available to workers and clients where appropriate. Social workers and all those providing care to clients should be able to help shape policy development to ensure consistency with client and worker needs and protection. Policies must address the following:

- Appropriate confidentiality, consent, and information protection
- Case management and supervision
- Cultural competency guidelines
- Professional development and ongoing trainings
- Anti-discriminatory/diversity practices

Components of Case Management

Clients frequently experience difficulty navigating everyday life problems and systems. One of the roles of a social worker is to help link clients with needed services and resources. To perform this role effectively, social workers must have a thorough knowledge of available local resources to aid the client.

When acting in the case manager role, social workers help clients define, locate, and access needed services and resources. Additionally, social workers must often interact with other professionals, including external resources to ensure the client's needs are met. In the case management role, social workers also make referrals directing the client to the appropriate resource for needed services. The worker acts as a manager, following up with the client on a regular basis to ensure the client is following through with his or her case plan. Workers may also serve as an advocate in this role, working on behalf of the client if any barriers to resources are met.

Process of case management:

- Assessing needs and client engagement
- Creating an intervention plan of care that includes goals, needed services, and timelines
- Administering the plan
- Monitoring progress and reassessing the plan at fixed intervals

148

- Termination of services
- Evaluation and follow-up

Case Recording, Documentation, and Management of Practice Records

Accurate case recording is an integral part of social work practice. It is necessary to accurately document clients' information for effective treatment and protection of confidentiality. It is also required to protect the agency from possible legal ramifications and to ensure reimbursement from funders. Client records should be kept up-to-date, objective, and completed as soon as possible to ensure accuracy of information. Social workers should assume it is always possible that records may be requested as part of legal proceedings. Treatment notes should always be clearly written and only include information necessary to the client's treatment to protect confidentiality as much as possible. Social workers must also adhere to any state or federal legal requirements related to storage, disclosure of information, release of client records, and confidential information.

Establishing Service Networks or Community Resources

Due to limited funding and resources and a rapidly growing demand for services, establishing service networks to maximize community resources has become a necessary part of social work practice. Social workers and social service agencies frequently create partnerships, collaborations, or networks to bridge gaps in service and provide a comprehensive system of care for clients. These collaborations can be formal with the use of a comprehensive intake process and service or memorandums of agreements between programs. Partnerships can also be informal in which workers routinely refer clients to specific providers. When establishing new community resources, social workers must first perform a community assessment, which involves examining existing resources, community needs, and demographics.

Employee Recruitment, Training, Retention, Performance Appraisal, Evaluation and Discipline

Employee recruitment, training, retention, performance appraisal, evaluation, and discipline are primary responsibilities of an organization's human resources department. However, a worker's direct supervisor, manager, or other team leader plays a role in these aspects as well. An effective team leader will know which skillsets and personality traits are needed to fill roles on the team. The leader will communicate this need to human resources, which will then develop a job posting and pursue recruiting and interviewing efforts to find a competent candidate. Once a candidate is selected, offered a job, and has accepted the job, human resources will normally provide generalized training about the organization (such as more detail about the mission and vision, employee benefits, company culture, ethics courses, and so on). The team leader or a lateral colleague will provide on-the-job training and support until the new employee is established. Depending on the job, extra training may also be required (such as certification or licensures) during a specified period after hire. When so much time and resources are committed to a new employee, retention becomes important for preventing waste. Retaining employees begins in the hiring process, by ensuring the candidate is truly a good fit for the role and the workplace culture. Retention continues by ensuring the employee remains satisfied with their job, work environment, and compensation. Performance appraisals and evaluations should take place at regular intervals to review the employee's current work and future goals and to keep organizational expectations transparent. If an employee is performing poorly or acting inappropriately, disciplinary measures such as coaching, demotion, suspension, or termination of the employee may be required from both the team leader and a representative of human resources.

Case Recording for Practice Evaluation or Supervision

Social workers must document their practice with the client. Social workers document sessions with clients as well as client legal mandates, such as visitation with minors in state custody. Documentation may be a combination of narrative and quantitative descriptions, depending on agency requirements. Records should be kept confidential either electronically or in a physical location. New laws require that all records be electronic, and they are called an electronic health records. These records must be confidential as stated in the Health Insurance Portability and Accountability Act of 1996 (HIPAA). It is crucial for the social worker to maintain accurate documentation.

Evaluating Agency Programs

Different types of evaluation methods can be used to evaluate agency programs. A needs assessment looks at existing processes and services to determine whether a need exists. This needs assessment is usually a systematic investigation utilizing concrete planning strategies, evidence, case studies, interviews, and other methods of information synthesis. A need can be defined as perceived (what is believed to be needed), expressed (what is asked for), or relative (this term used primarily in the context of socioeconomic inequities between classes, races, genders, or other defined groups). A formative or summative assessment is usually conducted on a pilot study of a program, or during the planning phase of a program, to ensure that it will likely produce the desired outcomes. If it appears that the program will not produce the desired outcomes during the formative evaluation, changes can be made or the program can be discarded before further resources are unintentionally wasted. A cost effectiveness evaluation examines various ways a program could be conducted to determine which route minimizes the resource cost while maximizing desired results. This is a way to minimize or eliminate unnecessary costs and maintain lean processes. A cost-benefit analysis examines all associated monetary costs over a set period of time in order to determine whether the associated costs outweigh the projected benefits in the end, or vice versa. An outcomes assessment examines a program for the effects that resulted in participants. Often, desired effects are listed as part of the program objectives during the planning phase. Outcomes assessments may check if program objectives were met. They may also look at program effects on a broader scale, such as whether the program is considered an overall success and should be repeated.

Effects of Program Evaluation Findings on Services

Often the urgency of immediate client services takes precedence over program evaluation, but evaluation is a necessary step in ensuring that an organization provides effective and affordable services for clients. Program evaluation can be conducted during the formative stage of a program, in order to establish the best objectives and methods, but it can also be summative, evaluating outcomes of the program at a later stage. Summative evaluations can be used to determine what changes should be made or even if the program should continue.

Needs assessments, which explore the needs of constituents or clients, play a pivotal role in developing programs. Needs assessments provide evidence for the necessity of a program trying to obtain funding and measure program usefulness. Cost-effectiveness looks at whether programs are being conducted in a way that makes the best use of the available money. Cost-benefit analysis is a process of comparing the beneficial outcomes of a program to the amount of money spent on them to see if the benefits are worth the cost. Both of these cost-related aspects of program evaluation are important, especially for grant proposals. Ultimately, program evaluation seeks to do outcomes assessments, something

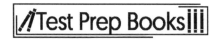

frequently requested by funding agencies. Outcomes assessments look at the program's effectiveness at meeting its objectives and in making the expected changes.

<u>Techniques Used to Evaluate a Client's Progress</u>
There are several techniques to evaluate client progress, including self-reporting by the client, quantitative measures that are collaboratively discussed by the social worker and the client, and narrative approaches that utilize a textual basis for describing progress. Social workers may ask client scaling questions to measure client mood and/or progress. Client progress should be measured at regular intervals in order to assist with treatment planning and intervention efficacy. Clients should be informed of progress, and social workers should develop progress notes to reflect client progress. Social workers need to be aware of client progress and compliance in order to accurately measure the steps the client is taking to move forward.

Quality Assurance

In social work, quality assurance is the practice of ensuring that services rendered meet established criteria and deliver intended, beneficial outcomes. Quality assurance practices review procedures in place to ensure they lead to high caliber service delivery, to identify gaps that need to be addressed, and to prevent errors before they are made.

Methods of quality assurance include program assessments, benchmarking, social worker evaluations, and internal and external audits. Program assessments and social worker evaluations are often conducted off a list of standardized best practices; actual processes are compared to the standardized best practices to determine compliance. Benchmarks are clear, quantitative indicators of performance that serve as a standard for outcomes. Program evaluations may compare program outcomes to benchmark metrics to determine how well the program is performing. If there is a large gap, the program may undergo quality improvement procedures (such as a gap analysis r root cause analysis) to determine what is causing the discrepancy. Once this has been determined, a plan-do-study-act cycle (PDSA, a quality-oriented test of change) can be implemented to see whether benchmark indicators improve.

Auditing is a regular practice in the social work field. Auditing is conducted both on processes performed, as well as on the actions of the social worker to ensure ethical conduct and high levels of competence. For example, during licensure application and renewals, social workers' educational histories are audited to ensure they meet licensure and continuing education requirements. Audits may be conducted internally by the organization in which the social worker is employed; they will also be conducted by external regulatory bodies. The NASW performs comprehensive audits nationally, while state or local appointed boards and associations may audit for other requirements.

Consultation and Interdisciplinary Collaboration

Leadership and Management Techniques

Leading and managing teams requires a range of organizational and interpersonal skills. An effective leader can clearly develop a vision for a preferred future state, as well as develop strategies to make the vision a reality. An effective leader must also be able to identify key stakeholders who are necessary to reach the vision, and be able to keep them actively engaged throughout the operational process. These tactics require that the leader is self-motivated, able to think uniquely to solve problems, and has a desire to develop and attain a feasible end result. However, a single leader cannot accomplish a vision alone. Therefore, leaders must be able to communicate the vision and motivate their team to take the actions that are necessary to reach the desired goal.

Leaders should be individuals who the team can trust and feel comfortable supporting. The most effective team will be one where leadership vision and team motivation align; however, this arrangement may not always be the case in a work setting. Therefore, a leader must know how to make projects seem of value to the employee, know which tasks are a good fit with an employee's personality type, and understand what motivates a team member's work. When managing a team, leaders may fall on a spectrum of laissez-faire (hands-off and relatively unstructured) to autocratic (which involves a high-level of micromanaging). Most successful leaders manage their teams by falling somewhere in the middle—establishing clearly defined goals and strategies and hand-selecting appropriate workers to execute tasks, but allowing their team members have to a sense of autonomy and creativity over their delegated responsibilities.

Models of Supervision and Consultation

In social work, supervision takes place when a more experienced professional mentors or coaches an emerging professional in fieldwork, practical application, or other service delivery setting. This requires strong interpersonal skills, a sense of respect, and open communication between both parties. The supervisor should be able to provide supportive instruction and guidance without arrogance and condescension; the supervisee should be receptive to instruction and have an honest desire for professional growth and learning. Some commonly used models of supervision in the social work setting include individual-oriented types of supervision, in which the supervisor may ask the supervisee to reflect upon their interactions with different clients or their personal judgments and biases that may have arisen during a session. The supervisor may also present the supervisee with different forms of research and data, and ask the supervisee to utilize the evidence to structure interventions. Finally, the supervisor may provide coaching related to the supervisee's development, by establishing small objectives that lead to larger professional goals.

In peer-oriented and group-oriented approaches, lateral-level colleagues (perhaps with the aid of one or two supervisors) learn from one another by sharing clinical experiences and lessons, new research and literature, or other professional development opportunities. This may take the form of team meetings at the beginning or end of the day, social events where work can be discussed, or conference settings. In some workplaces, individual, peer, and group models may be integrated to provide a more holistic sense of supervision.

Consultation can take place in any interaction that a social worker has with a client, regardless of setting or context. Consultation can primarily be divided into organizational, program, educational, mental health, and clinical cases. These can take place one-one-one with an individual or in group therapy settings.

Educational Components, Techniques, and Methods of Supervision

Social workers should expect to continuously learn. Educational components include staying abreast of new and emerging research and methodology in the field, brushing up on less-used skills, learning from mentors and more experienced social workers, and ensuring that one's practical expertise is up to the most recent standards. Supervisors or managers may choose to ensure that social workers who report to them have the time and resources to continuously learn, that they can learn materials for their needs, and that they feel comfortable addressing any gaps in their education with their superiors in order to resolve the discrepancies.

Techniques for learning may include visual techniques (such as books, videos, newspaper articles, and journal articles), listening techniques (such as lectures, seminars, podcasts, and audiobooks), or hands-on techniques (such as field work or practicums with a mentor). Some learning opportunities include tactics from all three learning techniques.

Supervisors may choose to be more involved in their approach to their team's education, or may be more distant and allow their team members to pursue their educational goals and requirements independently. An effective supervisor will allow their team members to introspect as to what may be the best educational route for them, and provide space coupled with guidance and support to support their team members in achieving their goals. Effective supervisors will also ensure that the professional goals individual team members are seeking serve the goals of the group, as well.

The Supervisee's Role in Supervision

Although the focus is often on the supervisor's role of ensuring that clients are provided with ethical services by training and evaluating the supervisee, the supervisee's role in supervision is not passive. The social worker should fully engage in the process of supervision and use this relationship to grow and improve. In order to do that, the supervisee must be willing to discuss areas of ethical or legal concern that have arisen in their interactions with clients. They must also be ready to honestly address their own struggles and identify their learning needs, and seek the help and advice of the supervisor. This can only happen effectively through genuine self-assessment, which flows from a real desire to become a better social worker. The process of self-assessment in supervision can help them see any biases or weaknesses that may be holding them back from fully meeting their clients' needs. If the social worker is defensive or resistant to the supervisory relationship, then they will make little progress.

Factors to consider when receiving feedback during supervision/consultation:

- Social workers can benefit from feedback during supervision or consultation, especially with difficult clients/cases or at significant times in treatment, such as termination.

- When discussing cases, client confidentiality should be protected as much as possible, and client consent to release information should be acquired.

Identifying Learning Needs and Developing Learning Objectives for Supervisees

Supervisors must ensure that their team members are competent and ethical, that they deliver service effectively, and that they are satisfied with their performance and work environment. Supervisors may audit or review performance with their team members to ensure standard competency and operational requirements are met. If gaps exist, supervisors may choose to develop trainings that address them. Speaking directly with team members individually or as a group can also help supervisors to find out where personal learning concerns or interests lie. In general, supervisors should ensure that their team is knowledgeable about current literature and able to deliver social service to the highest acceptable quality, that their team understands the legalities and risks of their work, and that all team members perform professional and ethically in any given situation.

When choosing to develop learning objectives that are not based on any existing gaps, supervisors may focus on new and emerging research, skillsets, or modalities that their team may want to use in their practical work. They may also choose to focus on improving current processes to enhance the client experience; often, this practice may focus on areas that are important but may not regularly get attention in the day-to-day routine tasks (such as writing competence, leadership skills, business skills, and so on). Supervisors may choose to teach learning objectives in a workshop or other interactive format, conduct online trainings, or engage in field work as a learning modality.

Elements of Client System Reports

Elements of client reports may include developmental history, family history, substance use information, medical history, presenting problem, and recommendations. There are a variety of elements of client reports that may be required by the agency. With the advent of electronic records, client reports are often built into the software that the agency uses. Client reports may also be in DAP (data, assessment, plan) format or in the model of SOAP notes (subjective, objective, assessment, and plan). Reports are at the agency's discretion and the social worker should use the format that is required by the agency to develop client reports.

Elements of a Case Presentation

Elements of a social work case presentation may include identifying data, the presenting problem, history of the presenting problem, medical/psychiatric information, significant personal and/or social information, impressions and summary, and recommendations. This format is only one model to choose from. There are many formats for a case presentation, and the social worker needs to make sure that they are following their agency's or organization's case presentation format.

Principles and Processes for Developing Formal Documents

Social workers may need to develop formal documents that are used for a broad range of functions; therefore, it is important to develop writing and communication skills that can be employed in a variety of professional contexts.

Social workers may be expected to write grant and research proposals, used for securing external funding for practical and applied work. They may need to write brochures or pamphlets that advertise their practice (especially if they are running their own business), explain types of interventions, or promote community initiatives. Social workers may need to communicate through letter or email correspondence regarding a client's progress. In these instances, they must be careful to explain clinical concepts in ways the client can understand from simply reading the correspondence without the social worker there to answer any potential questions.

Additionally, written correspondence with the client must always remain appropriate and be mindful of HIPAA compliance and other privacy concerns. Social workers may be required to provide their superiors with weekly, monthly, or annual reports about the work they performed. They may also need to maintain regular reports of individual client progress updates or milestones. Social workers can be expected to provide evaluation reports on processes and outcomes utilized in their cases. Depending on the field of work (such as government agency, private institution, medical setting, et cetera), the requirements for reporting and evaluation may vary significantly.

Finally, today's social workers can expect to maintain some degree of technological capability and have the ability to leverage web platforms and social media. Web platforms can provide an avenue for blogging or other information sharing that makes people aware of the work of social institutions. Social media posts can provide this avenue as well, and they can also serve as another point of connection for clients and colleagues. Social media can be an important tool in business-building and networking. It is imperative that social workers maintain a respectful, professional online presence that maintains both the trust and privacy of their potential clients.

Consultation Approaches

Although it may lead to possible conflict due to differing perspectives, opinions, and approaches to treatment, the use of consultation assistance from an expert in a related field can be extremely beneficial to an individual's treatment. The NASW Code of Ethics (2.05) specifically addresses consultation with other disciplines. Accordingly, workers should seek consultations with other areas when it benefits clients. When seeking consultation, social workers should maintain client confidentiality to the greatest extent possible, only releasing necessary information. When seeking consultation, the worker should seek competent colleagues and only consult with those who are appropriately qualified. Additionally, the worker should ensure the guidelines are clear for the consultation process by defining goals, the presenting problem, and the role of the consultant(s). In line with the code of ethics, social workers also may provide consultation or supervision. When providing consultation, workers must also be knowledgeable in the focus area and always maintain appropriate and culturally sensitive boundaries.

Methods of Networking

Networking in social work can be defined in different ways. One type of networking occurs when social workers connect with colleagues and other professionals to improve services and skills. External collaboration with community resources and colleagues with similar goals enables social workers to learn about available resources and to provide opportunities for developing relationships with others who have a similar purpose.

Additionally, social workers may also help develop connections between clients, organizations, or other groups. This networking assists with the acquisition of support, skill development, and the facilitation of ongoing learning related to resources. Networks are typically more informal than official organizations and can therefore sometimes be more easily accessed by individuals.

Interdisciplinary and Intradisciplinary Team Collaboration

Interdisciplinary team collaboration refers to a group of professionals with different skillsets and perspectives working toward a common goal (such as a social worker, a psychiatrist, a job counselor, and a life coach working together to support an unemployed client). Intradisciplinary team collaboration refers to a group of professionals from the same field but with varying backgrounds working together (such as a team of three veteran clinical social workers and two entry-level clinical social workers who are establishing a new program in their organization).

Interdisciplinary teams can support a client holistically. Because they work together, they may offer smoother operating processes than a client would experience if they sought the services of each team member individually. Social workers may be placed in interdisciplinary teams by their superiors, or they may refer clients to colleagues in different fields and voluntarily choose to collaborate on the client's intervention. Regardless, communication channels and communication itself must be clear, open, and purposeful when working with other professionals. All team members should be clear about their roles in the client's intervention, and the client's positive outcomes should be the primary goal of the collaboration. Intradisciplinary teams may tend to understand each other's perspectives better. This type of team dynamic most commonly occurs in organizational shifts or in supervisory or mentoring relationships.

Basic Terminology of Other Professions

Social workers may need to work with professionals in a number of other fields to support their clients. Therefore it is important to have a basic understanding of some of the terminology that is used in the professions with which social workers most commonly collaborate. These include the criminal and legal fields, since social workers may often support legal cases such as those of abuse, negligence, divorce, and child custody. Social workers should understand basic legal terms so that they can provide relevant support to the clients as well as to the other professionals involved in the case.

Socials workers often collaborate with educators in the school setting, and they work with children who may be in a vulnerable position. In these contexts, social workers should understand the values of the school system, the laws that school systems must follow when working with children, and ensure that social work does not detract from the child's educational experience.

Social workers may commonly collaborate with or refer patients to professionals in the medical field. They may need to understand basic medical and health terminology associated with their client's conditions. They may need to understand the impact that clinical issues may have on both the client's current behavior and desired outcomes. For example, a social worker may see a client who has severe depression linked with alcoholism. A physician may diagnose the client with stage 4 cirrhosis; the social worker will need to understand the severity of this diagnosis and how it will impact the client's depression and future sessions with the social worker. When in doubt, the social worker should ensure that their working relationships allow clarifying questions to be asked. Asking questions as needed will allow the social worker to fully understand any unfamiliar contexts and to serve the client.

Influencing Organizational and Social Policy

Social workers may act in a macro capacity for the common public good and serve as policy advocates, or provide leadership in the policy change process. There are many types of societal influences that can affect social policy.

Cultural
Societal perceptions or beliefs can shape policy. For instance, a general belief that children should have access to health care can aid in the development of child health care laws. Additionally, the media can bring problems/issues to the forefront and have a huge impact on public opinion, which can then influence policy development.

Economic
Lack of or an availability of resources has a significant impact on policy development. Additionally, those who control the resources also impact how policy is shaped.

Institutional
The capabilities, resources, and structure of government offices affect policy development. The institutions that create and implement policies have to be able to do so in an effective manner for those policies to be successful.

Social

The social environment, including events or situations such as recessions, wars, or poverty, all affect how policies are developed.

Legal

Existing laws and policies can influence future trends in policy development. New policies may or may not be adopted, depending on how they complement those already in existence and the current social climate. Legal events may also influence new policies.

Political

The political climate directly influences social policy, since the parties in control of governing bodies directly affect which policies and laws are implemented and repealed.

Availability of Community Resources

There is a wide range of community resources available, making it confusing for some clients to navigate the system and identify what would be most helpful for them. Therefore, a case manager plays a critical role in helping the client to find and utilize the community resources that would be most beneficial. When seeking resources, it is useful to look at the different domains of life—physical, psychological, emotional, spiritual, and educational—and then compile a collection of resources that may be useful for the client in each of these domains.

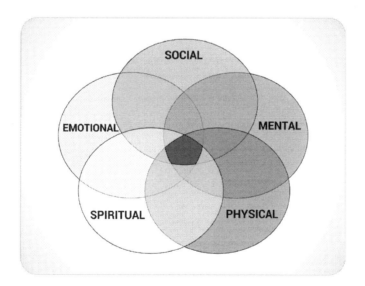

Physical needs can include food, shelter, clothing, or medical care, and there are many government programs available for these needs, such as free health care, affordable housing, and food stamps. For the elderly or disabled, their greatest need may be related to the accessibility of physical resources. In that case, the delivery of meals through Meals on Wheels or transportation services may be the most appropriate recommendation. Another help would be prescription assistance programs offered by some pharmaceutical companies to those with low income, which provide medications for free or at reduced cost. Other resources for the elderly can be accessed through the Administration on Aging and other local departments for elder care.

Ensuring the provision of adequate emotional and psychological services would first involve making sure the client is receiving emotional support from family and friends, or getting involved in support groups with others who have similar struggles. For the elderly, there may be community centers with programs to help seniors connect with each other and stay active. When it comes to finding the right psychological resources, both therapeutic and psychiatric, there are many options, so the client must be involved in the process of deciding what type and format of therapy would be best.

An often-overlooked area of whole-person care is the spiritual needs of the client. In addition to providing spiritual support, religious organizations are often nonprofits that can assist the client in physical or emotional ways as well. Fraternal organizations may provide similar benefits to a person, offering emotional, social, and spiritual components.

Educational resources should not be disregarded, especially in the case of someone who has mental or physical health needs. Whether formal training or informal learning through the library or online, there are many resources for gaining knowledge in almost any area. As discussed, education related to the individual's specific health needs is a crucial element of self-management care, client activation, and empowerment.

Calling United Way's helpline at 211, checking the U.S. government website, or conducting an internet search are easy and effective means of identifying the relevant community resources in the client's locality. Collaborating with other service providers can also make use of those who already know the client and can also prevent overlap in the provision of services. Finally, and perhaps most important, help the client to find resources through the people and organizations with whom they are already connected. Not only does this encourage self-determination and empowerment by helping the client see how many resources they already have in their life, but many clients will be most comfortable with places and people they already know.

Techniques for Mobilizing Community Participation

Limited resources in communities make community member participation in social change movements vital to the success of the community. Mobilizing community members is an important part of creating macro-level change. The community develops a sense of self-determination when it takes an active role in removing barriers, creating needed services and resources and advocating for the rights of its members. Members are encouraged to participate in problem identification, goal setting, and resource mobilization to create change. When community members become engaged in the change process, the overall sense of community empowerment increases. There are some challenges with community participation in which social workers can assist. Community members may lack necessary skills, or there may be barriers created by institutions that operate in the community. Social workers can serve the role of educator to help community members develop needed social organizational skills. The worker may also serve as an advocate to overcome barriers created by larger systems and institutions. Workers must engage a community and mobilize its strengths, resources, and supports systems to create positive changes.

Establishing Program Objectives and Outcomes

When developing a social work program, objectives should be developed for each process that is used or evaluated and for each outcome that is desired or evaluated. Often, a funding source will require that certain process and outcome objectives are evaluated in order for the organization to receive funds; this often provides a practice with some objectives to manage. When objectives are not tied to a funding source, programs may decide to develop them based on a needs assessment, or the program's service interest and capacity. These may be inspired by evidence-based research, successful outcomes in other programs, from data collected from focus groups, or may be tailored to a specific case. A logic model is a useful tool to map out what the program hopes to achieve, the inputs it requires, and the expected outputs. It can also be used at the end of a program to map out the actual intervention, and analyze how it compared to the expected plan.

Process objectives set standards for procedures, activities, and other implementation constructs of the social work program. Outcome objectives set standards for what exactly the program hopes to achieve. All objectives should follow SMART criteria. This means that any objective that is set forth should be Specific (it is clear what the action will be taken and who will it), Measurable (changes can be measured and analyzed), Achievable (the objective is realistic for the client, the social worker, and the available resources), Relevant (the objective relates to the desired overall goal), and Time-bound (the objective can be achieved in a specified time period).

Governance Structures

The National Association of Social Workers (NASW) is considered the most reputable association for the field of social work. NASW sets the tone for the field's standards, competency requirements, and public and legislative initiatives. It also provides a resource for social workers to stay current on emerging research and news, and resources with which to continue their social work education.

Other important governance structures in the United States that social workers may deal with depend on their field of practice. Social workers who work in a small, private setting may only have a single office manager to whom they report. If a social worker owns their own practice, they may choose how they establish the organization's reporting hierarchy. Social workers who work as part of a large government agency, such as a case worker for a state's Department of Child and Family Services, may work with a more bureaucratic structure that involves a supervisor, manager, division director, agency director, and the state governor. Social workers who work as part of a national non-profit may have a large, hierarchical governing structure similar to that of a state or federal agency, whereas social workers who work in local non-profits may be part of a lateral leadership system.

Often, non-profit and government groups will collaborate with one another or with private companies to lead social work initiatives. Therefore, social workers may need to be flexible in how they adapt to the governance structures of the organization they are serving while still maintaining the standards established by the NASW.

Formal and Informal Power Structures in the Decision-Making Process

Organizations are typically run as hierarchies of power. The higher in power level a position is, the more likely it is to be involved in decision making. Formal power structures are those that are listed in the organizational chart, such as the chief executive officer of an organization. The higher on the chart the position is listed, the more power that position has in decision-making. In small organizations where workers are more close-knit, this structure may be less strict. However, there are likely to be distinguished key players who primarily execute decisions (such as the company founder, or the person who is in charge of all operations). In informal power structures, key power wielders may not be officially listed as having high-ranking positions on an organizational chart, but they can still influence important decisions or the opinions of formal power structures. For example, informal wielders of power could be a mid-level employee who oversees a critical project, business associates who refer the most clients to the organization, or an entry-level employee who has the most knowledge about a niche topic in the field.

Accreditation and/or Licensing Requirements

In the United States, social work accreditation and licensure requirements vary by state. Therefore, aspiring social workers should ensure they follow standards set forth in the state in which they hope to practice.

The Council on Social Work Education (CSWE) is the main accrediting body for higher education programs in social work, and the majority of states require that social workers receive undergraduate or graduate degrees from universities whose social work curriculum is CSWE-accredited in order to become a licensed professional. CSWE-accredited programs ensure that coursework includes not only informational related to competencies established by the NASW, but that an emphasis is placed on ethics, professionalism, and practical application. Most states do not allow aspiring social workers to take board examinations without proof of a CSWE-accredited degree.

Other licensing information pertains to the type of social work a person hopes to do and the education they have received. Clinical social workers have different licensing requirements. Some states require post-graduate education in social work before licensure can be obtained. Other levels of licensure require practical and field work for a designated period of time. While board scores may be transferred across state lines, licensure is a separate process in each state that reviews both the worker's education and working experience comprehensively.

Practice Questions

1. Which therapeutic modality uses the miracle question?
    a. Cognitive behavioral therapy
    b. Psychodynamic therapy
    c. Solution focused brief therapy
    d. Person centered therapy

2. If a client is in immediate danger of self-harm or harm to others, what is the social worker's responsibility to the client?
    a. No responsibility
    b. Send the client home immediately
    c. Continue the therapy process with the client
    d. Direct the client to the nearest emergency room

3. Goal setting is used in which phase of the social work process?
    a. Termination of services
    b. Treatment planning
    c. Contracting
    d. Developing rapport with the client

4. Which two phases indicate client readiness for change?
    a. Pre-contemplation and contemplation
    b. Action and termination
    c. Contemplation and preparation
    d. Maintenance and recycling

5. If a social worker and a client are breaking down a goal into smaller steps for the client to proceed, what is this called?
    a. Fragmentation
    b. Partialization
    c. Step work
    d. Fractionalization

6. Which therapy modality is favored by insurers and managed care companies as more evidence based?
    a. Cognitive behavioral therapy
    b. Psychodynamic therapy
    c. Person centered therapy
    d. Narrative therapy

7. Being able to relate to the client's experiences as if one is in their shoes is called what?
    a. Sympathy
    b. Pity
    c. Empathy
    d. Relatedness

8. Which of the following is harmony and agreement in communication with the client?
   A. Congruence
   B. Affluence
   C. Way of being
   D. Being in tune

9. The acronym for the Health Insurance Portability and Accountability Act of 1996 is what?
   A. HIPPO
   B. HIPAA
   C. HIPPAA
   D. HI1996

10. The acronym ICWA stands for what?
    A. Inclusive Change for Women
    B. Indian Child Warfare Association
    C. Indian Change for Welfare Agency
    D. Indian Child Welfare Act

11. When a client is resistant to change and not thinking about change as an option, they are at what stage of change?
    A. Contemplation
    B. Action
    C. Pre-contemplation
    D. Maintenance

12. A group of clients who are in group therapy where the group cannot be altered and the group does not allow new members is called a(n) _____ group.
    A. Closed
    B. Open
    C. Stagnant
    D. Gated

13. What kind of therapy involves the revelation of unconscious drives, such as sex or aggression?
    A. Psychodynamic
    B. Solution focused brief therapy
    C. Cognitive behavioral therapy
    D. Rational emotive behavior therapy

14. What does the biopsychosocial model stand for?
    A. Biorhythm, psychotic, social welfare
    B. Biological, psychological, social
    C. Biotine, psychological, socioeconomic
    D. Biotrons, psychomatic, sociocultural

15. Cognitive approaches of psychotherapy address cognitive _____.
    A. Distractions
    B. Disenchantment
    C. Distortions
    D. Tracking

16. The goal of crisis intervention is to bring the client back to what?
    A. Eloquence
    B. Equilibrium
    C. The house
    D. Justice

17. What therapy modality was developed by Steve de Shazer and Insoo Kim Berg?
    A. Psychodynamic therapy
    B. Cognitive behavior therapy
    C. Rational emotive therapy
    D. Solution focused brief therapy

18. Out-of-home placements are mostly a result of which of the following?
    A. Abuse and neglect
    B. Abuse and murder
    C. Neglect and comfort
    D. Legal issues and responsibility

19. Physical _____ is an anger management technique that clients may use to reduce overwhelming emotions.
    A. Regulation
    B. Responsibility
    C. Exercise
    D. Repression

20. Which of the following involves a written and signed agreement concerning client behavior?
    A. Negotiating
    B. Contracting
    C. Mandating
    D. Mediating

21. Clients may need what kind of team approach if they have complex problems, such as medical, legal, or psychological issues?
    A. Honorary
    B. Upheld
    C. Eminent
    D. Interdisciplinary

22. Social workers need to be adept at _____ communication styles in order to function in a multidisciplinary environment.
    A. Written
    B. Haggling
    C. Negotiating
    D. Multilingual

23. Social welfare _____impacts social work practice by shaping laws and policies that affect client functioning in the social environment.
    A. Policy
    B. Legislation
    C. Communication
    D. Observation

24. If a client threatens the life of a specific person, the social worker becomes a what?
    A. True hero
    B. Mandatory historian
    C. Mandatory reporter
    D. Practice agent

25. Client reports may be in the format of what kind of notes?
    A. DIP and SOAR
    B. DAP and SOAP
    C. Subjective and objective
    D. Case history and recommendations

26. The first stage of the therapeutic process is what?
    A. Change
    B. Termination
    C. Commitment
    D. Storming

27. If a client needs the services of an expert in another field, the social worker may _____ the client for these services.
    A. Refer
    B. Absorb
    C. Terminate
    D. Assist

28. What kind of teams may consist of medical, legal, psychological, and other disciplines?
    A. Multilayered
    B. Multiordered
    C. Multidisciplinary
    D. Metadisciplinary

29. It is critical that social workers provide clients with verbal _____ because the client needs affirmation, reflective listening, and treatment information from the social worker.
    A. Demands
    B. Feedback
    C. Consultation
    D. Knowing

30. Social workers may _____client services so that the client is not overwhelmed by service providers and the services provided are appropriate for the client.
   A. Coordinate
   B. Provide
   C. Display
   D. Verbalize

31. In the elements of a case presentation, the social worker should always include the presenting what?
   A. Goal
   B. Solution
   C. Problem
   D. Side issue

32. If a client needs a social worker to discuss their situation with another agency or professional, they need to sign which of the following?
   A. Release of conditions
   B. Developmental disability waiver
   C. Contract
   D. Release of information

33. _____ centered approaches usually involve behavioral modification and may be broken down into steps for the client.
   A. Goal
   B. Task
   C. Partialization
   D. Client

34. The psychodynamic approach originated with which one of the following?
   A. Skinner
   B. Jung
   C. Freud
   D. Ellis

35. If a social worker overidentifies with the client or views the client as an important figure in their life, the social worker is encountering what?
   A. Countertransference
   B. Transference
   C. Negative transference
   D. Nullification

36. Which approach theorizes that thoughts and behaviors influence emotions?
   A. Cognitive behavioral
   B. Psychoanalytic
   C. Miracle approach
   D. Dialectical behavior therapy

37. Who is one of the founders of family centered therapy?
    A. Sigmund Freud
    B. Carl Jung
    C. Salvador Minuchin
    D. Albert Ellis

38. What kind of group allows prospective members into the group most of the time, does not have specific beginning and end dates, and group members are not heavily vetted before being permitted into the group?
    A. Closed
    B. Open
    C. Archaic
    D. Affluent

39. A person may experience which of the following when they are overly involved in the life of another person and do not differentiate themselves from that person?
    A. Escarpment
    B. Enmeshment
    C. Boundary flaws
    D. Concretization

40. A juvenile minor may be placed for adoption if there has been a _____ of parental rights.
    A. Justification
    B. Stopping
    C. Formation
    D. Termination

41. What provides social workers with additional resources for their clients and within their scope of practice?
    A. Socializing
    B. Networking
    C. Partying
    D. Conversations

42. What kind of records are required today in social work practice and social workers should become proficient at using them within the scope of their practice?
    A. Economic
    B. Political
    C. Electronic
    D. Paper

43. Which BEST describes a definition of client advocacy?
    a. Helping clients recognize and then use their strengths, resources, and systems to obtain goals
    b. Working on behalf of clients to remove barriers and obtain needed resources and/or services
    c. A short-term treatment usually lasting four to six weeks and is implemented when a client enters treatment following some type of traumatic event that causes significant distress
    d. Helping to link clients with needed services and resources

44. Which is NOT a method of working with involuntary clients?
    a. Helping clients to recognize participation is still a choice
    b. Including a client's goals in a service plan along with mandated goals
    c. Protecting a client's right to self-determination
    d. Refraining from getting a client's consent in treatment, since participation is mandatory

45. Which of the following is an aspect of the psychosocial approach to treatment?
    a. Unique to the field of social work and allows it to stand out from other professions
    b. Used when clients experience a state of disequilibrium, are out of balance, and can no longer function effectively
    c. Emphasizes the concept of problems of living
    d. Short-term, practical, and evidence-based intervention

46. Which component of the problem-solving process is left out of these steps?

    1. Assess, define, and clarify the problem
    2. Examine options and select/implement a solution
    3. Evaluate and adjust

    a. Emphasize contracting and carefully planned task implementation.
    b. Determine possible solutions.
    c. Social worker functions as a collaborator to assist the client in identifying smaller tasks.
    d. Social worker identifies issues, strengths, and resources.

Answer Explanations

1. C: Solution focused brief therapy includes the miracle question, scaling questions, exception questions, and past success questions. Solution focused brief therapy is often used because it is time sensitive and allows clients access to self-direction.

2. D: The client should be directed to the nearest emergency room for assessment and treatment if they are an immediate danger to themselves or others. Social workers are at liability if the client harms themselves or others and has indicated this to the social worker. If client is at risk for self-harm, the social worker should instruct them to contact the nearest emergency services.

3. B: Goal setting is used during the treatment planning phases of service to the client. However, goal setting may be initiated during any phase of treatment and added to the treatment plan. Goal setting is a vital part of the treatment process in order to allow the client to visualize where they are going.

4. C: Contemplation and preparation indicate that the client is ready to make changes. Pre-contemplation indicates resistance and unwillingness to change. Action phases suggest that the client is already engaged in the change process and not contemplating or preparing.

5. B: Partialization is the breaking down of a goal into smaller steps so that it is more manageable for the client. Partialization is especially useful when approaching complex problems. Clients should be encouraged to learn partialization methods so that they can eventually break down their goals into smaller steps without the assistance of the social worker.

6. A: Insurers and managed care companies sometimes consider cognitive behavioral therapy as the most evidence based therapy for practice. Insurers are becoming more and more time focused and are favoring brief therapies and evidence-based therapies for practitioners.

7. C: Empathy is being able to relate to the client as if in their shoes while also remaining objective. If a social worker cannot be empathetic toward a client, then the social worker should work through the issue or refer the client to another worker.

8. A: Congruence is harmony or agreement in communication with the client. Congruence is an important part of social work practice because it may determine treatment success with a client. If there is not congruence in communication with a client, the social worker and client must work on developing this process.

9. B: HIPAA is the acronym for the Health Insurance Portability and Accountability Act of 1996. All social workers need to be familiar with this Act because it affects electronic record confidentiality for the client.

10. D: The Indian Child Welfare Act (ICWA) provides regulations and guidance for the placement of Native American children. Social workers who are located in areas where there is tribal governance should be familiar with the Act because it directs placement and treatment of children in tribal custody.

11. C: The client is in the pre-contemplation stage of change and is resistant to the idea of change and doesn't want to change during this time. The contemplation phase is when the client is actively thinking about changing, and the action phase is when the client is taking action to change. The maintenance phase occurs when the client has completed the change and is reiterating the change in their life.

12. A: A closed group is formed when clients are specifically chosen by the agency, and new clients cannot enter the group. Open groups permit the fluctuation of new members who are welcome during each meeting.

13. A: Psychodynamic therapy involves the recognition of sexual and/or aggression drives. Psychodynamic therapy originated with psychoanalysis and the "talking cure" with Sigmund Freud. Modern psychoanalysis is often referred to as psychodynamic therapy.

14. B: The biopsychosocial model is a common model used in social work practice today to encompass multiple areas of a client's life. Spiritual and gender aspects may also be included in this model.

15. C: Cognitive distortions are cognitive aberrations that the client uses to hinder progress and change. Clients are often involved in fallacious thinking patterns and need assistance in changing these distortions into more constructive thought patterns.

16. B: The goal of crisis intervention is to bring the client back to pre-crisis equilibrium and physical and emotional stability. The first treatment goals of crisis intervention are to assure the physical and emotional safety of the client.

17. D: Solution focused brief therapy was developed by Steve de Shazer and Insoo Kim Berg. This brief therapy involves changing cognitive perceptions through Socratic style questioning techniques. Clients are allowed self-direction in the change process and reduction of symptoms may be viewed as a success instead of elimination or abstinence.

18. A: Abuse and neglect are the most common reasons for out-of-home placements concerning juveniles and adults. Child protective services and adult protective services investigate these issues and petition the courts for out-of-home placements. These agencies attempt to utilize out-of-home placements as temporary, but they sometimes become permanent if there is no change in family dynamics. Often these agencies will attempt to place the juveniles with relatives if parental rights are terminated but in cases where such placement is not an option, non-relative placements are sought.

19. C: Physical exercise may assist in reducing anger. There are several anger management techniques, but physical exercise may be one of the more effective techniques for clients in states of emotional fluctuation. Before engaging in strenuous exercise, it is recommended that clients obtain a physician's approval.

20. B: Contracting with a client involves a written and signed document to alter the behavior of the client. No-harm contracts and safety plans may be contractual documents that the client agrees to by signature. Contracts are not usually legally binding but may assist the client in behavior management and motivation.

21. D: Clients may require an interdisciplinary team approach if they have complex issues. Social workers need to know how to interact with other disciplines because they need to view the client as a whole person with biopscychosocial spiritual needs.

22. A: Social workers need to be proficient at written communication styles to function in a multidisciplinary environment. Social workers interact with many professions in the course and scope of their work and need to be able to communicate to have constructive client outcomes.

23. B: Social welfare legislation influences social work practice outcomes because it shapes agency policy and practices. Social workers need to be aware of agency policies shaped by legislation in order to follow legal mandates. Social workers may be advocates of social welfare legislation in their practice because they can shape legal policies for the benefit of their clients.

24. C: The social worker is a mandatory reporter to a prospective victim of client violence. This mandate originated with the Tarasoff case involving a client who was not reported to the prospective victim and then proceeded to kill her. Social workers must report threats to life to the authorities and the potential victim.

25. B: Client reports may be in the format of DAP or SOAP notes depending on the agency. Other agencies may use an entirely different format for their reports, though DAP and SOAP are probably the most common formats.

26. C: The first stage of the therapeutic process is commitment, and the client needs to be committed to change and taking action within the therapeutic framework. The client's commitment to therapy and change are probably the most important elements of the therapeutic alliance. This phase also involves ensuring that the social worker and client are a good fit based on the client's needs and the social worker's skills and expertise.

27. A: The social worker may refer the client for services outside the area of their expertise. Clients often need referrals to a multitude of services in complex cases. Referrals may be made for legal, psychological, and/or medical purposes.

28. C: Multidisciplinary teams consist of experts within different fields who are providing services, or advocating, for the social work client. Some clients need extensive multidisciplinary teams to return to a sufficient level of social functioning.

29. B: Clients require verbal feedback from the social worker because they need affirmation and information concerning their issues. Feedback should be combined with empathy for the client.

30. A: Social workers often coordinate so that there is a smooth continuity of services for clients. Social workers may research and obtain services for clients when necessary. Many clients have complex issues that require coordination of services.

31. C: The social worker should always include the presenting problem in a case presentation. There may also be data concerning medical/psychiatric information, significant personal and/or social information, impressions and summary, and recommendations.

32. D: Clients need to sign a release of information waiver for each agency or professional the social worker will speak to on behalf of the client. A release of information waiver is also required for family members and friends of the client that the social worker may speak to.

33. B: Task centered approaches may assist the client in behavioral modification and the client may engage in partialization in order to carry out tasks in a step-by-step approach. Task centered approaches may be beneficial for more concrete thinkers.

34. C: Sigmund Freud is the father of psychoanalysis or the "talking cure," from which psychodynamic theories originated. Freud's follower and disciple, Jung, took a different approach to psychoanalysis and had a major falling out with Freud. Skinner and Ellis are better known for cognitive behavioral techniques of psychotherapy.

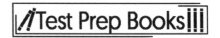

35. A: The social worker is encountering countertransference when they over identify with a client. This needs to be worked through by the social worker or addressed in supervision. Countertransference can be destructive if left unaddressed or it can become a beneficial experience if the social worker recognizes it and can come to terms with their role in the social worker/client relationship.

36. A: The cognitive behavioral approach most commonly suggests that thoughts and behaviors influence emotions. The psychoanalytic approach focuses on drives and past events. The miracle approach does not exist, and dialectical behavior therapy uses some cognitive behavioral approaches, but also focuses on mindfulness and emotional self-regulation.

37. C: Salvador Minuchin is one of the founders of family therapy. Social workers who work with families may want to be familiar with his techniques. Minuchin's work is seminal to the field of family therapy and many family therapy models are based on Minuchin's ideas.

38. B: An open group allows membership to ebb and flow and usually does not have a distinct starting point or closing point. Members are permitted to enter as they wish and there is not as homogenous a criterion to enter the group as in closed groups.

39. B: Enmeshment occurs when a person is overly involved in the life of another person and loses differentiation with that person. Enmeshment is considered unhealthy and needs to be addressed in the social work process. If enmeshment can be deconstructed, a healthier relationship may be formed. When enmeshment is present it is due to the lack of boundaries. By helping the client to establish healthy boundaries, the enmeshment can be deconstructed.

40. D: If there is a termination of parental rights by the state, the minor may be placed for adoption. Sometimes the foster parents may wish to adopt the child or the child may be placed for outside adoption by the state. Parental rights are often terminated when parents are not deemed fit to parent the child over a long period of time and have made no progress with their treatment plan. Occasionally, parents will opt to terminate rights rather than participate in a treatment plan to make the home safe for their child.

41. B: Networking may provide social workers with additional resources to assist their clients. Networking may be performed at conferences, meetings, and trainings. Networking may also be interdisciplinary in nature and the worker may network with medical, legal, and psychological professions. The social worker may network within the capacity of their employment scope. Networking is a vital part of social work. It can be helpful to reach out to those met while networking during difficult cases.

42. C: Electronic records are required today in the social work field. Social workers should be familiar with electronic health records and prepare to use them in today's environment. Medical records in all fields are now electronic, and the systems of documentation vary. Some electronic health records are software based and others are Internet based. Social workers should have some computer proficiency in order to use electronic records systems.

43. B: Client advocacy is working on behalf of a client to remove barriers and obtain needed resources and/or services. Choice A, client empowerment, is helping clients to recognize and then use their strengths, resources, and systems to obtain goals. Choice C, crisis-intervention approach, is a short-term treatment usually lasting four to six weeks and is implemented when a client enters treatment following some type of traumatic event that causes significant distress. Choice D, case management, is helping to link clients with needed services and resources.

44. D: It is important that social workers always acquire client consent, even when working with involuntary clients. Guidelines about client consent are mentioned throughout the NASW Code of Ethics. When working with involuntary clients, social workers should help clients to recognize participation is still a choice, include a client's goals in a service plan along with mandated goals, and protect a client's right to self-determination.

45. A: The psychosocial approach is unique to the field of social work and allows it to stand out from other professions. Choice *B* is related to the crisis intervention theory, whereby clients experience a state of disequilibrium and are out of balance. Choices *C* and *D* are related to Task Centered Practice, which emphasizes concepts of living and is a short term, practical, and evidence-based intervention.

46. B: Determining possible solutions is the second step in the problem-solving process. Choices *B, C* and *D* are components of Task Centered Practice, which includes: contracting and carefully planning task implementation, along with the social worker functioning as a collaborator to help client identify issues, strengths, resources, and smaller tasks.

Professional Values and Ethics

Professional Values and Ethical Issues

Legal and Ethical Issues Related to the Practice of Social Work

Social workers are, by nature, helping professionals. In theory, they are much like other helping professionals such as counselors or family therapists. The goal of the field of social work is not only social justice, however, but improving the lives of individuals through empowerment and advocacy. Social work maintains a person-focused perspective that stipulates that the profession strives to "meet people where they are," not forcing ideals and decisions onto those in need, but instead using their own values to empower them to make changes.

The social work profession has a set of values that governs how social workers do their jobs. These values are the root of the social work profession and lay the groundwork for everything that social workers do. These six values are: service, social justice, dignity and worth of the person, importance of human relationships, integrity, and competence.

In order to meet the needs of the various populations served by social workers, there are certain rules and regulations regarding ethics that social workers must follow. The National Association of Social Workers (NASW) has a Code of Ethics that serves to educate social workers on how they should conduct themselves.

The NASW Code of Ethics has six core purposes. These purposes are:

- To establish the core values on which the mission of social work is based

- To provide a set of ethical standards for social workers, as well as specific information regarding different ethical dilemmas

- To help identify information that social workers should take under advisement when ethical conflicts may exist or when an ethical dilemma presents itself

- To provide standards that can be used by others to ensure accountability and responsibility by those in the profession

- To inform new social workers about core issues relating to the mission of social work and to the ethical standards of the field

- To provide the rules and standards that social workers can use to evaluate the conduct of others in the profession

Ethical Dilemmas

Ethical dilemmas occur when three different conditions are met in a situation. The first is that the practitioner must make a decision. If the situation does not require that a decision be made, then there isn't an ethical dilemma. The second is that there are different decisions that could be made or different actions one could take. The third condition is that an ethical ideal will be conceded no matter what decision is made.

One type of ethical dilemma occurs when you have a situation in which two ethical principles are conflicting. This is a pure ethical dilemma because either choice of action involves conceding one of these principles, and there is no way to keep both principles intact. Another type of ethical dilemma occurs when ethical principles conflict with values and/or laws. In these types of situations, a social worker's values may conflict with an ethical principle, and a decision must be made.

Once you have determined which kind of ethical dilemma you are facing, there are steps to take in order to reach a conclusion and, ultimately, the resolution of the dilemma. The NASW lays out steps that should be taken when attempting to resolve an ethical dilemma.

Determine: Is there an ethical dilemma?

Identify: What are the core standards and values involved?

Rank: Rank values and ethical principles in order of importance.

Develop: Make a plan.

Implement: Put the plan into place.

Reflect: Evaluate the ethical decision-making process.

The Client's Right to Refuse Services

As per the NASW Code of Ethics, the client has the right to refuse all or a portion social work services and utilize self-direction at any point. Social workers should address this possibility with the client during the intake process, as well as inform the client fully about the possible ramifications of refusing services. Clients may need outside service linkages from the social worker during the termination process; they may also choose to continue service but decide to work with a different social worker or in an entirely different social or health field.

Social workers should be respectful of clients who terminate services before completing the problem-solving process, and they should remain detached and objective during the termination without taking any critical feedback too personally. Rather, this can be viewed as a learning opportunity to understand different types of clients better. It is important to note that not all clients can voluntarily cease services. For example, court-appointed social work sessions often cannot be terminated by the client. In these cases, the social worker may have difficult interactions with the client and face resistance, especially if the client truly does not want to be in the session. Additionally, clients who are unable to make decisions due to a medical reason (such as a mental condition that inhibits decision-making) may voice opposition to the treatment, but they cannot be the actual person who terminates treatment. This is usually left to a proxy, such as a legal representative or family member.

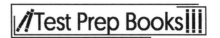

Professional Boundaries

Difficulties in Setting and Maintaining Professional Boundaries in Social Work
Professional boundaries in social work are clearly defined limits on the practitioner-client relationship that provide a space for the creation of safe connections. Some helpful things to keep in mind include: the line between being friendly and being friends; being with the client versus becoming the client; and understanding the limits and responsibilities of the social worker role.

Conflicting values occur when the social worker's values and knowledge about best practices are at odds with the client's values, history, relationships, or lifestyle. *Vicarious trauma* may happen when a social worker experiences symptoms of trauma after listening to a client's experience. These symptoms may arise due to the practitioner sharing a similar history of trauma. Boundaries may be difficult to maintain if the social worker feels that they need to rescue the client due to an unhealthy attachment to positive results in practice. This is termed the *rescuer role*. Professional boundaries may also be difficult to set and maintain if there is poor teamwork between colleagues in the social work organization. This is evident when social workers assume the roles of other team members because they believe they are not fulfilling their responsibilities to the client.

Professional boundary issues occur when social workers have multiple types of relationships with a client. This may include a professional, business, or personal relationship. For example, it is permissible to see a client out in public at a restaurant, but not to invite a client to dinner for business or personal reasons. When encountering a client in public, the relationship with the client must be kept confidential. However, if the client chooses to say hello, saying hello in return and quickly ending the encounter would be acceptable.

There are several boundary issues that come with working with clients. These issues are:

- Intimate contact: This refers to things such as hugging a client at the end of a working relationship, or patting a client on the hand during a crying session. Sexual contact also falls into this category.

- Personal gain: This refers to instances in which a social worker engages in activity with a client that results in a monetary (or otherwise valuable) benefit to the social worker. This could involve situations such as referring a client to a business owned by the social worker or a friend/family member of the social worker, selling something to a client, or even asking a client for professional suggestions.

- Emotional and dependency issues: This refers to instances in which a social worker's own personal issues cause the social worker to have impaired judgment, possibly resulting in other boundary issues, such as a dual relationship with the client.

- Altruistic instincts: In some instances, a social worker's own good intentions and concerns for a client can result in boundary violations and confusion about the relationship between the social worker and the client. An example of this would be going to a client's bridal shower or retirement party.

Strategies for Setting and Maintaining Professional Boundaries in Social Work
Despite these difficulties, social workers must set and maintain boundaries with their clients and colleagues to ensure an effective practice. Practitioners should consistently monitor how their

professional boundaries enhance or harm relationships with clients, colleagues, supervisors and administrators. They must also gauge the impact of their boundaries on the amount of time they devote to work, their ability to cope with stress at work, and the amount of time and energy that they spend on extraneous activities and relationships.

There are several strategies for building and maintaining appropriate professional boundaries and relationships. First, practitioners should examine their motivations for giving extra time and attention to a client. If a social worker treats one client differently, this indicates that the boundary may be overextended. Social workers can manage this situation by determining whether the services provided are in line with the client's care plan, the organization's mission, the job description, and scope of practice.

Social workers should also avoid encouraging clients to contact them through personal channels. Clients should use the channels of communication set in place by the organization, such as work email, voicemail, cell phones, pagers, receptionists, on-call staff, and procedures for after-hours referrals to 911, emergency rooms, or mental health crisis centers. Extending the professional boundaries of the social worker role puts colleagues and the organization at risk for failure. It also sets an unfair expectation that other colleagues will extend their professional boundaries. If boundaries are inconsistent between colleagues and within the organization, then clients may become confused and distrust the entire organization.

A third strategy for building appropriate professional boundaries is establishing clear agreements with clients during the initial sessions about the role of a social worker and the dynamics of a client-practitioner relationship. When warning signs indicate that healthy boundaries may be in jeopardy, social workers must address the issues with the client clearly, quickly, and sensitively. This involves clarifying the roles and boundaries with the client and asking the client to restate these boundaries to ensure understanding.

A fourth strategy is limiting self-disclosure about the social worker's personal life to information directly related to the client's goals. If there is a dual relationship between the social worker and client, the practitioner must preserve the client's confidentiality, physical security, and emotional well-being in social situations.

A fifth strategy is avoiding social media within professional practice. Practitioners should not connect with clients on social media. This includes adding clients as friends on Facebook or following clients on Twitter. Social workers should use discretion and limit the amount of online information that is made available to the public or social network connections to prevent conflicts of interest. Social workers also shouldn't attempt to access online information about clients without prior informed consent. Finally, practitioners shouldn't post negative information about colleagues or the organization online.

A sixth strategy is for social workers to foster strong work relationships with their colleagues at the organization. These connections will help practitioners cope with stresses, think through questions of ethics and professional relationships, and help maintain a sense of humor. Practitioners should be sensitive to signs of bullying in the workplace, as each practitioner deserves respect and dignity to ensure social justice for others. It's important that social workers use appropriate channels of supervision and consultation to determine appropriate boundaries in difficult situations. Supervision can also be useful when trying to remedy concerns with existing organization procedures that address or inhibit client needs.

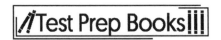

A final strategy for maintaining professional boundaries is ensuring appropriate self-care. This includes taking time for nurturing oneself throughout the workday, maintaining a regular work schedule, and taking time away from the office each day to refocus. Practitioners should limit communication when they are away from work to ensure time for rejuvenation, especially during vacations or personal time. They must also be aware of how they handle work stress and monitor how often they take work home. This includes physical work, emotional strain, or hyper-vigilance about work situations. If a practitioner consistently struggles to maintain professional relationships and work boundaries, they should seek supervision or outside mental health counseling.

Ethical Issues Related to Dual Relationships

Dual relationships are clearly outlined in the NASW Code of Ethics. The Code of Ethics states that social workers should not engage in dual relationships with clients or former clients in which exploitation of the client may occur. The Code of Ethics does recognize that there might be situations where dual relationships are unavoidable. For example, a social worker might have two jobs, one of which involves providing group therapy to survivors of sexual abuse. It is possible that a member of the aforementioned therapy group could become an employee or client at the social worker's second place of work. In these types of situations, the Code of Ethics suggests that the social worker establish clear boundaries that are sensitive to the client/former client.

Under no circumstances should a social worker ever become involved in a sexual relationship with a client. In addition, the Code of Ethics establishes that social workers must avoid sexual relationships with anyone who is related to or has a close personal relationship with a client or former client. The Code of Ethics also states that social workers should not become involved in sexual relationships with former clients because of the high risk of harm that may occur with such relationships. If, however, a social worker does become involved in a sexual relationship with a former client, the social worker is responsible for demonstrating that the former client entered into the relationship without manipulation or exploitation. The Code of Ethics also specifies that, due to the obvious risk of harm, a social worker should not provide professional services to anyone with whom the social worker has had a previous sexual relationship.

Situations called "boundary crossings" are when a social worker does not intend to create a dual relationship but inadvertently does so, as would be the case were a clinician to self-disclose personal information during a therapy session. This is distinguished from a boundary *violation*, which occurs when a dual relationship is established that is inherently coercive or manipulative and therefore harmful to the client. What are some clues about whether a boundary crossing is unethical?

- It hinders the social worker's care
- It prevents the social worker from being impartial
- It exploits or manipulates the client or another person
- It harms clients or colleagues

Dual relationships are sometimes unavoidable in practice, particularly in small communities. However, it is possible to avoid dual relationships that involve boundary violations and ethical violations.

Self-Disclosure Principles and Applications

To build professional boundaries, it is recommended that social workers limit self-disclosure about their personal lives to information directly related to the client's goals. If there is a dual relationship between the social worker and client, the practitioner must preserve the client's confidentiality, physical security, and emotional well-being in social situations.

Obtaining Informed Consent

When disclosing information due to legal requirements, it is always important to discuss the situation with the client. It should be noted that the social worker should evaluate their own safety when discussing disclosure of confidential information with the client. If the social worker believes the situation to be unsafe if/when the client learns of the disclosure, then it is not necessary to alert the client prior to disclosing the confidential information. This is something that should be discussed in detail with clients during the informed consent process and throughout the relationship.

One of the difficulties associated with breaking confidentiality to protect a third party is that the threat isn't always clearly established. If a client discloses during treatment that he is going to go home and stab his neighbor, this is clearly a plan of intended harm. However, what about an HIV-positive client who fails to warn sexual partners of her HIV status? What if the client fully understands the risk to her partners and has no intention of disclosing her status? This is a situation that would require thorough documentation, thoughtful debate, and possibly conferencing with colleagues to decide upon the best course of action.

Confidentiality also becomes more complicated when a social worker is working with two or more people, either in a family or group session. All participants must agree that any information shared within the context of treatment will be kept confidential and not shared with others. However, the social worker should stress with clients that they cannot force other members to abide by the confidentiality agreement and that breach of confidentiality is a risk.

Documentation

Keeping accurate client records has many purposes, such as documenting the history and treatment of a client, getting insurance reimbursement, and providing social workers a historical account of client sessions. The information contained in a client record can also be used to evaluate the effectiveness of services. Client records, when combined with other evaluation tools (e.g., client satisfaction surveys, reactions to treatments, accomplishments of goals), can be an effective method of evaluating treatment progress. Supervisors may review client records to evaluate the effectiveness of the treatment process, social worker performance, and client progress, or to ensure documentation is being completed accurately and on time. When reviewing client records for evaluation, ethical standards must always be upheld.

The NASW Code of Ethics specifically addresses guidelines for using client information for evaluation, including:

- Protecting confidentially to the fullest extent possible
- Accurately reporting information
- Protecting clients from harm
- Obtaining required client consent for all uses of their information (e.g., supervisory review, reimbursement)
- Making clients aware that the consent can be withdrawn without punishment

Termination

Termination of the relationship occurs when the client and the social worker have reached treatment goals. Even though the relationship is terminated, the client may feel warmly toward the social worker, and congruence and empathy may still be part of the relationship. Some clients may require maintenance sessions to continue stability, but when termination is the next clear stage in the relationship, psychotherapy sessions should end.

In the case of a client choosing to prematurely terminate services, the social worker should clearly explain the risks to the client and also carefully document all meetings and interactions to protect against legal ramifications. Abandonment, which refers to the social worker terminating services prematurely without adequate reason or in an improper manner, is considered malpractice and can lead to lawsuits. When the social worker decides to end the working relationship, they must ensure that the client is adequately prepared and warned about the end of services, and that the client is emotionally equipped to deal with the termination. Social workers can refer clients to other types of providers, who can continue working with the client after their own services have ceased. If a social worker needs to terminate services early, such as in the case of leaving a job, they should connect the client to a new social worker who can continue to provide the same level of services.

Death and Dying

Some clients have documented clear wishes about their death and dying (advance directives), while others do not. In these cases, social workers may be called upon to provide information and counsel to the client and client system. This can be an emotional process, and social workers should show compassion, sympathy, and respect as the client and the client system adjust to the news. Terminal clients are allowed to take comfort measures, such as hospice services, but are not allowed to take any external measures that would intensify or speed up the dying process (such as requesting a lethal medication dose).

Terminal clients may choose to refuse treatment and pass away naturally; while this process may hasten death, it is considered a natural and acceptable alternative to prolonging the dying experience with intervention, and it is also considered the client's choice. Terminal clients may choose this route if they have made peace with the decision and with their family and friends, if they want to remove a physical and financial burden from loved ones, and if they are ready for the process. Still, in such a case a social worker could provide guidance to ensure the client truly understands the process and consequences of their decision. With a do not resuscitate (DNR) order, a client chooses to refuse services if their cardiopulmonary system ceases to work.

In clients who are unable to make decisions (such as those who are in a permanent vegetative state), the next of kin or a legal appointee may make medical decisions on the client's behalf. This may include taking the client off life support, if applicable. This can be a highly contentious situation if family members or legal proxies do not agree on the best course of action. This situation can be avoided by preparing advanced directives, which document the client's wishes in such contexts.

Research Ethics

Research performed on living creatures, especially humans, is always scrutinized for ethical concerns. Such research often uses experiments for which the outcomes are unknown. Therefore, it is possible that any research performed on a person may have unintended, unwanted, or otherwise harmful psychological, physiological, emotional, or social effects. Research ethics are intended to protect participants, ensure that research is being conducted for some public benefits, and ensure that participants who are involved have been provided with informed consent. Informed consent involves explaining to an individual, in as much detail possible, the processes of the experiment or study, all potential side effects or outcomes, and the opportunity to make an educated decision independently about participation in such a study. Informed consent also documents the fact that the participant may leave the study at any time. Informed consent paperwork is usually signed by the participants, the researcher, and an independent third party. Some controversy still exists over research that affects vulnerable populations, such as those with psychological disorders, the elderly, children, the poor, and others who cannot easily make objective decisions or could be persuaded by experiment incentives (such as gift cards or the like).

An Institutional Review Board (IRB) is any independent group that reviews research and clinical trial designs that have human participants to ensure there are no potential ethical violations. IRBs are accredited by the US Food and Drug Administration. These groups can request changes, additions, and eliminations to any study proposal; they can also completely deny a proposal for approval. Without IRB approval, research designs cannot come to the experiment phase. While research is in session, IRB committees conduct regular audits to ensure compliance is still intact. Noncompliance can result in heavy fines, penalties, criminal investigation, and termination of a study.

Supervision and Management

Supervisors and managers should always be aware of the hierarchical power they wield over subordinates, and they should ensure that their leadership does not take advantage of this dynamic. Behaviors that would be unsuitable in a lateral colleague may be ignored in a supervisor if a subordinate feels their job or work environment would be in jeopardy should a complaint be filed.

Interpersonal work dynamics between supervisors and subordinates should ensure that the supervisor treats subordinates with professional respect and support, even when they are challenging them to grow professionally or learn more. It is critical to not become domineering in this regard. Additionally, if a supervisor needs to coach a subordinate on performance, this should be done privately rather than in front of other colleagues. On the other hand, supervisors also need to make sure that their relationships with subordinates do not become overly friendly or intimate. Supervisors should avoid confiding overly personal details to subordinates or pursuing romantic relationships in the workplace. Not only could this cause extreme discomfort for colleagues, it could also be reported for harassment. When in doubt, supervisors can refer to the NASW Code of Ethics to drive not only their service delivery, but also their interactions in the workplace.

Social Worker Safety

Social workers are often in high-risk situations, working with high-risk populations. The threat of violence or other personal safety issues is relatively high compared to other fields of work. Implementing policies and procedures that help protect social workers during their workday can help mitigate some of this risk. This includes the provision of an avenue to report unsafe settings or clients, and if necessary, to terminate working relationships in which the social worker does not feel safe without fear of workplace reprisal. Reviewing the daily processes of service delivery can help identify areas where risk management techniques may be necessary.

Since social workers work in a number of different places—office settings, jails, courtrooms, family homes, community centers, hospitals, and so on—they should treat each session individually and assess safety risks each time. This assessment may include an overview of the location, the ability to receive emergency services quickly, other available workers who may be able to help in an emergency, and the state of the client at each visit (even if it is someone the social worker has treated for some time). Social workers should also protect their personal boundaries, such as not allowing clients to call or visit them at home, not sharing personal information in person or online, and maintaining protocols to address client emotions that could lead to violence. (Examples include shouting at or threatening the social worker. While these are not physical assaults, they are still verbal and emotional violence toward the social worker, and they could escalate.)

Confidentiality

Use of Client Records

Issues relating to confidentiality include the storage and maintenance of records and charts. All confidential material should be kept in a secure location and locked at all times. For example, if a social worker takes a clipboard into client rooms to make notes for later documentation, that clipboard should be locked in a drawer when not in use so that no one can turn it over and see confidential information when the social worker is away from their desk. With the use of electronics and computers, there should be policies in place to lock computers when away to avoid anyone seeing notes or other confidential information. Collaboration between colleagues in which clients may be discussed should be done behind closed doors to avoid anyone else hearing the conversation.

Social workers are to provide clients with reasonable access to records. Social workers are permitted, however, by the Code of Ethics to withhold all or part of the client record from the client if the social worker determines there is a great risk of harm in releasing the information. In these cases, it is important to fully document the request, whether the records were released, and the rationale for either releasing or not releasing them.

There may be instances in which a social worker is sued for malpractice. In these cases, the Code of Ethics states that it is permissible for the social worker to share confidential client information to aid in self-defense, but only so far as is necessary to adequately defend oneself.

Throughout the development of a professional relationship in social work, it is important to keep case notes and records for several reasons. Case notes are important in the process of conceptualizing the case and the client's needs. They can help the practitioner pull together his or her thoughts when making a diagnosis. Case records also serve as a measure of the standard of care and subsequently can be used in court to show adequate client care. They help social workers determine whether clients have made progress, remember what the client said from visit to visit, and can be used when a practitioner seeks supervision about the case. In addition, case notes are needed by insurance companies, agencies, and schools to support the treatment that is provided to clients.

Legal and Ethical Issues Regarding Confidentiality

Social workers have a duty to protect confidential information of clients. Ethically, client information should not be discussed with anyone other than the client. Legally, a client has a right to keep their medical and therapeutic information confidential. The Health Insurance Portability and Accountability Act of 1996 (HIPAA) requires that medical information (including therapeutic and mental health information) be protected and kept confidential. However, there are certain limitations to confidentiality. These generally involve risk of harm to the individual being served, as well as others.

Social workers are not as protected as some other professionals when it comes to confidentiality and often find themselves being called to testify in court cases related to their clients. There are also certain situations in which social workers may have to release confidential information to protect the client or satisfy the duty to warn.

Providing services to minors can be challenging when it comes to confidentiality issues, especially since the legal rules and regulations vary from state to state. At times, there can be a conflict between the social worker's feeling of ethical responsibility to maintain the privacy of the minor and the legal right of parents to be informed of issues discussed. Adolescents in particular may discuss concerns with a social worker that they do not want their parents to be aware of, and it can be a violation of trust if these issues are subsequently revealed to parents. It is imperative that at the start of treatment, the expectations of the social worker's relationship with each person are discussed with the parents and minors, as well as the benefits and limits of confidentiality. Minors should never be promised confidentiality when the social worker cannot keep that promise, but the privacy and individuality of the minor should be maintained as much as possible. In cases where private information about the minor is going to be revealed, social workers should always inform the minor. This holds true regardless as to whether it is with the client's consent, mandated reporting, or due to the parent utilizing their right to information.

With technology being utilized extensively by helping professionals, confidentiality of electronic information is another important issue. Counseling sessions are now being provided by telephone, video chat, and online simulation, and these media open new possibilities for information abuse. If a practitioner provides a video therapy session, they should be aware that it is possible for the client to have someone else in the room, off-camera, without informing the clinician or other participants. The same could be true with electronic communication such as texting or email. There is no way to know if a client is forwarding electronic information to third parties without the clinician's knowledge.

Mandatory Reporting

Some clients may disclose intent to harm themselves. It is necessary in these situations to fully assess suicidal intent and determine if the client is serious about carrying out a plan for self-harm. It might be sufficient, in cases where a client has considered self-harm but has no clear plan, to complete a safety plan with the client. The safety plan will outline what the client agrees to do should they begin to experience the desire to engage in self-harm. However, if the client has a clear plan of action and access to items necessary to carry out the plan, then confidentiality should be broken to protect the client. This would involve notifying police and having the client committed for observation for their own protection.

In addition to protecting clients from themselves, social workers also have a duty to warn third-party individuals if there is threat of harm. Duty to warn was established by the 1976 case Tarasoff vs. Regents of the University of California. In this case, a graduate student at the University of California-Berkley had become obsessed with Tatiana Tarasoff. After significant distress, he sought psychological treatment and disclosed to his therapist that he had a plan to kill Tarasoff. Although the psychologist did have the student temporarily committed, he was ultimately released. He eventually stopped seeking treatment and attacked and killed Tarasoff. Tarasoff's family sued the psychologist and various other individuals involved with the university. This case evolved into the duty to warn third parties of potential risk of harm. Satisfying the duty to warn can be done by notifying police or the individual who is the intended victim.

Because ethical dilemmas can involve legal situations, they may also have legal consequences for a social worker or necessitate involving the legal system. For example, a client may disclose that he frequently drinks large amounts of alcohol and then drives his children to school. Ethically, there is an obligation to keep what the client has said in confidence. However, the client's children are being placed in a situation in which they are in great danger of being injured or harmed. Due to laws protecting the welfare of children, the social worker would need to make a report to Child Protective Services. In some states, if someone has a good faith reason to believe that a child is being neglected or abused, and does not report the situation, that person may face a civil lawsuit and even criminal charges.

It's important to note as well that social workers are considered mandated reporters in all states. This means there is a legal and ethical obligation to break confidentiality to report any signs and symptoms of child and elder abuse. In some cases, it will be impossible to know for sure if abuse or neglect is happening. Often the social worker will have only a small amount of information that may raise concerns, but must make a report so that an investigation can occur. A social worker cannot be held liable for reports made in good faith to Child Protective Services or Adult Protective Services.

Liability is another legal issue that social workers may sometimes face. Clients can sue a social worker for malpractice. When a social worker is sued, the liability does not stop with the social worker. In lawsuits, a social worker's supervisor can be named as a defendant, and liability can extend as far as the head of the agency that employs the social worker. Agencies that provide social services carry malpractice insurance for this very reason. It is good practice, however, for individual social workers to also carry malpractice insurance for extra protection.

Ethical and Legal Issues Regarding Mandatory Reporting of Abuse

Mandatory reporting laws require social workers, and other professionals, to report any suspected abuse or neglect. This means that any professional who has a suspicion of abuse or neglect of a child or a vulnerable adult must legally make a report to either Child Protective Services or Adult Protective Services. Note that some states, such as Tennessee, have laws that require all citizens to report suspected abuse or neglect, making everyone a mandated reporter.

Often when abuse or neglect is suspected, the concern about breaking confidentiality is at the forefront of the mind of the social worker. During informed consent, this requirement to report any signs of abuse or neglect should have been disclosed to the client. When such breaks in confidentiality occur, they can damage the relationship. In some cases, it may be necessary or appropriate to disclose to the client that a report is being made. For example, if a new mother has tested positive for cocaine and the infant has tested positive for cocaine while in the hospital, the infant will remain in the Neonatal Intensive Care Unit due to withdrawal. Disclosing to the mother that a report is being made, and why it's being made, could prepare her and create an opportunity to speak further with her about treatment options and other important considerations. It's important to note that social workers who fail to report suspected abuse or neglect can be subject to civil penalties and/or prosecution.

Professional Development and Use of Self

Professional Values and Principles

Values are ideas or beliefs that guide an individual's thoughts and actions. The values that a person holds have their basis in the moral foundation to which they were exposed in childhood and adolescence. Moral foundations can include anything from family-specific beliefs and religious moral codes to the ethics and laws of society. As an individual gets older, they are increasingly exposed to new value systems that coincide or challenge their existing values. When someone must consider adopting one value system over another, this is called a *value conflict*. Value conflicts may occur when someone makes new friends, engages in romantic relationships, joins a new community, attends a new school, and accepts a new job.

The process of acquiring values is important for social workers to keep in mind when working to understand where their own values and their clients' values originated. Social workers should be aware of their own moral codes, values, biases, and prejudices to avoid conflict with the treatment they are providing to clients. The process of acknowledging and controlling personal values in social work practice is called *value suspension*. Self-awareness is a vital part of ensuring that one's personal values and beliefs do not intrude on the social worker/client relationship. It may be necessary to seek consultation from a supervisor or colleague in situations where one's personal values or beliefs conflict with those of the client and when those feelings cannot be resolved. In extreme cases where consultation and self-reflection cannot remedy the conflict, termination of the social worker/client relationship and referral to another therapist may be necessary.

All professions are built upon a foundation of values and guided by ethical codes. At times, these values trump that profession's empirical knowledge base. The focus of the social work profession is providing care and improving society rather than simply defining and explaining existing problems. To these ends, social workers must apply the knowledge and skills in other fields, including sociology, philosophy, law, and psychology.

Social workers must distinguish between and cater to social and individual morality. Individual morality describes the behavior of one person in private or specific people in public roles. Social morality is the wide range of behaviors that create and contribute to public life and impact greater society. Social workers must recognize the interplay between these types of morality and advocate when their absence creates social injustice.

Below are the three main values in social work.

Preserving Human Rights

Social workers are charged with preserving the rights of all people. This means taking a compassionate, holistic view of the individuals that social workers serve and advocating for them when society cannot meet their needs. Still, it's important that clients retain the power to make decisions about the direction their lives will take. The social worker can guide clients, but the clients maintain the ultimate decision. Only when clients pose a risk to the well-being of others should social workers intervene on their behalf. Social workers should take a strengths-based approach in their practice and help their clients develop and use their personal strengths to achieve their goals and compensate for weaknesses. The ultimate goal of social work is to provide clients with the tools they need to empower themselves to make their own decisions and enhance their personal health and the well-being of their family, community, and the greater society.

Advocating for Social Justice

Social workers advocate for justice and fair treatment for those they serve. Practitioners should challenge prejudice and discrimination against their clients to model good moral judgment and to uphold anti-discrimination laws. Practitioners must also inform those in power when they become aware of policies that violate anti-discrimination laws or unethical practices. In this role, social workers are agents of social change who help improve society for future citizens.

Social workers should celebrate the diversity of their clients and the communities where they work. This includes identifying differences and similarities between cultures and maintaining an "open door" policy to all individuals in need of assistance. These practices are intended to promote a society inclusive to all individuals and groups, regardless of their personal characteristics, values, or beliefs. Practitioners must identify resources in their community and their own organization to best serve their clients. Social workers should use good moral judgment to make sure that these resources are given equally to their clients and are tailored to the specific needs of those they serve.

Following the Ethics and Morality of the Profession

Practitioners must follow the profession's code of ethics and act with honesty, compassion, and dignity. Social workers should be familiar with the most recent version of the social work code of ethics, which contains the values and principles endorsed by the practitioners and researchers in the field. They should apply these principles in practice and evaluate how they can be tailored to their specific communities. Practitioners should also be respectful of clients and colleagues by acting with sincerity and good moral judgment. This includes setting and following professional boundaries with clients and coworkers, following the profession's ethical code, and taking responsibility for their actions.

Professional Objectivity

While social workers should show empathy toward a client, it is also important that they remain objective and do not become enmeshed in the social worker/client relationship. Enmeshment occurs when the social worker is overly involved with the client's emotional life, and it may harm the client. Social workers must demonstrate professional objectivity with the client to avoid countertransference, which occurs when a social worker redirects their emotions onto the client. In addition, social workers can engage in professional objectivity by recognizing that the client is the party who needs to do the majority of the work in the relationship. It is difficult to maintain professional objectivity when enmeshment occurs, and social workers should seek supervision if they cannot maintain professional objectivity with the client.

Social workers must also ensure that they're competent to fulfill any job that they are assigned before practicing with clients. This includes being a life-long learner and reviewing relevant research literature related to their therapeutic approaches and the clients they serve. Practitioners should also use evidence-based practices in their work with clients whenever possible. Practitioners should behave in morally responsible ways, advocate for their clients when they are faced with discriminatory practices or policies, practice self-care to ensure that they are effective in their work, and should only work within the scope of their practice.

Protecting Client Self-Determination

Social workers realize that clients have a right to lead their lives as they see fit, making their own decisions based on their values. Issues may arise when the values of clients do not align with how others believe clients should behave or live. Social workers must advocate on the behalf of clients with other professionals to ensure that their values are at the core of any plan. It is the job of the social worker to work with the client to aid in goal creation and identification that is congruent to the client's values.

There are situations where promoting client self-determination may cause conflict between the client, social worker, and other professionals. For example, if a client has entered a hospital due to medical issues arising from alcohol abuse, healthcare professionals may recommend that the client attend an alcohol and drug rehabilitation facility for treatment. However, if the client does not wish to seek treatment, then the social worker should advocate on their behalf and help to devise a plan that honors the client's wishes. Exceptions to this value would be when a client needs protection from self-harm or harming others. In this situation, the social worker must act in accordance with legal and ethical standards to do no harm versus promoting the self-determination of the client.

Client Competence and Self-Determination

Social workers realize that clients have a right to lead their lives as they see fit, making their own decisions based on their values. Issues may arise when the values of clients do not align with how others believe clients should behave or live. Social workers must advocate on the behalf of clients with other professionals to ensure that their values are at the core of any plan. It is the job of the social worker to work with the client to aid in goal creation and identification that is congruent to the client's values.

There are situations where promoting client self-determination may cause conflict between the client, social worker, and other professionals. For example, if a client has entered a hospital due to medical issues arising from alcohol abuse, healthcare professionals may recommend that the client attend an alcohol and drug rehabilitation facility for treatment. However, if the client does not wish to seek treatment, then the social worker should advocate on their behalf and help to devise a plan that honors the client's wishes. Exceptions to this value would be when a client needs protection from self-harm or harming or others. In this situation, the social worker must act in accordance with legal and ethical standards to do no harm versus promoting the self-determination of the client.

Social Worker's Own Values and Beliefs on the Social Worker-Client Relationship

Social work as a profession prides itself on practitioners putting personal values aside, even when those values conflict with client values. Social workers must not engage in discriminatory practices or condone the discriminatory practices of others. For example, if a social worker is personally uncomfortable with same-sex relationships, but has a gay or lesbia client, the social worker will need to take steps to evaluate their own values and beliefs. The social worker must ensure that personal feelings are put aside in order to appropriately meet the client's needs. Self-awareness is a vital part of ensuring that one's personal values and beliefs do not intrude on the social worker/client relationship. It may be necessary to seek consultation from a supervisor or colleague in situations where one's personal values or beliefs are in conflict with the client and when those feelings cannot be resolved. In extreme cases where consultation and self-reflection cannot remedy the conflict, termination of the social worker/client relationship and referral to another therapist may be necessary.

Social Worker's Own Values and Beliefs on Interdisciplinary Collaboration

Reflecting on one's personal values and beliefs in order to maintain objectivity and reduce biases when providing treatment for clients is a fundamental component of the NASW's Code of Ethics. Providing treatment as part of an interdisciplinary collaboration (such as part of a team consisting of medical professionals, allied health workers, financial experts, legal experts, and other professionals that support a client) is becoming more common in the field of social work. It can be difficult to manage all competing interests, as each professional on a collaborative team will bring a different perspective with different ideas for the most effective treatment. While a social worker may focus primarily on psychosocial factors that influence a client's life, a doctor may focus more on the client's physical health, and a financial expert may focus on providing the client with better financial resources. Therefore, working in collaborative groups requires keeping the client's desired outcomes for the intervention as the primary goal of the interdisciplinary team. Documenting the client's goals and mapping out each professional's objectives can help mitigate the effects of professional and personal biases. Additionally, a documented plan can help establish clear job roles for each professional so that a single set of values does not take over the full scope of the intervention. When interdisciplinary collaboration accounts for these factors, the benefits of providing the client with multiple skillsets and perspectives can be tremendous.

Transference and Countertransference in the Social Worker-Client Relationship

Transference occurs when the client consciously or unconsciously relates to the social worker because the social worker reminds the client, in some way, of a person from a past relationship. Transference by clients toward the social worker often occurs during the course of treatment and the client needs to be made aware of transference issues and how to reduce them. If clients are experiencing transference with the social worker, they may also be experiencing transference in other relationships in their lives, and this needs to be addressed. Transference is a common occurrence for many clients and can be a useful tool in therapeutic treatment to develop both healthier relationships and a productive relationship with the social worker.

Countertransference occurs when the social worker identifies the client with someone from the social worker's past. Social workers must work through countertransference issues while assisting the client in recognizing and coping with transference situations. If social workers recognize countertransference, they may want to seek the assistance of a supervisor to work through countertransference issues. Transference and countertransference may be useful for the social worker and client to experience because they may impact other areas in the relationships of both.

Transference and Countertransference Within Supervisory Relationships

Transference and countertransference are used to describe how projections occur in an interactive relationship. Transference occurs when supervisees project certain attitudes, values, beliefs, or feelings onto their supervisors; countertransference occurs when supervisors project certain attitudes, values, beliefs, or feelings onto their supervisees. Depending on the intensity or type of projections that take place, transference and countertransference experiences may impact the boundaries, mentoring relationship, or professional collaboration that takes place between supervisors and supervisees. Transference and countertransference experiences may also occur as a result of temporary situations the supervisor or supervisee find themselves in, and interactions that occur afterward may have a long-lasting impact. For example, a supervisee may have heard from a colleague a long, emotional story about harassment from another supervisor. Upon meeting with their personal supervisor, the supervisee may project irrational feelings of anger, fear, or resentment on the supervisor for the rest of their working relationship. Additionally, supervisors must take care to examine supervisees when they are working with clients. Transference and countertransference can take place unexpectedly between social workers and their clients, and it can have similar impacts on the intervention process. Finally, overly positive transference and countertransference experiences can be somewhat problematic as well.

They may unwittingly place one person on a pedestal, result in an insincere mentoring relationship, or cause feelings of disillusionment in supervisees when they see their supervisors make an error.

Transference and countertransference experiences can be minimized by openly discussing their potential in the beginning of a professional relationship. By discussing the fact that both parties are vulnerable to this experience, both parties can become more self-aware and reflective about occurrences and how to handle them. This sets the stage for professional and collaborative growth, transparency, and effective communication.

Safe and Positive Work Environment

Social workers have an emotionally and physically taxing job; therefore, a safe and positive work environment is crucial in supporting social workers in their jobs and in doing their best work. A safe and positive work environment is characterized by processes that foster work-life balance, good boundaries between work and personal life, a culture of respect and ethical behavior toward colleagues and subordinates, just compensation for tasks performed, support for the social worker's personal and professional development, and a zero-tolerance policy for threats, violence, harassment, or bullying in the workplace. Additionally, a documented process that allows social workers to express when they feel unsafe (whether with coworkers or with clients) and established avenues for resolution are other ways to ensure a positive and safe work environment. Social workers should feel comfortable employing these avenues without fear of consequences from colleagues or supervisors. Finally, leadership should ensure their workers feel comfortable communicating their professional goals, successes, and obstacles; leadership should also provide opportunities that support professional goal achievement or resolution to overcome obstacles.

Social Worker Self-Care Principles and Techniques

Due to the highly emotional, interpersonal, and empathic demands of the social work field, social workers must employ and sustain self-care practices to protect their personal health. Without self-care, social workers are highly susceptible to burnout and compassion fatigue, two risks that occur when working in a field that often provides exposure to disheartening humanitarian situations, abusive intrapersonal relationships, and cases that, for bureaucratic or personal reasons, take a long time to resolve. Unchecked, these experiences can lead the social worker to feel detached from work and hopeless toward cases, or to consistently experience the ill effects of chronic stress. Self-care practices may include establishing boundaries between one's work and personal life, having a regular meditation practice or other mental exercises that are shown to soothe the nervous system, eating a healthy diet and engaging in regular physical exercise (as these behaviors decrease inflammation in the body and reduce stress hormones), and having a trustworthy support system of friends and colleagues. Introspective exercises, such as daily journaling, can provide the social worker with a better understanding of which activities bring stress to their lives and which activities bring peace. By knowing these, the social worker can bridge the gap to reduce stress in areas they can control (such as setting a clear cut-off time for answering emails, or scheduling personal activities that bring them joy). They can adopt healthy coping mechanisms for the areas in which they are unable to control factors that might contribute to their stress (such as an emotional case or external funding issues).

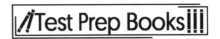

Burnout, Secondary Trauma, and Compassion Fatigue

Sometimes it may be necessary to seek supervision if the social worker experiences burnout, secondary trauma, compassion fatigue, countertransference or the inability to develop a trusting relationship with the client. Although the focus is often on the supervisor's role of ensuring that clients are provided with ethical services by training and evaluating the supervisee, the supervisee's role in supervision is not passive. The social worker should fully engage in the process of supervision and use this relationship to grow and improve. In order to do that, the supervisee must be willing to discuss areas of ethical or legal concern that have arisen in their interactions with clients. They must also be ready to honestly address their own struggles and identify their learning needs, and seek the help and advice of the supervisor. This can only happen effectively through genuine self-assessment, which flows from a real desire to become a better social worker. The process of self-assessment in supervision can help them see any biases or weaknesses that may be holding them back from fully meeting their clients' needs. If the social worker is defensive or resistant to the supervisory relationship, then they will make little progress.

Factors to consider when receiving feedback during supervision/consultation:

- Social workers can benefit from feedback during supervision or consultation, especially with difficult clients/cases or at significant times in treatment, such as termination.

- When discussing cases, client confidentiality should be protected as much as possible, and client consent to release information should be acquired.

Impairment is a professional issue that should be addressed swiftly. Impairment occurs when a social worker's personal problems (e.g., mental health conditions, difficult life circumstances, or alcohol/drug use) have an impact upon their practice. The Code of Ethics states that social workers should seek to rectify their impairment by consulting with colleagues or supervisors, seeking their own treatment, limiting work, and/or terminating client relationships until the impairment has been fully addressed. In the event that a colleague is suffering from some sort of impairment, a social worker should address the concern with the colleague and encourage the colleague to rectify the issue. If the issue continues without proper attention, the social worker should go through appropriate channels to seek additional help for the colleague and to prevent consequences to clients. The same is true if the social worker feels there has been unethical behavior by a colleague. The social worker should discuss the behavior with the colleague and possibly with a supervisor. If a colleague is unfairly accused of unethical behavior, assisting the colleague in rectifying the situation is the best course of action.

Evidence-Based Practice

Social workers can use Evidence-Based Practice methods to ensure effective treatment for clients. This type of practice uses both research and clinical knowledge. Social workers using evidence-based practice will choose interventions that have scientifically documented effectiveness. With this method, workers also evaluate chosen interventions throughout treatment to ensure a successful outcome.

Research Terms

Independent variable: a factor changed or controlled when conducting an experiment or research

Dependent variable: a factor dependent on the independent variable and is observed for changes as the independent variable is manipulated

Randomized controlled trial (RCT): a quantitative study that uses participants or subjects who are chosen randomly to participate

Reliability: the consistency of a measure, or the likelihood the same result will be achieved each time a measure is used

Validity: reflects whether a test, tool, or study is measuring what it intends to measure

External validity: the ability of a study to be generalized to other people or circumstances

Internal validity: refers to cause and effect; one question that can be posed: Are the effects of the study caused by the intervention?

Professional Development Activities

Professional development activities are a vital component of continuing education and ensuring social workers remain competent over the course of their careers, especially as public needs and norms shift. Social workers can find a plethora of continuing education courses, seminars, and trainings at the college or university from which they received their degree. Often, these are free or discounted for alumni. The NASW provides various free to for-cost opportunities on their website, including a portal which allows the user to filter opportunities by date, topic, location, and cost. The web site also provides online courses that can be done at home, free teleconferences in which to learn from peers, online articles, and links to new scholarly literature. The NASW also invites professionals to write and advocate for issues on behalf of the organization, which allows social workers to hone research and writing skills while also promoting themselves professionally and serving causes about which they are personally passionate. Networking and conferences are another way to meet and learn from peers and develop professionally. Additionally, employers may provide free or discounted opportunities for social workers to pursue professional development activities. This may include activities such as in-house workshops or sponsoring employees to attend conferences or trainings.

In order to maintain licensure, social workers must pursue a certain number of continuing education hours per designated time cycle. Therefore, all social workers can inherently expect to continuously develop as professionals as long as they are continuing to renew their licenses. The specifics of continuing education are determined by the state issuing the license and the type of license that is held. Certain licenses may also require that all or a portion of the continuing education credits cover specific topics.

Practice Questions

1. The NASW Code of Ethics has six core purposes. Which of the following choices are included in those core purposes?

> I. To provide the rules and standards that social workers can use to evaluate the conduct of others in the profession
> II. To help identify information that social workers should take under advisement when ethical conflicts may exist or when an ethical dilemma presents itself
> III. To inform new social workers about core issues relating to the mission of social work and to the ethical standards of the field
> IV. To relate the vision of social work in a standard way throughout the profession
> V. To establish the consequences of violating the ethical standards of social work
> VI. To ensure that collaborating professions are aware of the expectations to which social workers are held

   a. I, II, and III only
   b. I, IV, and V only
   c. II, III, and VI only
   d. III, IV, and VI only

2. Claudia is coming to therapy for the first time. She meets her therapist, Susan, a licensed clinical social worker, and Susan tells her what she can expect from treatment. Claudia says that she understands the process of therapy, as well as the risks, and that she is excited to begin. Susan makes a note of their discussion and begins her assessment. Has Susan satisfied the informed consent requirement, and why or why not?
   a. Yes. Susan discussed the process and risks of therapy, and the client agreed.
   b. No. Susan didn't ask Claudia if she understood everything fully.
   c. No. Susan did not have Claudia sign a consent form.
   d. Yes. Susan made a note that Claudia agreed as part of her documentation.

3. Susan's husband is employed in the IT sector and is looking for a new job. Susan's client, Claudia, mentions during their therapy session that her husband is an IT recruiter. At the end of their session, Susan asks Claudia for her husband's contact information. She says she would like her husband to reach out to Claudia's husband in order to find a better IT job. What boundary issue does this represent?
   a. Dependency
   b. Personal gain
   c. Dual relationship
   d. Altruism

4. Janelle is a social worker who just got a referral for a new client. The client's name seems familiar, but she isn't sure why. When she meets the client, Jeremy, she realizes that she had a brief sexual encounter with him years ago at a party early in college. Jeremy shows no signs of recognizing or remembering her. Janelle isn't sure if she should continue to provide services to Jeremy or not. If Jeremy does not remember the encounter, is it okay for Janelle to continue to provide therapy?
   a. No. Janelle should have refused to speak to Jeremy as soon as she recognized him.
   b. Yes, but only if Jeremy continues to have no memory of the encounter.
   c. No. Janelle should address the situation and refer Jeremy to another practitioner.
   d. Yes, but only if she reminds Jeremy of the encounter, and he agrees to continue with services.

5. What are the components of an ethical dilemma?
   a. Conflicting values; the social worker must decide between different courses of action; the social worker may have to terminate with the client
   b. Ethical principles are at odds; the social worker can either make a decision or not; the situation is troubling to the social worker
   c. Different courses of action exist; ethical principles are at odds; the social worker can either make a decision or not
   d. The social worker must make a decision; different courses of action exist; no matter what choice of action is made, an ethical ideal will be compromised

6. There are steps to resolving an ethical dilemma that have been outlined by the NASW Code of Ethics. What is the correct order of these steps?
   a. Consider, Specify, Rank, Establish, Implement, and Enforce
   b. Consider, Specify, Rank, Establish, Implement, and Reflect
   c. Determine, Identify, Rank, Develop, Implement, and Reflect
   d. Determine, Identify, Rank, Develop, Implement, and Enforce

7. Susan has been seeing a client, Christine, for about six months. Christine has three young children and a previous drug addiction. Susan suspects that Christine may be using again and decides to confront her at their session. When Christine arrives, she appears to be under the influence, and she has her two-year-old with her. Susan also notices that the two-year-old is covered in bruises. When she comments on the bruises, Christine becomes defensive. Christine has disclosed in the past that she sometimes gets so angry at her small children that she feels like she could beat them, but that she never would. What is the ethical concern?
   a. Christine has disclosed past drug abuse and violent thoughts toward her children. Susan now suspects both are occurring, but would have to break confidentiality to report her suspicions.
   b. Christine may be on drugs again, but she's already been defensive with Susan, so it will be difficult for Susan to bring it up without damaging their relationship.
   c. Christine has made disclosures in the past regarding drug use and also seems to need childcare so she can go to therapy. Susan knows a good babysitter who can help, but also knows that would be establishing a dual relationship.
   d. Christine seems to be neglecting her children. Christine could possibly use education about parenting issues. Susan isn't sure if Christine would be open to a referral for parenting classes.

8. Janelle is a therapist at a nonprofit agency, and she is supervised by Susan, who meets with the Executive director each month to alert her of any issues. Janelle has been seeing Brad for over a year for individual therapy. Brad wanted to focus on marital issues, but his wife refused to join him, telling him the issues in their marriage were because of his own personal problems. Brad told Janelle he wanted to improve himself to be a better husband. Last week, Brad's wife moved out and filed for divorce. She told him he had not improved himself during the last year of therapy. Brad believes this is Janelle's fault and has filed a malpractice lawsuit against Janelle. Legally, could Brad do anything else in regard to malpractice?
   a. No. You can't sue someone because your wife left you.
   b. Yes. Brad could also file suit against Janelle's supervisor and go up the chain of command, naming even the Executive director in the lawsuit.
   c. Yes. Brad can also file suit against Janelle's direct supervisor.
   d. No. Brad can only sue Janelle, because she was his therapist.

9. Brad has filed his malpractice lawsuit against his therapist, Janelle. The agency for which Janelle works has liability insurance. What options are available to social workers like Janelle, to protect them from malpractice lawsuits such as this one?

    a. If a social worker's agency has liability insurance, the social worker is covered by the agency insurance.

    b. A social worker needs their own liability insurance, because the agency insurance will only cover supervisors and the director.

    c. If the informed consent document states that the client holds the therapist harmless, then the therapist is protected from claims of malpractice.

    d. It is good practice to have personal liability insurance even if the agency one works for also has liability insurance.

10. There are clues to help social workers determine whether a "boundary crossing" has become an ethical violation. What is one of these clues?

    a. The social worker is consistently late to work.

    b. The social worker plays on his computer instead of completing documentation.

    c. The social worker cannot be impartial.

    d. The social worker has conflict with coworkers.

11. Client information is protected by confidentiality. However, in the instance where a client makes a threat against another individual during treatment, the social worker is required to warn the individual, thus breaking confidentiality. What court case established the duty to warn?

    a. Tarasoff vs. Regents of University of California

    b. Regents of University of California vs. Bakke

    c. Blonder-Tongue vs. University of Illinois

    d. Fisher vs. University of Texas

12. When required by law to disclose confidential information about a client, the social worker should always discuss the disclosure with the client before the disclosure occurs. Is this true or false? Why?

    a. False. At the time of the informed consent, the client should have been told about legal requirements that cause the social worker to break confidentiality, and therefore, the social worker never needs to discuss a specific disclosure with the client.

    b. True. The social worker has to get the client to sign a new informed consent form stating that the client understands the disclosure will be made.

    c. False. The social worker should assess any threat to their personal safety, or the safety of others, and should only discuss the disclosure with the client if no one appears to be at risk of harm.

    d. True. The social worker has a duty to tell the client that a disclosure is being made and that confidentiality is being broken.

13. When working with a group, confidentiality is _____ group members.

    a. guaranteed by

    b. fluid within

    c. true for

    d. dependent upon

14. Jane works in an agency providing individual therapy. She has an office that she shares with another social worker. Their office door has a lock on it, and they both have a key to the office. Jane keeps her records in a filing cabinet under her desk and does not lock it because her office door is always locked, even if she is in the building. Is Jane providing enough security for her records?

    a. No. Even though Jane keeps her office locked, she should still lock her filing cabinet.

    b. Yes. If Jane's office is locked, she is doing her part to keep her records secure.

    c. Yes. because Jane and her office mate work for the same agency, the office mate is not a risk.

    d. No. Jane should advocate for records to be kept in a single location in the agency with a separate locked door.

15. Which of the following is the most important element when a social worker is dealing with record requests and disclosures of confidential information due to legal requirements?

    a. Follow through

    b. Documentation

    c. Consultation with colleagues and supervisors

    d. Informed consent

16. Social workers are considered _____ by all states.

    a. Legal consultants

    b. Social service experts

    c. Mandated reporters

    d. Knowledgeable about resources

17. Amy is a social worker for a home health company. She has been visiting her seventy-five-year-old client, Sofia, for about six months. Lately, Sofia's daughter has seemed on edge when Amy is visiting. As Amy approached the house for her most recent visit, she could hear Sofia's daughter yelling at her, along with what she believed to be sounds of Sofia being hit. Amy then observed Sofia holding her arm and saw red marks when Sofia moved her hand. Amy attempted to speak to Sofia about her home life, but Sofia simply shook her head "no." Amy also noticed that Sofia has lost some weight over the last couple of months. Amy has concerns about Sofia's well-being. What should Amy's course of action be?

    a. Amy should continue to observe Sofia and make notes regarding what she sees.

    b. Amy should make a report to Adult Protective Services.

    c. Amy should look at the nursing notes to find out what other health care professionals have observed.

    d. Amy should drop in more often to see if she can catch Sofia's daughter in the act.

18. Which of the following is NOT one of the five core values of the social work profession?

    a. Independence

    b. Dignity and worth of the person

    c. Importance of human relationships

    d. Competence

19. Ethically, social workers are required to maintain confidentiality when working with clients. Legally, HIPAA requires that social workers keep psychotherapy notes confidential. What does HIPAA stand for?

    a. Health Information Personal Acceptability Act

    b. Health Insurance Personal Acceptability Act

    c. Health Information Perpetuating Accountability Act

    d. Health Insurance Portability and Accountability Act

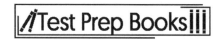

20. Due to mandated reporting laws, social workers must report any suspected abuse or neglect. Those who fail to report can be held to both civil and criminal lawsuits. Social workers cannot be held responsible for reports made in what?

a. Earnest
b. Good faith
c. Concern
d. Private

21. Jane is working with a client whose goals are based on his personal values. Jane finds her own values in direct conflict with the client's values. Jane has tried to self-reflect and work through this issue, but she finds herself having a harder time putting her own values aside each session. What should Jane's next step be?

a. Termination
b. Consultation
c. Speaking to the client about the conflict she is having
d. Personal exploration

22. Social workers strive to consider cultural impact on individual values. How should cultural differences and values be addressed?

a. Cultural values and differences should be pointed out so that the client knows the social worker is aware of them.
b. Cultural values and differences should be learned by the social worker and worked around when issues arise.
c. Cultural values and differences should be learned by the social worker and used as strengths and to empower change.
d. Cultural values and differences should be compared to the greater society to find similarities.

23. Social workers have a set of core values that shape the profession. One of these values is service. What does this mean for a social worker?

a. Service means that the social worker will address social problems and help those in need. Service also means that social workers will provide pro bono or volunteer work when not at a paid position.
b. Service means that the social worker will provide the best client service possible and always look for ways to improve.
c. Service means that the social worker will try to help as many people as possible, often working in more than one position.
d. Service means having pride in how social workers serve their clientele.

24. The field of social work has a set of core goals for the profession. What are these core goals?
    I. Improve social function
    II. Consult with colleagues
    III. Resolve problems
    IV. Put the client first
    V. Achieve desired change
    VI. Meet self-defined goals
    VII. Challenge wrongs
    VIII. Make a difference

    a. II, IV, VII, and VIII only
    b. I, II, IV, and VII only
    c. III, IV, VI, and VII only
    d. I, III, V, and VI only

25. When a social worker's own mental health issues, such as anxiety or depression, begin to interfere with their ability to serve their clients, what is this called?
    a. Self-awareness
    b. Interference
    c. Impairment
    d. Personal problems

26. A client's right to live life according to their own values and beliefs is supported by social workers in a way that it is not by other professions. What is this right called?
    a. Personal responsibility
    b. Self-determination
    c. Self-guided
    d. Self-rule

27. Sexual relationships between social workers and colleagues or co-workers are _____.
    a. not permissible under any circumstance.
    b. permissible if the colleague is not at the same agency.
    c. not permissible unless the social worker was in the relationship prior to employment.
    d. permissible except when one person is in position of authority over the other.

28. Interdisciplinary collaboration is commonplace in social work. To avoid conflict, there are steps that can be taken to promote a smooth working relationship. The first step is to advocate. What does this mean within the context of interdisciplinary collaboration?
    a. Educating team members about the role of the social worker
    b. Standing up for the social workers when other team members try to keep them from being heard
    c. Making sure everyone on the team hears what the social workers have to say
    d. Asking team members to remember that everyone has strengths they bring to the table

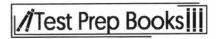

29. At every level of professional development, it is important to continually participate in education opportunities. Why is this important to the values of social work?

a. Continuing education is necessary in order to maintain a level of competence in the area of expertise that the social worker practices.

b. Continuing education is required to maintain licensure, and licensure ensures that the social worker is regarded as a capable professional.

c. Conferences and learning situations provide networking opportunities that can aid in interdisciplinary collaboration.

d. Education is an ongoing personal journey.

30. Alex is a social worker in the Emergency Room where Lucas, who is homeless, frequently visits for ailments of varying severity. The Emergency Room staff advise Alex that he must find somewhere for Lucas to go. Alex speaks at length with Lucas, who states that he has no friends or family with whom he is in contact. Lucas tells Alex that he has lived at shelters before and that he doesn't like the rules that must be followed. Lucas declines a bed at the local shelter. Alex discusses this with Lucas' doctor and nurse and both become adamant that Lucas must go to a shelter; sleeping on the street is not acceptable. Alex facilitates a discussion between medical personnel and Lucas in which Lucas maintains that he does not intend to go to a shelter. Eventually, Alex asks to speak privately with the medical personnel, and he advocates strongly on Lucas' behalf, stating that Lucas has made his decision. Was Alex's course of action correct?

a. No. If the doctor felt that a shelter was necessary, then Alex's responsibility was to listen to the doctor and to convince Lucas to go to the shelter.

b. Yes. Having a private conversation with the medical staff was the best solution, so that Lucas didn't hear the discussion.

c. Yes. By advocating on Lucas' behalf, Alex was protecting his right to self-determination.

d. No. Alex should have asked to call Lucas' relatives on his behalf to convince them to take him in.

31. When working in an interdisciplinary collaboration, what should be kept in mind to ensure a seamless working relationship?

a. Educate, Communicate, Experience, Skill levels, Conflict

b. Advocate, Understanding, Common Ground, Differences, Conflict

c. Advocate, Communicate, Experience, Skill levels, Closure

d. Educate, Understanding, Common Ground, Differences, Closure

32. What is the purpose of the emphasis on understanding systems within the field of social work?

a. To help increase the amount of field experience that a social work student participates in because only so much can be learned in the classroom.

b. To better understand a client's place in society so that the social worker can help increase social understanding and make connections.

c. To learn about diversity within family and social systems so that all clients receive unbiased and respectful care.

d. To help the social worker advocate for clients on the local, state, and national levels by understanding the programs available.

Answer Explanations

1. A: The six core purposes of the NASW Code of Ethics are:

- To establish the core values on which the mission of social work is based

- To provide a set of ethical standards for social workers, as well as specific information regarding different ethical dilemmas

- To help identify information that social workers should take under advisement when ethical conflicts may exist or when an ethical dilemma presents itself

- To provide standards that can be used by others to ensure accountability and responsibility by those in the profession

- To inform new social workers about core issues relating to the mission of social work and to the ethical standards of the field

- To provide the rules and standards that social workers can use to evaluate the conduct of others in the profession

2. C: No, informed consent has not been satisfied. Susan did not have a document outlining what therapy would entail, including the risk and limitations. She also did not have Claudia sign such a document to become part of the chart. Documentation of informed consent protects both the client and the social worker.

3. B: Personal gain refers to instances in which a social worker engages in activity with a client that results in a monetary (or otherwise valuable) benefit to the social worker. This could involve situations such as referring a client to a business owned by the social worker or a friend/family member of the social worker, selling something to a client, or even asking a client for professional suggestions.

4. C: The Code of Ethics does not specify the length of a prior relationship—only that if a sexual relationship existed, services should not be provided. A risk of harm could still exist. It is best if this situation is avoided. Janelle should address the situation with Jeremy, acknowledge her professional limitations, and refer him to another social worker.

5. D: In order to have an ethical dilemma, three conditions must be met. The first is that the practitioner must make a decision. If the situation does not require that a decision be made, then there isn't an ethical dilemma. The second is that there are different decisions that could be made or different actions one could take. The third condition is that an ethical ideal will be conceded no matter what decision is made.

6. C: The steps to resolving an ethical dilemma are as follows:

Determine: Is there an ethical conflict or dilemma?

Identify: What are the core standards and values involved in the situation?

Rank: Take the values and ethical principles and rank them in order of importance in regard to the situation.

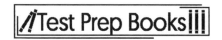

Develop: Make a plan that correlates with the values and principles that were previously ranked as important to this situation. This may involve collaborating with colleagues or supervisors. When outlining the plan, identify any potential risks or adverse effects.

Implement: Put the plan into motion taking care to use social work practice skills that allow for ultimate sensitivity.

Reflect: Evaluate the ethical decision making process. How did all involved agencies and individuals fare? It is not uncommon for social workers to make use of ethical review committees or ethical consultations when facing dilemmas to gain assistance and perspective.

7. A: Susan has knowledge that Christine has a history of drug abuse. Christine has shown signs of possible relapse. Susan also has safety concerns for Christine's children based on what she has seen and the way Christine has behaved. Due to her concerns, a good faith report is warranted, which will require that Susan break confidentiality to report the suspected child abuse and neglect.

8. B: During malpractice suits, the liability goes all the way up the chain of command. This means that not only the social worker at the heart of the lawsuit, but also any supervisors or persons above them, can be held liable and named in the lawsuit.

9. D: Although the agency has liability insurance, it's always best practice for a social worker to carry their own liability insurance. The liability insurance of the agency is going to protect the agency first and foremost. The social worker should always look out for their best interest in cases involving questions of malpractice or the risk of lawsuit.

10. C: When a social worker fails to maintain impartiality and maintains a bias that cannot be overlooked, an ethical violation has occurred. The situation needs to be reviewed, and consultation should be sought.

11. A: Tarasoff vs. Regents of University of California is the correct answer. In this 1976 case, the therapist failed to notify the intended victim of the threat of harm. After the client had stopped seeking treatment, he then attacked and killed Tarasoff, prompting her family to sue the University and therefore establishing the duty to warn. None of the other cases directly relate to duty to warn.

12. C: False. A social worker should always assess their own personal safety, as well as the safety of others, when deciding if a confidential disclosure should be discussed with the client. For example, a social worker is working with someone who has a history of violence toward women, and he discloses that he has been contemplating harming his neighbor who has turned down his advances. In this instance, it would be safer if the social worker didn't discuss the disclosure with the client. Given his history of violence, discussing the disclosure might put both the therapist and the neighbor at risk.

13. D: When working with a group, confidentiality is dependent upon group members. In a group therapy situation, everyone must agree to keep confidential any information that is discussed in the group. It is impossible, however, for the social worker to guarantee that each group member will abide by that agreement and maintain confidentiality.

14. A: Records must be kept in a secure and locked environment. Despite the fact that the office is always locked, a second form of security would be best. It is important to remember that cleaning staff or other individuals might have access to the office when neither social worker is there.

15. B: Documentation. Documentation is the social worker's best friend. If it isn't documented, it didn't happen. Social workers deal with very sensitive situations, some of which end up in a court of law. If there is no documentation that something happened, there is no proof. Documenting any requests from clients—as well as whether or not those were honored and why or why not—is just as important as what happens during sessions.

16. C: Mandated reporters. Social workers, along with other professionals such as doctors, teachers, and nurses, are considered mandated reporters by all 50 states. Mandated reporting laws state that any professional in a human service industry with reasonable suspicion of abuse or neglect must make a good faith report to the correct agency so that an investigation can occur.

17. B: Amy should make a report to Adult Protective Services. Amy's job is not to prove or disprove that abuse or neglect is occurring; that is the job of Adult Protective Services. Amy has enough information to be concerned that something is not right about the situation and that Sofia may not be safe. A report should be made.

18. A: The five core values are: service, dignity and worth of the person, importance of human relationships, integrity, and competence.

19. D: HIPAA refers to the Health Insurance Portability and Accountability Act of 1996. HIPAA establishes that psychotherapy notes must be kept confidential by mental health professionals. This includes notes made during individual or group sessions, notes regarding conversations, notes pertaining to disclosures, and even notes that analyze situations involving the client.

20. B: Good faith means that the social worker has a reasonable suspicion and has no alternative reasons for reporting other than concern.

21. B: If Jane has been unable to rectify the situation through self-assessment, she should then turn to consultation with colleagues regarding her values conflict. If the consultation proves ineffective, she may ultimately need to consider termination and referring the client to another social worker.

22. C: Cultural values and beliefs should be researched and learned when working with clients from a different culture. These values should then be used as strengths during goal development to aid the client in making the changes they desire.

23. A: Service means addressing social problems. This refers both to individual problems and problems in the broader society. Social workers are encouraged to provide some services pro bono as a way to give back to society and to help those who otherwise could not afford services. It also means that social workers should volunteer in some aspect outside of their paying positions.

24. D: The core goals of social work are to improve social function, to resolve problems, to achieve desired change, and to meet self-defined goals. While some of these goals are in regard to clients, they also apply to social workers themselves.

25. C: Issues involving a social worker's personal mental health are considered a form of impairment. Alcohol and drug addiction also fall into this category. With any issues regarding professional impairment, the social worker should seek consultation from colleagues and supervisors. It may be necessary to lessen the workload, and possibly to terminate some client relationships and make referrals.

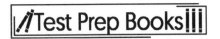

26. B: Self-determination refers to everyone's right to live the life they choose. This doesn't mean that the choices made and life lived will be relatable or understood by others. Social workers strive to preserve self-determination, to allow clients to decide their own goals, and to assist clients in achieving those goals.

27. D: Sexual relationships between colleagues are permitted by the Code of Ethics. The only exception is that a sexual relationship between a supervisor and supervisee is not permissible because of the obvious authority and power that one individual has over the other.

28. A: In this context, *advocate* means that the social worker will educate the rest of the team about the role of the social worker. Often the professional goals and vision of social work differs from that of other disciplines. The social worker should educate team members about this and attempt to gain understanding.

29. A: Competence is the reason that social workers need to be continually educated. This is important so that the social worker can provide the services in which they are trained and remain up-to-date on research and practice.

30. C: Alex was correct in protecting Lucas' right to self-determination. Lucas had made it clear several times that he had tried going to a shelter in the past and did not like the restrictions. He preferred a freer life that allowed him permission to do as he pleased. If Lucas had been suffering from some sort of medical issue that would make him unsafe, then Alex would have needed to explain all the information to him so that he understood his choices. If Lucas still decided to avoid the shelter, then that would have been his right.

31. B: The things to remember when working with an interdisciplinary collaboration are Advocate (educating team members about the role of the social worker), Understanding (striving to understand the other disciplines by asking questions about their roles, functions, and goals), Common Ground (attempting to find things in common that would contribute to better collaboration), Differences (recognizing that differences exist between disciplines and their goals and approaches), and Conflict (striving to approach conflict directly and with sensitivity and respect).

32. B: The field of social work places an emphasis on understanding systems because once the practitioner understands a client's place in society, then he or she can help increase the client's social understanding and make connections to help meet treatment goals. Understanding the client from an individual, family, and social system perspective sets the foundation for an understanding systems. The other choices describe other emphases in the field of social work, such as the emphasis on field experience, the emphasis on advocacy at the local, state, and national levels, and the emphasis on maintaining effectiveness in practice.

Dear ASWB Clinical Test Taker,

We would like to start by thanking you for purchasing this study guide for your ASWB Clinical exam. We hope that we exceeded your expectations.

Our goal in creating this study guide was to cover all of the topics that you will see on the test. We also strove to make our practice questions as similar as possible to what you will encounter on test day. With that being said, if you found something that you feel was not up to your standards, please send us an email and let us know.

We have study guides in a wide variety of fields. If you're interested in another one of our products, try searching for it on Amazon or send us an email!

Thanks Again and Happy Testing!
Product Development Team
info@studyguideteam.com

FREE Test Taking Tips DVD Offer

To help us better serve you, we have developed a Test Taking Tips DVD that we would like to give you for FREE. **This DVD covers world-class test taking tips that you can use to be even more successful when you are taking your test.**

All that we ask is that you email us your feedback about your study guide. Please let us know what you thought about it – whether that is good, bad or indifferent.

To get your **FREE Test Taking Tips DVD**, email freedvd@studyguideteam.com with "FREE DVD" in the subject line and the following information in the body of the email:

   a. The title of your study guide.

   b. Your product rating on a scale of 1-5, with 5 being the highest rating.

   c. Your feedback about the study guide. What did you think of it?

   d. Your full name and shipping address to send your free DVD.

If you have any questions or concerns, please don't hesitate to contact us at freedvd@studyguideteam.com.

Thanks again!

Made in the USA
Middletown, DE
02 November 2020